New York at the Lou
Exposition, St.
Report of the New York State
Commission

DeLancey M. Elli

Alpha Editions

This edition published in 2022

ISBN: 9789356784895

Design and Setting By

Alpha Editions

www.alphaedis.com

Email - info@alphaedis.com

Contents

CHAPTER I
Introduction and Historical Sketch
HISTORICAL SIGNIFICANCE

[ILLUSTRATION]

The Louisiana Purchase Exposition was held in the city of St. Louis in 1904, in commemoration of the acquisition in 1803 of the vast territory west of the Mississippi, then called Louisiana. The transfer is generally regarded as one of the most important events in our national history and stands on record as the greatest acquisition of territory ever made by peaceful methods. An American historian of great prominence says: "The annexation of Louisiana was an event so portentous as to defy measurement; it gave a new face to politics and ranked in historical importance next to the Declaration of Independence and the adoption of the Constitution."

The territory was ceded to France by Spain by the secret treaty of San Ildefonso in 1800. This aroused to intense excitement the people of the West, who were inclined to give credit to the rumor that the army of forty thousand men sent by Napoleon (who was responsible for the negotiation of that treaty) were in reality to take military possession of Louisiana and the Floridas instead of to suppress the insurrection in San Domingo, the ostensible object. France and England had been struggling for many years for supremacy in the Western Continent, and in the possession of this vast territory Napoleon foresaw a prosperous New France. But there were many complications arising at home. Important political questions demanded attention, and the great Napoleon soon realized that he could not hope to cope successfully with the two great problems lying at such a great distance apart.

NEGOTIATIONS FOR TRANSFER OF TERRITORY

At that time our country was interested in procuring possession of the site of New Orleans and the free passage of the Mississippi river forever for all American citizens, and negotiations were opened for their purchase by Thomas Jefferson, author of the Declaration of Independence, and at that time third President of the United States.

During the negotiations Napoleon suggested the transfer of the whole Louisiana territory and the transaction was brought to a most successful conclusion, the signers of the treaty being James Monroe, Robert R. Livingston, and F.B. Marbois, the representative of Napoleon. It was a significant bargain. By it Napoleon formed closer bonds of friendship between France and the United States, and prevented any possibility of the territory falling into the hands of Great Britain. He prophesied that this Republic would eventually become a world power and a commercial rival to England. How completely his prophecy was fulfilled. Our country attained possession of a vast territory embracing more than a million square miles, an area greater than the combined areas of the British Isles, France, Germany, Spain, Belgium, the Netherlands and Italy, the consideration being a figure less than that representing the value of a single square block in any one of our great cities, or an amount much smaller than has been yielded by any one of many mines within the boundaries of the territory. Twelve flourishing states and two territories have since been carved out of Louisiana, and the center of our population is rapidly moving towards that region which was once known as the wilderness of the West.

ROBERT R. LIVINGSTON

It is a matter of the utmost gratification that the State of New York played so important a part in this great event in the person of Robert R. Livingston, who was then United States Minister to France. Dr. Livingston, the title of LL.D. having been conferred upon him by the University of the State of New York, was one of the leading statesmen of his day. A graduate of Kings (now Columbia) College, he began his career in the practice of law in New York city, and was made Recorder of the city in 1773. Elected to the Continental Congress in 1775, he was appointed one of a committee of five to draft the Declaration of Independence, but enforced absence from Philadelphia made it impossible for him to sign the document. He was soon after elected Chancellor of the State of New York, and as such administered the oath of office to George Washington as first President of the United States. His previous training in public affairs admirably fitted him for assuming the important duties leading to the transfer of the Louisiana territory, and to him as much as to any individual belongs the credit for the successful consummation of the transaction.

At the Exposition a handsome statue of Livingston, by Lukemann, was erected in the Cascade Gardens, on the approach to the West Pavilion. Upon the front of the New York State Building appeared this legend: "Robert R. Livingston of New York, Minister to France 1801-1805, inaugurated the negotiations for the Louisiana Purchase and was the first to sign the treaty."

ORIGIN OF THE EXPOSITION

The first action looking towards the commemoration of the Louisiana Purchase was taken at a meeting of the Missouri Historical Society in September, 1898, when a committee of fifty citizens was appointed to take the preliminary steps looking to the observance of the occasion. This committee recommended the submission of the question to a convention of delegates, representing all the Louisiana Purchase states, and at this convention, which was held at the Southern Hotel, St. Louis, January 10, 1899, it was decided to hold a World's Fair as the most fitting commemoration of the one hundredth anniversary of the acquisition of the Louisiana territory. An executive committee, with the Hon. David R. Francis as chairman, was appointed to carry out the undertaking, and this committee determined that at least $15,000,000, the amount paid to France for the territory, would be needed.

ACTION BY CONGRESS

Congress passed a bill in June, 1900, carrying a provisional appropriation of $5,000,000, and pledging governmental support if the city of St. Louis raised $10,000,000. The people went to work with a will and had raised $5,000,000 by popular subscription early in January, 1901, and the following January thirtieth an ordinance was passed by the St. Louis Municipal Assembly authorizing the issuance of $5,000,000 in city bonds. On March twelfth President McKinley appointed a National Commission of nine members, and in August issued a proclamation inviting all the nations of the world to participate in the Exposition. Owing to labor difficulties and delay in securing construction material it soon became evident that it would be impossible to hold the fair during the year 1903, as originally planned. Legislation being necessary in order to provide for the necessary postponement, a bill was passed by Congress and approved by President Roosevelt June 25, 1902, authorizing the holding of the fair in 1904 instead of 1903, as originally determined.

Beginning with the basic appropriation of $15,000,000, [Footnote: In the winter of 1904 a bill was passed by Congress authorizing a Government loan of $4,600,000 to the Exposition Company, to be repaid in instalments from the gate receipts. The loan was entirely canceled early in November, 1904.] as described above, to which had been added $1,000,000 appropriated by the State of Missouri, the great enterprise was projected on a $50,000,000 basis. It was planned to make the universal Exposition at St. Louis the most comprehensive and wonderful that the world had ever seen. How well its projectors succeeded is a matter of recent history. How completely all previous expositions were eclipsed has been told many times in picture and in print.

THE SITE

The site chosen for the Exposition included the western portion of Forest Park, one of the finest parks in the United States. Its naturally rolling ground afforded many opportunities for effective vistas, which were quickly embraced by the Exposition Company's landscape artists. Containing 1,240 acres, it was a tract approximately two miles long and one mile wide.

The grounds might be said to have been divided into two general sections, the dividing line being Skinker road. To the east was the main picture, so called, which was formed by the grouping of eight magnificent exhibit palaces around Festival Hall, the Colonnade of States and Cascade Gardens.

THE MAIN PICTURE

Festival Hall stood upon a rise of ground well above the principal exhibit palaces, and its majestic dome surmounted by a gilded figure of "Victory," the first "Victory" to take the form of a man, was visible from most any part of the grounds. The grouping of the exhibit palaces was geometric in arrangement, in shape like an open fan, the ribs of the fan being the waterways and plazas between which the exhibit palaces were located.

THE ARCHITECTURE

The architecture, while varied and in some instances striking, was still so modified as to make a most harmonious whole. For purity in architecture the best example was the Palace of Education, which was built on the lines of the Italian Renaissance. For most striking architectural effects the Mines and Metallurgy building was invariably pointed out. It was of composite architecture, comprising features of the Egyptian, Byzantine and Greek. The stately obelisks which guarded its entrance ways and the bas-relief panels which formed its outer facade, were objects of universal interest.

To the southeast of the main group of buildings, and gracefully clustered among the trees, were the state pavilions. Along the extreme northern portion of the grounds for a mile stretched the amusement highway, known as the Pike.

OTHER FEATURES

To the west of Skinker road were located the Administration buildings, and, with one or two exceptions, the pavilions of foreign governments, the Agriculture and Horticulture buildings, the Philippine Reservation and the Department of Anthropology. The Intramural railroad, seven miles in length, passed the principal points of interest and enabled visitors to get about the grounds with speed and comfort.

To convert this great tract of land into a beautiful park with well-kept roadways embellished with velvety lawns and magnificent flower beds, would seem to be a task greater than man could perform within the short space of time available for the completion of the Exposition. That it was done, and well done, is a matter of history.

PROCESSES AS WELL AS PRODUCTS

It was early determined that the great Fair should be one of processes, as well as of products; wherever possible there should be life and motion; that the exhibits should answer the question, "How is it done?" as well as "What is it?" The result was that the Exposition became a constantly changing scene of moving objects and an educational force many times greater than any of its predecessors. The student of Mechanics, Electricity, Pedagogy, the Applied Arts, and other kindred subjects could obtain here within a limited area valuable data, which otherwise could only be collected at the expense of much time and considerable money.

DEDICATION CEREMONIES

The formal dedication ceremonies covered three days, beginning April 30, 1903, the actual date of the Centennial Anniversary of the signing of the treaty, and one year previous to the opening of the Exposition. Our commonwealth was fittingly represented at that time, a special appropriation of $50,000 for the same having been made by the Legislature. Governor Odell and staff, State officers, a joint committee from the Legislature and the members of the Louisiana Purchase Exposition Commission attended. There were also present a provisional regiment of infantry of the National Guard, under command of Colonel S. M. Welch, N.G., N.Y.; a provisional division of the Naval Militia under command of Lieutenant E.M. Harman, Second Battalion; and Squadron "A" of New York, under command of Major Oliver H. Bridgman.

THE FIRST DAY'S PROGRAM

The program for the first day consisted of a grand military parade in the morning and exercises in the Liberal Arts building at two o'clock in the afternoon, followed by fireworks in the evening. The day was cold and unpleasant, and a chill wind blowing from the north caused visitors to seek comfort in heavy wraps.

The Governor of the State of New York and her troops met with a continuous ovation along the line of march of the great military parade, and from every side compliments and felicitations were bestowed upon the State's representatives for so hearty and imposing a participation in an event a thousand miles from home.

The occasion was graced by the presence of the President of the United States, Theodore Roosevelt, and by ex-President Grover Cleveland, both of whom made extended remarks at the afternoon exercises.

ADDRESS OF PRESIDENT ROOSEVELT.

The address of President Roosevelt was replete with historical allusions and pointed epigrams. He drew many lessons from the valor and patriotism of the early settlers of the west, and said, among other things:

"Courage and hardihood are indispensable virtues in a people; but the people which possesses no others can never rise high in the scale either of power or of culture. Great peoples must have in addition the governmental capacity which comes only when individuals fully recognize their duties to one another and to the whole body politic, and are able to join together in feats of constructive statesmanship and of honest and effective administration. ... We justly pride ourselves on our marvelous material prosperity, and such prosperity must exist in order to establish a foundation upon which a higher life can be built; but unless we do in very fact build this higher life thereon, the material prosperity itself will go for but very little. ... The old days were great because the men who lived in them had mighty qualities; and we must make the new days great by showing these same qualities. We must insist upon courage and resolution, upon hardihood, tenacity, and fertility of resource; we must insist upon the strong, virile virtues; and we must insist no less upon the virtues of self-restraint, self-mastery, regard for the rights of others; we must show our abhorrence of cruelty, brutality, and corruption, in public and in private life alike."

ADDRESS OF EX-PRESIDENT CLEVELAND

Ex President Cleveland delivered an eloquent panegyric and in closing said:

"... We may well recall in these surroundings the wonderful measure of prophecy's fulfillment, within the span of a short century, the spirit, the patriotism and the civic virtue of Americans who lived a hundred years ago, and God's overruling of the wrath of man, and his devious ways for the blessing of our nation. We are all proud of our American citizenship. Let us leave this place with this feeling stimulated by the sentiments born of the occasion. Let us appreciate more keenly than ever how vitally necessary it is to our country's wealth that every one within its citizenship should be clean minded in political aim and aspiration, sincere and honest in his conception of our country's mission, and aroused to higher and more responsive patriotism by the reflection that it is a solemn thing to belong to a people favored of God."

THE SECOND DAY'S PROGRAM

The second day was designated "Diplomatic Day," and was devoted to a luncheon to the visiting diplomats in the Administration Building, followed by exercises in Festival Hall, at which time addresses were made by Honorable John M. Thurston of the National Commission, who was president of the day; Honorable David R. Francis, president of the Exposition Company; M. Jean J. Jusserand, the French Ambassador, and Senor Don Emilio de Ojeda, the Spanish Minister. In the evening a brilliant reception was given to the Diplomatic Corps at the St. Louis Club.

THE THIRD DAY'S PROGRAM

The third day, Saturday, May second, was officially designated "State Day," and the exercises consisted of a huge civic parade, which consumed two hours in passing a given point, and exercises at two o'clock in the Liberal Arts building, over which ex-Senator William Lindsay of the National Commission presided. Addresses were made by Governor Dockery, who welcomed the governors and delegations from the various states and by Governor Odell of New York, who responded. His brilliant address, which was frequently punctuated by applause, follows:

ADDRESS OF GOVERNOR ODELL

"Governor Dockery, Ladies and Gentlemen:

"There is no phase of American history which should inspire us with greater pride than the consummation of the purchase of the Louisiana tract, an event which opened the pathway to the West, and made possible the powerful nation to which we owe our allegiance. Trade, the inspiration for travel, which brought about the discovery and civilization of the Western Hemisphere, would have demanded inevitably the cession to the United States of the vast regions beyond the Mississippi. Except, however, for the peaceful and diplomatic measures adopted through the wisdom of Thomas Jefferson, this territory could only have been acquired by the sacrifice of human life and the expenditure of untold treasure. That Robert Livingston, a citizen of the Empire State, became the ambassador of the great commoner at the court of France and that it was due to his skill and intelligence that Napoleon was brought to an understanding of the conditions as they existed and of the determination of our then young Republic to prevent the building up of foreign colonies at our very threshold, is a cause for congratulation to the people of the State I represent, and renders the duty which has been assigned to me, therefore, doubly pleasant. Memorable as was this event, and of great importance to the future growth of the Republic, it left its imprint not only upon America, but upon Europe as well. Through it the Napoleonic ambition to develop a vast plan of colonization which threatened the peace of the world was thwarted. The dismemberment of the French possessions which soon followed resulted in the grouping together of the various states of Europe into vast empires whose relations with our country are such that encroachment or territorial aggrandizement upon this hemisphere are forever impossible. Spain, whose waning power was then apparent, was no longer a menace, and thus rendered possible the acquisition of the remaining stretch of territory which made our possessions secure from the Gulf to the Canadian line. While, therefore, as Americans we are prone to the belief that if the necessity had arisen we should have been able to wrest this rich and fertile territory from even the strongest hands, it is well for us to understand, however, that even the diplomacy of which we boast would have been futile except for the failure of Napoleon in San Domingo and his pressing need of funds to permit him to face the enemies of the French. 'Westward Ho!' was the cry of the Old World. From the time when the genius of Columbus accepted the theories of the earlier astronomers the imagination and cupidity of adventurous spirits had been excited by tales of 'far off Cathay.' One hundred years ago the protocol for this territory was signed; one hundred years of history has been written; a nation of three millions has expanded into an empire of eighty millions of souls. Our country has not only become a power among the nations of the world, but has taken an advanced position in the progress and work of civilization. A westward passage to India was sought by Columbus and was still the aim of La Salle in his adventurous voyage along the mighty Mississippi. To-day the American flag floats at the very gates of China, and almost in sight of its walls, placed there by American valor and by American arms in a struggle for human rights, and liberty. Trackless forests and undulating prairies have become the highways for the speeding engines bearing the burdens of traffic to the Orient. No longer are they the pasturage for the buffalo, but the source of food supply for the whole world. Treasures of untold value have been laid bare by the ingenuity of man, but far beyond this wealth are the products in grain and lowing kine which add their hundreds of millions to the resources of our country, extending even beyond the dreams or the imagination of those who sought only the precious metals with which to return with a competence to their native land.

"This is but the span of a century and to commemorate its glories we come from the eastern section, from the earlier colonies to congratulate the people of the West upon the results which we as a nation have achieved. So few the years, yet how notable the history. Upon this soil began those battles which ended in the emancipation of the slave. From this border, and almost from within this territory, came the great Emancipator, a man who struggled with the vicissitudes of fortune in early life, who aided in developing the great West, and whose name will be forever enshrined as the one who in his act as chief magistrate of this country removed the stain which the earlier Dutch had fastened upon our body politic like a 'festering sore.' The past, with all of its achievements, with all of its successes, is to us but an incentive and guide for the future progress of our country. America still beckons to the oppressed of all lands and holds out the gifts of freedom, and we at this time, and upon this occasion, should renew our adherence to those policies which have made us great as a nation. The future is before us, and the patriotism and self-sacrifice of those who made the country's history so glorious should be an inspiration to us all for higher ideals of citizenship. Through the golden gates of commerce pours an unceasing stream of immigration, which must be amalgamated with American ideas and American principles. From the earlier settlers has come a blending of the vigor of the Anglo-Saxon with the Teutonic and Latin races, resulting in that composite type which we are wont to recognize and regard as the type of the true American. Aside from the commercial and industrial results which followed the acquisition of this vast and fertile territory, and the building up of the large marts and towns which everywhere blend with its magnificent scenery, the definition of the power and extent of our Constitution was most important. At its inception, coming at a time when the framers of the Constitution were not only able to interpret their work, but to give to it their moral force and support, it was demonstrated that no constitutional limitations should retard the onward growth, the onward rush of American civilization, until it should have reached the farthermost bounds of the far-off Pacific. The barriers to human progress were by this interpretation removed and ranges of new States have given effect to the democratic principles of our great Republic, and have made of our country a Union—not of weak, impotent States— but a commonwealth of nations, bound to each other through a centralized government by ties of allegiance, common interest and patriotism, where freemen rule and where suffrage is more esteemed than wealth.

"These rights and their protection should receive our earnest thought. The battles of the past have been for freedom and liberty, and the struggles of the future will be for their preservation, not, however, by force of arms, but through the peaceful methods which come through the education of our people. The declaration which brought our Republic into existence has insured and guaranteed that liberty of conscience and that freedom of action which does not interfere with the prerogatives or privileges of a man's neighbors. Capital and labor are the two great elements upon which the prosperity and happiness of our people rest, and when, therefore, aggregations of the one are met by combinations of the other, it should be the aim of all to prevent the clashing of these great interests. The products of toil are worthless unless there be some means by which they can be substituted or transferred for that which labor requires. The concrete form in which these transactions are conducted is the money power or the capital of the land. Without work all of these fertile fields, these teeming towns, would have been impossible, and without a desire to benefit and elevate humanity, its onward progress would have been useless. To work, to labor, is man's bounden duty, and in the performance of the tasks which have been placed upon him, he should be encouraged, and his greatest incentive should be the knowledge that he may transmit to his children and his children's children a higher civilization and greater advantages than he himself possessed. Trade conditions which would permit to the toiler but a bare sustenance, the bare means of a livelihood, would be a hindrance to human progress, a hindrance not to be removed by all of the maxims of the philosopher or the theories of the doctrinaire. Promise without fulfillment is barren, but when you can place before the mechanic the assured fact that the performance of his duty means success in life, and that his non-performance means failure; when you can show him that this law is immutable, you have made of him a useful citizen and have instilled into his mind a firm belief that the freedom and liberty of which we boast is not an inchoate substance to be dreamed of and not enjoyed. But this desired result cannot be secured if combinations of capital, which produce the necessaries of life cheaper and better, are assailed as the enemies of mankind. There is always a mean between those who seek only a fair recompense and return for that which they produce, and those who seek undue advantages for the few at the expense of the many. The laws which have been enacted, if properly executed, are sufficient in their force and effect to encourage the one and to punish the other, but in our condemnation let us not forget that with the expansion that has come to our country, an expansion of our business relations is also necessary. This growth has brought us into intimate contact with the markets of the world, and in the struggle that is always before us, the competition of trade, if we are to hold our own among the world's producers, we should encourage and not hinder those who by their energy, their capital and their labor have banded together for the purpose of meeting these new conditions—problems which our individual efforts alone cannot solve, but which require the concentrated force and genius of both capital and labor. Incentive for good citizenship would indeed be lacking if there were taken from us the opportunities for development, the opportunities for the young man to follow in the footsteps of those who have written their names in the history of our country as the great captains of industry. Success will always follow perseverance and genius. Every heresy, every doctrine which would teach the young man of this country differently, is an insult to the intelligence of our people, and is in the direction of building up a dangerous element in American society which in time would threaten not only the peace and prosperity we enjoy, but our very institutions themselves. When you have placed before the young man all of his possibilities, you have made it impossible to make of our Republic a plutocracy controlled by the few at the expense of the many. The individual should count for as much as the aggregation of individuals, because an injury to the one will lead to the destruction of the many. The question of adjusting and harmonizing the relations of capital and labor is the problem before us to-day and is one which will become more urgent in the future. Its solution must be along those lines of constitutional right which every citizen has been guaranteed. Every man is entitled in the prosecution of his work to the broadest possible liberty of action and the protection of law, of that law which is the outgrowth of necessity and which seeks to encourage and not to oppress. Such recognition can always be secured if there is a determination upon the part of those charged with the responsibility of government to have it. And who is not? Every man possessed of a ballot is responsible and has the power, not only to formulate but to criticise and to punish as well. If this right be properly exercised, an honest and efficient administration of our affairs can always be secured. To aid in this work we have given to the press the broadest possible liberty, a freedom which, however, should never be abused. It should never be used as the medium for the circulation of charges or of calumnies which are without foundation, and which please but the fancies of those in whose minds there always exists envy and discontent. Such a misuse of privileges should be condemned by all right-minded citizens. In its virtuous indignation with those who abuse public place and power, it should be careful to do exact justice because in our busy and active lives we have come to depend to a very great extent upon the wisdom and the honesty of these who edit our newspapers for the information rightly to judge of the conditions, events and necessities of our country. By means of the press, and with an intelligent citizenship, we may always feel sure that there will come into our public life influences for good which will render our government more stable, will add to its renown and to its glory and will insure for all the perpetuation of those principles which have come down to us through the wisdom of our forefathers and which have been amplified by the knowledge of succeeding generations.

"The greatest solvent for political heresies, for doctrines which are antagonistic to popular government, is education. To the educated mind there comes a conception of duty which is not possible to the ignorant. The great colleges and schools with which we are blessed are performing a vital work, and these institutions for developing a higher order of citizenship are of far more worth and of greater importance than all of the ships of war or the arms of the nation in maintaining and upholding those policies which have been adopted for our protection against foreign and domestic foes. But it is not alone a theoretical education which is necessary for this higher citizenship. It must be linked with the knowledge which comes of the study of the character, of the manner and methods of other nations than our own, which leads the artisan to inspect and to improve upon the ingenuity of his fellows of other lands. It is this feature in the exposition which is to take place upon this ground next year that is particularly significant and important in the solution of the problems to which I have referred. It is the contact, the friendly rivalry thus created, which brings about a betterment and improvement of conditions. It is appropriate, therefore, that at the one hundredth anniversary of this great event of our nation's history, we should gather here all of the ingenuity and the genius of the past and the present, that we may contrast and make note of our progress. This will be an inspiration for us in the performance of our duty, and will add to our affection for our native and adopted land, and thus make of America a still greater power for good. A patriotic people is possible only when there exists a love of country which has been inspired by the stories of the past. It is the stories of the glorious past which encourage us to grapple with the problems of the present and to look with disdain upon those who fail to solve them. What fills our mind with more gratitude; what inspires us with greater heroism; what instills more patriotism than the struggles of the early colonial wars? The Anglo-Saxon energy which swept from this continent the dominion of those who sought only wealth, and which substituted the thrift of the voyagers of the *Mayflower* and of the settlers of Jamestown— which Speaks of the battles with the Indians, which tells of the glories not only of victories but of the defeats of the heroes of the Revolution—all are incentives for purer and better citizenship. And so, too, as we recall the struggles to the death of the descendants of these earlier settlers in the greatest civil war that the world has ever known, let us to-day, both in charity and in patriotism, remember them all as heroes. While we may differ as to the principles for which they fought, there is no conflict of opinion, no divergence in thought, which bids us to-day to withhold our admiration for all those who took part in that great struggle. It was but a page in our nation's history, but a page shaded by human blood. It was but the working out the will of Divine Providence, so that from its baptism of blood our republic might emerge greater, stronger and more powerful than ever before, that there might thereafter be no sectional hate, no dividing line in the patriotism of our people. This it is which should inspire us to-day. More progress, a further advance in civilization, the extending of a helping hand to the afflicted and the welcoming word to the oppressed, should be concrete evidence of America's greatness and of the devotion of her people. Then it will be that our flag, now honored and respected, honored because of the power and the intelligence of our people, will take on additional lustre and additional significance as that of a nation that has accepted its duty to protect humanity at home and abroad, and to stand as the pacificator and preserver of the peace of the world."

At the conclusion of the afternoon exercises Governor Odell reviewed the New York State troops on the plaza in Forest Park. The review was held in the presence of a large assemblage and was an inspiring sight.

OPENING DAY

One year later, on April 30, 1904, the Exposition was formally opened to the public; elaborate exercises being held at eleven o'clock at the foot of the Louisiana Purchase Monument on the Plaza St. Louis. There were present a distinguished assemblage, including a delegation of the Senate and the House of Representatives, the National Commission, the Board of Lady Managers, representatives of foreign governments, Governors of States and their staffs, State Commissions, United States Government Board, Exposition officials, and others. The exercises were opened by a prayer by Rev. Frank W. Gunsaulus of Chicago, which was followed by an address by President Francis. The Treasurer of the Exposition, William H. Thompson, as chairman of the committee on grounds and buildings, introduced Isaac S. Taylor, who delivered the gold key to the buildings to President Francis and presented diplomas to his staff. An address followed by Director of Exhibits F.J.V. Skiff, who presented commissions to his staff, the chiefs of the various exhibit departments. Next followed addresses in behalf of the city of St. Louis by Hon. Rolla Wells, Mayor; in behalf of the National Commission by Hon. Thomas H. Carter, its President; in behalf of the United States Senate by Senator Henry E. Burnham; in behalf of the House of Representatives by Hon. James A. Tawney. New York State was especially honored in the selection of the president of her commission to speak in behalf of the domestic exhibitors. Hon. Edward H. Harriman was then introduced by President Francis.

ADDRESS OF PRESIDENT
HARRIMAN

After briefly complimenting the President and Directors of the Exposition, Mr. Harriman said:

"Our 'Domestic Exhibitors' could have no higher testimonial than that furnished by the magnificent buildings and grounds of this Exposition. We have here combined in brilliant variety the charms and beauties of garden, forest, lake and stream, embellished by these splendid structures, forming an harmonious whole certainly not equaled by any former Exposition. All credit is due the President and Directors, whose intelligence and untiring labors have conquered all obstacles and brought this World's Fair to a most auspicious and successful opening. One cannot view the result of their labors without being deeply impressed with the magnitude of their undertaking, and when we consider the exhibits which have been assembled within these grounds, we are led irresistibly to an appreciation of the multitude of forces which contributed to this great work, and particularly to the co-operation which must have existed to produce the result before us.

"I have the honor on this occasion to speak for our 'Domestic Exhibitors.' They are well represented by their works before you, and by these works you can know them.

"These exhibits represent in concrete form the artistic and industrial development of this country, and in viewing them one cannot but be impressed with the great improvement in the conditions affecting our material and physical welfare and with the corresponding advancement in our intellectual and esthetic life.

"Let us consider for a moment the processes by which this result has been reached. We have here collected the products of our artistic, scientific and industrial life. The raw materials of the farm, the vineyard, the mine and the forest have been transformed by the skilled artisan, the artist and the architect into the finished products before you. By the co-operation of all these resources, of all these activities, of all these workers, this result has been accomplished. From the felling of the trees in the forest, the tilling of the soil and the mining of the ore, through all the steps and processes required to produce from the raw material the complicated machine or the costly fabric, there must have been co-operation, and all incongruous elements and resistant forces must have been eliminated or overcome.

"The chief factor, therefore, which has contributed to these results is the co-operation of all our people. The first law of our civilization is the co-operation of all individuals to improve the conditions of life. By division of labor each individual is assigned to or takes his special part in our social organization. This specialization of labor has become most minute. Not only is this true in scientific and philosophic research, in professional and business life, but in the simplest and earliest occupations of men, such as the tilling of the soil, the specialist is found bringing to the aid of his industry expert and scientific knowledge.

"... In the division of labor and the resultant specialization of human activity we have necessarily different classes of workers, some of whom have adopted the co-operative idea by forming organizations by which they seek to better their conditions. No doubt each class of workers has its particular interests which may be legitimately improved by co-operation among its members, and thus far the labor organization has a lawful purpose, but while standing for its rights it cannot legitimately deny to any other class its rights, nor should it go to the extent of infringing the personal and inalienable rights of its members as individuals. On the contrary, it must accord to its own members and to others the same measure of justice that it demands for itself as an organization.

"In working out this problem there has been much conflict. Indeed, according to human experience, such conflict could not entirely be avoided, but in the end each class must recognize that it cannot exist independently of others; it cannot strike down or defeat the rights or interests of others without injuring itself. Should capital demand more than its due, by that demand it limits its opportunities, and, correspondingly, the laborer who demands more than his due thereby takes away from himself the opportunity to labor. No one can escape this law of co-operation. Self-interest demands that we must observe its just limitations. We must be ready to do our part and accord to all others the fair opportunity of doing their part. We must co-operate with and help our colaborer. We should approach the solution of each question which may arise with a reasonable and, better still, a friendly spirit. He who obstructs the reasonable adjustment of these questions, who fosters strife by appealing to class prejudice, may justly be regarded by all as an enemy to the best public interests....

"In conclusion, permit me to advert to the Louisiana Purchase, which we are now celebrating, and call attention to the importance of that event in securing to our people the fullest benefit of the co-operative idea. Manifestly, if our Government were restricted to the original territory of the United States, as defined by the Treaty of 1783, we must have encountered in many ways the opposition of governments, some of them European, which would have occupied the territory beyond our original south and west boundaries. Our trade and commerce moving from or to

our original territory would, necessarily, have been largely restricted by hostile foreign powers. The Louisiana Purchase not only more than doubled our territory by adding a country rich in material resources, but gave us control of the Mississippi river, and made possible the acquisition of the Oregon Territory, the Mexican cessions and the annexation of Texas.
...

"Though much has been done towards the development of this imperial domain, yet we may truly say that we have only seen the beginning of that development. The possibilities for the future are boundless. With a land of unparalleled resources, occupied by a people combining the best elements of our modern civilization and governed by laws evolved from the highest and best progress of the human race, no eye can foresee the goal to which a co-operation of all these forces must lead."

The Mexican Commissioner, A. R. Nuncio, spoke in behalf of the foreign exhibitors. The concluding address was made by Hon. William H. Taft, Secretary of War, who attended as the special representative of the President. At its conclusion the President of the United States, in the White House at Washington, pressed a key that started the machinery, unfurled the flags, set the cascades in motion, and thus opened the Exposition.

BENEFICENT RESULTS

To the question "Was the Louisiana Purchase Exposition a success?" the answer must be an unqualified affirmative. The value of any great exposition cannot be measured in dollars and cents any more than it can be measured in pounds and ounces. The great Fair at St. Louis was not projected as a money-making undertaking. It was held to commemorate a great event in American history and was designed to arouse a popular interest in the story of the acquisition of the Louisiana Territory and its glorious results; to more closely knit together the peoples of the earth in good fellowship and brotherly love; to give to all nations an opportunity to demonstrate to each other their progress in material things; to awaken in the American people a sense of civic pride and a determined resolution to maintain and advance the prestige which they now enjoy among the nations of the earth. Having fulfilled all this, who shall say that the Exposition has been a failure?

FAIR OFFICIALS FROM NEW YORK

The State of New York has every reason to be proud of her connection with the great Fair, not only in her official participation, which through the generous action and hearty support of the Executive and the Legislature was on a most liberal and comprehensive scale, but many of her sons were prominent in its building, in the creation of its artistic effects, and no less in the administration of its various departments. At the very inception of the work New York was honored in the appointment of Martin H. Glynn, of Albany, N. Y., as a member of the National Commission. Mr. Glynn was afterwards elected Vice-Chairman of the Commission and was one of its most active members. Laurence H. Grahame, of New York city, was Secretary of the National Commission. His genial personality, his wide acquaintance and his long experience in newspaper work admirably fitted him for the duties of the position, which he performed with fidelity. Mrs. Daniel Manning, of Albany, was President of the Board of Lady Managers. The position was one requiring marked executive ability, dignity and tact. Mrs. Manning performed the arduous duties falling to her lot with a grace and cordiality which won for her the love and esteem of the official delegates to the Exposition from throughout the world. She was signally honored on many occasions and is one of New York's most distinguished daughters. Judge Franklin Ferriss, the general counsel for the Exposition Company, and one of St. Louis' most eminent lawyers, went forth from our State many years ago to seek and find his fortune in the West.

CHIEFS OF EXHIBIT DEPARTMENTS

Of the thirteen chiefs of departments in the division of exhibits New York lays claim to six. The Department of Education and Social Economy, as well as the Department of Congresses, was under the direction of Dr. Howard J. Rogers, now Assistant Commissioner of Education of the State of New York, and formerly Deputy Superintendent of Public Instruction; also United States Director of Education and Social Economy at the Paris Exposition in 1900.

Milan H. Hulbert had charge of the great Department of Manufactures and Varied Industries. Mr. Hulbert is a native of Brooklyn and a graduate of the Brooklyn Polytechnic Institute. He was in charge of the Department of Varied Industries for the United States Commission to Paris in 1900. The Art Department was presided over by Professor Halsey C. Ives, now of St. Louis, but formerly of New York State. The old school house in which he received the ground work of his education still stands at Montour Falls, Schuyler county. Professor Ives was also Chief of Arts at the Columbian Exposition in 1893. The Chief of the Department of Machinery, Thomas M. Moore, is a native, and has always been a resident, of New York city. He was in charge of the Departments of Machinery, Transportation, Agricultural Implements, Graphic Arts and Ordnance at the Pan American Exposition in Buffalo.

Of late years Dr. Tarleton H. Bean, Chief of the Forest, Fish and Game Department, has been a resident of New York State. In 1895 he became the director of the Aquarium in New York city and rebuilt that establishment. He was Chief of the Department of Forestry and Fisheries for the United States at the Paris Exposition in 1900.

The Chief of the Department of Physical Culture, James E. Sullivan, has always been a New Yorker. He is an acknowledged athletic record authority and editor of the official athletic almanac. He was in charge of the American contingent that competed in the Olympic games at the Paris Exposition, and was also director of athletics at the Pan American Exposition.

SCULPTORS

The heroic equestrian statue "The Apotheosis of St. Louis," generally considered one of the finest works of its kind, which stood at the very gateway to the Fair grounds, symbolizing the cordial welcome extended by the city to her guests from every part of the world, was the work of Charles H. Niehaus, of New York city. The sculpture of the Louisiana Purchase monument, the surmounting figure typifying "Peace" and the base decoration of groups representing scenes connected with the purchase, was by Karl Bitter, chief of sculpture of the Exposition, another New Yorker. Just in front of the monument and looking upon the grand basin were four groups portraying frontier life, entitled "The Buffalo Dance", "A Step to Civilization", "Peril of the Plains", and "A Cowboy at Rest", all being the work of Solon Borglum, another New Yorker. The crowning artistic and architectural effects of the whole Fair were embraced in Festival Hall and the Cascades. These were the work of two New York men, Cass Gilbert and Emanuel S. Masqueray. Mr. Gilbert was the architect of Festival Hall and Mr. Masqueray designed the Cascades and the Colonnade of States. Mr. Masqueray had other notable pieces of work in evidence about the grounds.

The Palace of Manufactures, standing just to the east of the Plaza St. Louis, was the work of Messrs. Carrere and Hastings, also New Yorkers. It was regarded as one of the most successful structures upon the grounds from an architect's point of view and it was appropriate that to New York men should have been intrusted the construction of the building in which exhibits of manufactures were displayed, in view of the pre-eminence of our State from a manufacturing and commercial standpoint.

And so throughout all the departments of the great Fair and throughout the season, one constantly encountered those who by some tie were bound to New York. Many of her sons who had gone forth in their youth came back and called at the New York State building and recalled some pleasant incident of the old days or made grateful acknowledgment of some benefit which had come to them from their native state. One of the most delightful features of all the experiences of those who had the honor officially to represent the Empire State at St. Louis was the meeting of the sons and daughters who had long since left home.

CONCLUSION

The gates had scarcely closed for the last time when the work of destruction and demolition began. All of the beauties of the dream city which for seven months had been the admiration of thousands and an inspiration to all to do higher and better things, were swept away almost in a night and soon the whole scene will be restored to a park. To those who had come to love its majestic structures, its placid waterways, its attractive vistas and its fairy like illumination, comes a pang of regret tempered with the feeling of gratefulness that it ever existed and that it was their privilege to witness it secure in the knowledge that it shall always be theirs to remember and to dream of. Most effectually was the whole story told in an address on Chicago Day, by Ernest McGaphey, a poet from that city.

"In its truest sense this Exposition is epic and dramatic. The mere prose of it will come to lie neglected on the dusty shelves of statisticians, but its poetry will be a priceless legacy to generations that will follow. And thus there is one light only which may not fade from the windows of Time—one glint to illuminate the flight of the dying years—that gleam which lives in fancy and in memory.

"And when this vision of magic departs; when the ivory towers have vanished, and the sound of flowing waters has been stilled, there will exist with us yet the recollection of it all. And so at the end the most enduring fabric known to man is woven of the warp and woof of dreams. The canvas of the great painters will crumble, the curves of noble statuary be ground into dust by Time, and all this pageantry of art and commerce disappear. But memory will keep a record of these days as a woman will treasure old love letters, and in the last analysis the height and breadth, the depth and scope of this splendid achievement shall be measured by a dream."

CHAPTER II

The Louisiana Purchase Exposition Commission, State of New York

[ILLUSTRATION]

The first steps looking toward the official participation of the State of New York in the Louisiana Purchase Exposition were taken by the Legislature of 1902, which passed the following act, receiving executive approval on April 7, 1902:

CHAPTER 421, LAWS OF 1902

An Act to provide for the representation of the state of New York at the Louisiana purchase exposition at Saint Louis, Missouri, and making an appropriation therefor.

Became a law, April 7, 1902, with the approval of the Governor. Passed, three-fifths being present.

The People of the State of New York, represented in Senate and Assembly, do enact as follows:

SECTION 1. The governor is hereby authorized to appoint twelve commissioners to represent the state of New York at the Louisiana purchase exposition to be held at Saint Louis, Missouri, beginning on the first day of May, nineteen hundred and three, and ending on the thirtieth day of November, nineteen hundred and three, and for the purposes of this act such commissioners shall be known as the "Louisiana purchase exposition commission." Such commission shall encourage and promote a full and complete exhibit of the commercial, educational, industrial, artistic and other interests of the state and its citizens at such exposition, and shall provide, furnish and maintain, during the exposition, a building or room for a state exhibit and for the official headquarters of the state, and for the comfort and convenience of its citizens and its exhibitors.

2. The members of the commission shall receive no compensation for their services, but shall be entitled to the actual necessary expenses incurred while in discharge of duties imposed upon them by the commission. Such commission may provide a secretary whose compensation, to be fixed by it, shall be at the rate of not to exceed twenty-five hundred dollars a year for all services to be performed in carrying out the provisions of this act, and may also provide such other clerical assistance and office facilities as it deems necessary, but no salaries or expenses shall be incurred for a longer period than ninety days after the close of the exposition.

3. The sum of one hundred thousand dollars, or so much thereof as may be necessary, is hereby appropriated out of any moneys in the treasury not otherwise appropriated for the purposes of this act. Such money shall be

paid by the treasurer on the warrant of the comptroller issued upon a requisition signed by the president and secretary of the commission, accompanied by an estimate of the expenses for the payment of which the money so drawn is to be applied. Within ninety days after the close of the exposition, such commission shall make a verified report to the comptroller of the disbursements made by it, and shall return to the state treasury the unexpended balance of money drawn in pursuance of this act. No indebtedness nor obligation shall be incurred under this act in excess of the appropriation herein made.

4. The commission shall, as requested by the governor, from time to time, render to him reports of its proceedings.

5. This act shall take effect immediately.

THE COMMISSION

Pursuant to the provisions of this act, Governor Odell named as the twelve members of the Commission: Edward H. Harriman, of New York city; Louis Stern, of New York city; Edward Lyman Bill, of New York city; William Berri, of Brooklyn; Cyrus E. Jones, of Jamestown; Lewis Nixon, of New York city; John C. Woodbury, of Rochester; Frank S. McGraw, of Buffalo; John K. Stewart, of Amsterdam; James H. Callanan, of Schenectady; John Young, of Geneseo; and Mrs. Norman E Mack, of Buffalo.

A few months after the appointment of the Commission, Cyrus E. Jones, of
Jamestown, resigned, and the Governor named Frederick R. Green, of Fredonia, in his place.

The results accomplished by the Commission as attested by the number of awards received in all of the exhibit departments; in the beauty and utility of the State building; in the careful procedure as to the expenditure of State funds, all bear testimony to the wisdom of the Chief Executive in the appointment of a Commission, all of the members of which were of acknowledged prominence either in professional, business or social life.

Throughout its entire existence the Commission worked with a singular unanimity and with a hearty interest but seldom found in commissions of this character. It held twenty-five regular meetings and two special meetings, the aggregate of attendance at all meetings being two hundred thirty-one, making an average attendance of eight and fifty-nine hundredths at each meeting. When it is considered that each member had large personal interests, and that he served the State absolutely without compensation, only necessary expenses being allowed by statute, and that a majority of the members of the Commission were obliged to travel from 160 to 450 miles to attend the meetings, its record for faithfulness to duty as shown by the above figures is one in which it may take a pardonable pride.

THE ORGANIZATION OF THE COMMISSION

By virtue of being first named by the Governor, Edward H. Harriman, of New York city, became President of the Commission, which completed its organization as follows: Vice-President, William Berri; Treasurer, Edward Lyman Bill. Executive Committee: Louis Stern, Chairman; William Berri, Lewis Nixon, John K. Stewart and James H. Callanan. Auditing Committee: James H. Callanan and John K. Stewart.

There was but one name presented for Secretary of the Commission, that of Mr. Charles A. Ball, of Wellsville. He was unanimously elected, with compensation of $2,500 per annum, the appointment taking effect December 8, 1902. In its choice of this officer the Commission was most fortunate. Efficient, faithful and courteous and with a wide circle of acquaintances, particularly among the prominent men of the Empire State, Mr. Ball was peculiarly qualified for the duties of the position. He was popular with his superiors and his subordinates, and so directed the work of the several departments within the Commission's jurisdiction as to procure the very best results.

Anthony Pfau was later appointed bookkeeper and assistant to the Secretary, and in the handling of a vast amount of detail work displayed commendable skill and patience. Seward H. French, stenographer to the Secretary, was always at his post of duty and cheerfully and faithfully served the Commission at all times. Herman Kandt, assistant bookkeeper, completed the office force.

An informal meeting was held in September, 1902, shortly after the names of the Commission were announced by the Governor. At this meeting an invitation was extended on behalf of the Louisiana Purchase Exposition Company to attend the ceremonies in connection with the allotment of sites for the various State buildings. The President appointed Commissioners Stewart, Woodbury and Callanan a committee to represent the Commission on that occasion, and on behalf of the State of New York, to accept the site for its building. The ceremonies in connection with this occasion are described elsewhere. The first formal meeting of the

Commission was called on December 3, 1902, at 120 Broadway, New York city.

At this meeting the Commission determined to maintain offices at 120 Broadway, New York city, until such time as the New York State building was opened at St. Louis, and for the expedition of business the following by-laws were provided:

BY-LAWS

First. The officers of the Louisiana Purchase Exposition Commission of the State of New York shall consist of a President, Vice-President, Treasurer and Secretary.

Second. Regular meetings of the Commission shall be held in the rooms of the Commission in New York city on the second Wednesday of every month, at two o'clock P. M., and all members shall be notified by the Secretary one week in advance of such meeting.

Third. Three members of the Commission shall constitute a quorum at all regular meetings.

Fourth. An Executive Committee of five members, appointed by the Commission, shall choose one of their number for Chairman, who shall act also as Chairman at the meetings of the Commission in the absence of the President or Vice-President. The Executive Committee shall meet at least once a month, and shall report at the regular meetings of the Commission. Three members of the Executive Committee shall form a quorum for the transaction of business.

Fifth. Any three members of the Commission may call for a special meeting, through the Secretary, of the entire Commission, at any time, by giving one week's notice.

Sixth. There shall be an Auditing Committee of two, whose duty it shall be to examine and audit all bills and accounts when properly verified. Such Committee shall report to the Commission at each meeting the amounts of bills and accounts so audited, together with the total thereof.

Seventh. A Treasurer shall be appointed by the Commission, who shall pay all bills when they have been properly verified and audited by the Auditing Committee.

Eighth. The Secretary shall prepare and forward to each member of the Commission a copy of the proceedings of the previous meeting in his regular monthly calls for meetings.

Ninth. The order of business at monthly meetings shall be as follows:

1. Reading of minutes of previous meeting 2. Report of Executive Committee 3. Report of the Treasurer 4. Report of regular and special committees 5. Unfinished business 6. Communications 7. New business

A STATE BUILDING

These preliminary formalities over, the Commission began in earnest the work of preparation for the State's participation at St. Louis. Believing that the most conspicuous feature of the State's participation in the Exposition, especially so far as the impression which would be made upon visitors was concerned, would be her State building, the Commission gave its first attention to this feature. Having been assigned such a commanding site, the Commission kept in mind that it was incumbent upon them to erect upon it a building of appropriate dignity and dimensions. It soon became evident that, with the appropriation already made, it would be impossible to erect a suitable building, maintain it and make suitable exhibits in the great departments of the Fair in which the State of New York stands pre-eminent. Steps were, therefore, taken to procure an additional appropriation from the Legislature of 1903, the matter being placed in the hands of the Executive Committee.

THE ARCHITECT

At the April meeting Mr. Clarence Luce, of New York city, was appointed the Commission's architect, and the plans for a State building presented by him were accepted. On June thirtieth a special meeting was called for the purpose of considering bids for the erection of the building and hearing the report of a special committee, consisting of Messrs. Luce and Van Brunt, who had visited St. Louis to further the interests of the Commission in this matter.

THE CONTRACTORS

Bids were received from several firms of contractors, ranging from $80,000 down to the contract price of the building, viz., $56,518, at which figure Messrs. Caldwell & Drake, of Columbus, Ind., contracted to complete the building in accordance with plans and specifications of the architect. The construction work was immediately inaugurated and was pushed forward so rapidly that the December meeting of the Commission, which was held on the eighteenth of that month, took place in the New York State building on the World's Fair grounds. After inspecting the building and carefully noting the progress which was being made, the Commission adjourned to meet at the Planters Hotel at seven o'clock in the evening. Through the courtesy of Honorable George J. Kobusch, president of the St. Louis Car Company, the private car "Electra" conveyed the members of the Commission to the grounds and return.

EMBELLISHMENT AND FURNISHING

An offer from the Aeolian Company, of New York city, to install, at its own expense, a pipe organ in the building was accepted, and an appropriation of $3,500 was made for an ornamental case to contain the organ which would be a distinctive addition to the decoration of the entrance hallway. In the meantime the matter of furnishing the State building had been in the hands of a Furniture Committee, who had made an exhaustive investigation upon the subject. In March a contract was made with Herter Brothers, of New York city, for furnishing the State building, in accordance with specifications prepared by the Commission, for $18,000.

THE COMPLETION OF THE BUILDING

By dint of prodigous effort the building was completed, entirely furnished and ready for the reception of guests on the opening day of the Exposition, at which time the offices of the Commission were opened in the State building, the New York offices remaining open throughout the summer in charge of Harry A. Sylvester.

The architect was commended for the prompt completion of his work in the following resolutions:

"*Whereas*, in originality of design, perfection in detail and attractiveness in equipment, the New York State building at the Louisiana Purchase Exposition is thoroughly representative of the dignity and position of the Empire State,

"*Resolved*, therefore, that the thanks of this Commission be tendered to the architect, Mr. Clarence Luce, as a token of our appreciation of his skill, talent and artistic tastes in creating a structure which meets with the warmest approval of this Commission, and which is a fitting home for New York at the World's Fair of 1904.

"*Resolved*, that the secretary be instructed to forward to Mr. Luce a copy of these resolutions, suitably engrossed."

Throughout the entire Exposition period there were but very few days that from one to three Commissioners were not present at the State building.

By resolution the Commission determined that the lady Commissioner and the wives of Commissioners, assisted by the official hostess, should be hostesses of the State building during the period of the Exposition, and in the absence of those, that the official hostess should act in that capacity, and it was further determined that any Commissioner or a majority of the Commissioners present at the New York State building at any time should constitute a house committee, and have full charge of the State building.

PLANS FOR PARTICIPATION

During the earlier meetings of the Commission they were waited upon by representatives of the Exposition Company, and by committees or representatives of organizations within the State either offering to co-operate with the Commission in the preparation of exhibit material or requesting appropriations from the Commission's funds to enable them to prepare exhibits.

In February, 1903, Honorable George L. Parker, a representative of President Francis, addressed the Commission, urging them to see that New York State was properly represented. He, stated that the people of the West expected great things of New York State; that the city of St. Louis and the territory the acquisition of which was commemorated by the Fair, spent large sums of money in the city of New York alone, and for that reason it was hoped and expected that New York should lead the other States of the Union.

Later in the year, Dr. J. A. Holmes, chief of the Department of Mines and Metallurgy, appeared before the Commission by invitation and made some interesting remarks concerning the scientific exhibit, which he felt it incumbent upon the State to make. He stated that there was no geological survey, either national or State, as valuable as that of the State of New York, and strongly advocated that a model oil well derrick be erected.

The Legislature of 1903 passed two acts which affected either directly or indirectly the work of the Commission. The first act provided $50,000 for participation in the dedication ceremonies of the Exposition and is as follows:

CHAPTER 189, LAWS OF 1903

An Act making an appropriation for the due and appropriate participation by the state in the ceremonies attending the dedication of buildings of the Louisiana purchase exposition.

Became a law, April 22, 1903, with the approval of the Governor. Passed, three-fifths being present.

The People of the State of New York, represented in Senate and Assembly, do enact as follows:

SECTION 1. The sum of fifty thousand dollars, or so much thereof as may be necessary, is hereby appropriated out of any money in the treasury, not otherwise appropriated, payable to the order of the governor, as he may require the same, to be expended by him in such manner as he may deem proper, for the due and appropriate participation by the state in the ceremonies attending the dedication of buildings of the Louisiana purchase exposition, to be held on April thirtieth, and May first and second, nineteen hundred and three, in the city of Saint Louis; and for the transportation, subsistence and other necessary expenses of the commander-in-chief and his staff, and of such portion of the national guard or naval militia of this state as may be directed to attend, and for the replacement by purchase of such military property of the state, as may be rendered unserviceable by this duty; provided that officers and men performing this duty shall serve without pay.

§ 2. This act shall take effect immediately.

The second act amended the original act providing for State representation, and increased the Commission's appropriation by $200,000, making $300,000 in all.

The act follows:

CHAPTER 546, LAWS OF 1903

An Act to amend chapter four hundred and twenty-one of the laws of nineteen hundred and two, entitled "An act to provide for the representation of the state of New York at the Louisiana Purchase exposition at Saint Louis, Missouri, and making an appropriation therefor."

Became a law, May 11, 1903, with the approval of the Governor. Passed, three-fifths being present.

The People of the State of New York, represented in Senate and Assembly, do enact as follows:

SECTION 1. Sections one, two and three, of chapter four hundred and twenty-one, of the laws of nineteen hundred and two, are hereby amended so as to read as follows:

Section 1. The governor is hereby authorized to appoint twelve commissioners to represent the state of New York at the Louisiana purchase exposition to be held at Saint Louis, Missouri, beginning on the first day of May, nineteen hundred and four, and ending on the thirtieth day of November, nineteen hundred and four, and for the purposes of this act such commissioners shall be known as the Louisiana purchase exposition commission. Such commission shall encourage and promote a full and complete exhibit of the commercial, educational, industrial, artistic and other interests of the state and its citizens at such exposition, and shall provide, furnish and maintain, during the exposition, a building or room for a state exhibit and for the official headquarters of the state, and for the comfort and convenience of its citizens and its exhibitors. Such commission shall have power and authority, in their discretion, to sell or otherwise dispose of any building, furniture, fixtures or other property which shall have been acquired by it pursuant to the provisions of this section.

*§*2. The members of the commission shall receive no compensation for their services, but shall be entitled to the actual necessary expenses incurred while in discharge of duties imposed upon them by the commission. Such commission may provide a secretary whose compensation, to be fixed by it, shall be at the rate of not to exceed four thousand dollars a year for all services to be performed in carrying out the provisions of this act, and may also provide such other clerical assistance and office facilities as it deems necessary, but no salaries or expenses shall be incurred for a longer period than ninety days after the close of the exposition.

*§*3. The sum of two hundred thousand dollars, in addition to the sum of one hundred thousand dollars heretofore appropriated by chapter four hundred and twenty-one of the laws of nineteen hundred and two which is hereby reappropriated for the above specified purposes, or so much thereof as may be necessary, is hereby appropriated out of any moneys in the treasury not otherwise appropriated for the purposes of this act. Such money shall be paid by the treasurer on the warrant of the comptroller issued upon a requisition signed by the president and secretary of the commission, accompanied by an estimate of the expenses for the payment of which the money so drawn is to be applied. Within ninety days after the close of the exposition, such commission shall make a verified report to the comptroller of the disbursements made by it, and shall return to the state treasury the unexpended balance of money drawn in pursuance of this act. No indebtedness nor obligation shall be incurred under this act in excess of the appropriation herein made. No member of such commission, nor such officer, shall be personally liable for any debt or obligation created or incurred by him as such commissioner, or such officer, or by such commission, or any such officer.

*§*2. This act shall take effect immediately.

CHIEF EXECUTIVE OFFICER

The title of the Secretary was thereupon changed to that of Secretary and Chief Executive Officer, and he was clothed with all the authority and duties pertaining to the latter position, his salary being increased to $4,000 per annum. Later his duties were further prescribed by the following resolution:

"*Resolved*, that the Chief Executive Officer shall exercise such direction and management of the office as shall make effective the various agencies employed. He shall nominate to the Commission all clerks and employees in all the departments. He shall fix and establish all salaries of officers, clerks and employees, subject to the approval of the Commission. He shall in like manner have power to suspend, without pay, for cause, upon charges made in writing and filed in the office of the Commission, with such suspended officers, clerks or employees, and with the Chairman of the Executive Committee, any and all officers, clerks and employees of the Commission. Discharges or removals of such officers clerks or employees must be approved by the Executive Committee of the Commission. He shall have power to visit and examine the work and management of the several departments created by the Commission. It shall be his duty to make regular monthly reports to the Commission, and at such other times as the Commission may be in session or request such report."

CHIEFS OF DEPARTMENTS

At the meeting of the Commission held in June, 1903, the following chiefs of departments were appointed:

Charles H. Vick, of Rochester, Superintendent of Horticulture and Floriculture, to take effect July 1, 1903, at a salary of $2,000 per annum.

J. H. Durkee, of Florida, Superintendent of Agriculture, to take effect July 1, 1903, at a salary of $2,000 per annum.

DeLancey M. Ellis, of Rochester, Director of Education, to take effect June 15, 1903, at a salary of $2,000 per annum.

Later Mr. Ellis's title was changed to Director of Education and Social Economy, and he was placed in charge of the exhibits in the latter department in addition to those of the Department of Education.

APPROPRIATIONS FOR EXHIBITS

The following appropriations were made for exhibits:

Horticulture and Floriculture $20,000
Agriculture, including live stock and dairy products 25,000
Education 20,000
Social Economy:
  State Commission in Lunacy $1,800
  State Board of Charities 1,200
  State Department of Prisons 2,000
  State Department of Labor 1,000
  Craig Colony for Epileptics 500
  General expenses 1,000
           —————- $7,500
Forest, Fish and Game 18,000
Scientific 7,500
Fine Arts 10,000

———————

Total $108,000

In the departments of Agriculture, Horticulture, and Education and Social Economy the work was placed in charge of the chiefs above named. The Scientific exhibit was placed in charge of the Director of the State Museum. All of the above exhibits were subject to the supervisory control of the chief executive officer. The Forest, Fish and Game exhibit was placed under direct control of the chief executive officer, valuable assistance being rendered, however, by the Forest, Fish and Game Commission.

The Fine Arts exhibit was provided for in the following resolution:

"*Resolved*, that Mr. W. H. Low, of the Society of American Artists; Mr. H. W. Watrous, of the National Academy of Design; Mr. J. Carroll Beckwith, a member of the Art Commission of the city of New York; Mr. Louis Loeb, of the Society of Illustrators; Mr. Frank C. Jones, delegate to the Fine Arts Federation from the National Academy of Design; Mr. Grosvenor Atterbury, of the Architectural League of New York, and Mr. Herbert Adams, of the National Sculpture Society, be named as an executive committee on art for the State of New York, whose duty it shall be to aid the chief executive officer of this Commission to develop the New York State art exhibit at the Louisiana Purchase Exposition, said executive committee to serve without expense to this Commission."

By means of the various agencies provided for the preparation of exhibits, the work was pushed forward as rapidly as possible, the Commission keeping in touch with its progress through monthly reports filed with the chief executive officer by the heads of various departments.

ASSISTANCE BY EXPOSITION OFFICERS

By the time the Commission held its meeting in St. Louis in December space had been assigned for most all of the State exhibits. There was an evident disposition on the part of the Exposition Company to do all in their power to assist the State of New York in making its participation an unqualified success. In appreciation of this attitude the following resolution was passed at the meeting held in the city of St. Louis in December:

"*Resolved*, that the members of the New York Commission desire to express to the president of the Louisiana Purchase Exposition Company and the heads of the various departments with whom they have been brought in personal contact, their appreciation of the delightful courtesy extended them. It is obvious that there is a desire on the part of the Exposition authorities to facilitate the departmental work of New York in connection with the Exposition. We cannot fail to express our admiration of the gigantic task which the officers of this great international fair have carried to such a successful culmination. In the entire history of expositions, there has been evidenced no greater progress, and such work could not have been accomplished save through the most prodigious efforts on the part of the projectors of this vast enterprise. When St. Louis opens her exposition gates next year, it will be to invite the world to witness the greatest exposition in all history. And be it further

"*Resolved*, that the secretary be instructed to forward a copy of this resolution to President Francis and the heads of the various departments of the Exposition."

NEW YORK DAY

The Commission took considerable care in the choosing of a day to be known as "New York Day." It was considered important that a date should be named upon which it would be possible for the Governor to be present. Moreover it seemed essential that no date during the heat of the summer should be designated, as but few New Yorkers would be apt to be present at St. Louis at that time, and, therefore, after mature consideration, October fourth was designated as New York State Day.

The Legislature of 1904 passed an additional appropriation of $40,000, by chapter 640, which is given below:

CHAPTER 640, LAWS OF 1904

An act, to make an additional appropriation to provide for the representation of the state of New York at the Louisiana purchase exposition at Saint Louis, Missouri.

[Became a law May 9, 1904, with the approval of the Governor.

Passed, three-fifths being present.]

The People of the State of New York, represented in Senate and Assembly, do enact as follows:

Section 1. The sum of forty thousand dollars, or so much thereof as may be necessary, in addition to the money heretofore appropriated, is hereby appropriated out of any moneys in the treasury, not otherwise appropriated, for the purpose of providing for the representation of the state of New York at the Louisiana purchase exposition at Saint Louis, Missouri. The money hereby appropriated shall be applicable to the purposes specified in chapter four hundred and twenty-one of the laws of nineteen hundred and two, as amended by chapter five hundred and forty-six of the laws of nineteen hundred and three, and shall be paid out in accordance with the provisions of such act, by the treasurer on the warrant of the comptroller issued upon a requisition signed by the president and secretary of the commission, accompanied by an estimate of the expenses for the payment of which the money so drawn is to be applied.

*§*2. This act shall take effect immediately.

This made possible the elaboration of some of the plans which the Commission had in mind.

HISTORY OF THE EXPOSITION PERIOD

The history of the Exposition period will be found in other chapters of this report. A description of the State building, detailed accounts of the dedicatory exercises and the exercises upon State Day, as well as other important functions, are given. The exhibits in the various departments are fully described, and the results of the inspection by the juries are given.

Throughout the entire life of the Commission death did not enter its ranks, nor the ranks of its attaches, nor did any untoward incident arise, although early in the morning of November twenty-first a catastrophe was narrowly averted. In the middle of the night a fire was found smouldering in the basement of the building, which, through the prompt action of the watchman on duty, was extinguished without doing extensive damage. Many were asleep in the building at the time, and but for the presence of mind and courage of those on duty the consequences might have been too fearful to contemplate.

DISPOSITION OF EXHIBITS

At a meeting of the Commission, held just before the close of the Exposition, the following resolution was passed:

"*Resolved*, that the Louisiana Purchase Exposition Commission of the State of New York hereby authorizes the Secretary and Chief Executive Officer, Charles A. Ball, to turn over to the Lewis and Clark Exposition Commission of the State of New York any of the exhibits, or such part thereof as the latter may desire in the various exhibit departments working under the auspices of the Louisiana Purchase Exposition Commission of the State of New York for the use of said Lewis and Clark Exposition Commission, State of New York, with the proviso that in the case of individual exhibits forming a part of said exhibits the Lewis and Clark Exposition Commission, State of New York, must get the consent of the owners of said exhibits and relieve the Commission of all responsibility relating thereto and return said individual exhibits to their owners at the close of the Lewis and Clark Exposition, it being understood, however, that said Lewis and Clark Exposition Commission must take possession of these exhibits not later than December 15, 1904."

Upon requisition from the latter Commission the Secretary and Chief Executive Officer turned over to the Lewis and Clark Exposition Commission the following material: The complete exhibit of the State in the departments of Education and Social Economy; the complete exhibit in the Department of Forestry, Fish and Game, with the exception of the Log-cabin and the Forest Nursery and a portion of the State exhibits in the departments of Mines and Metallurgy and Agriculture.

ACKNOWLEDGMENT TO PRESIDENT FRANCIS AND OTHERS

President Francis and the Exposition officials generally throughout the entire Exposition period extended to the Commission every courtesy and evinced a hearty interest in the work of New York, endeavoring to further the interests of the Commission in every possible direction. Desiring to express in suitable terms its appreciation of these courtesies the Commission also passed the following resolutions at its meeting held at the close of the Exposition:

"WHEREAS, the Empire State is about to close its official connection with this, the greatest of World's Fairs; and,

"WHEREAS, the members of the Louisiana Purchase Exposition Commission of the State of New York, appointed by the Governor, desire to express to the officials of the Fair their sincere appreciation of the hearty co-operation which they have rendered the members of this Commission, in every way facilitating the work of New York in each department of State representation; and,

"WHEREAS, in all of the Commission's relations with the officers of the Exposition, not only has every courtesy been shown the Commission, but there has been a friendly desire to promote their interests; therefore, be it

"*Resolved*, that the cordial thanks of this Commission be extended to the President of the Louisiana Purchase Exposition Commission, Honorable David R. Francis; to the Secretary, Honorable Walter B. Stevens; to the Director of Exhibits, Honorable Frederick J.V. Skiff; to the Director of Works, Honorable Isaac S. Taylor, and to the chiefs of each exhibit department of the Exposition, with whom the Commission or its representatives have been brought in contact; be it further

"*Resolved*, that these resolutions be spread upon the permanent records of the Commission and a copy of the same forwarded to each of the above named Exposition officials."

COMMENDATION FOR STAFF

With the exception of closing up its affairs, this marked the end of the Commission's work and before adjournment the following resolutions commending the efficiency and faithfulness of its employees were spread upon the minutes, and a copy was sent to each attache:

"WHEREAS, this Commission is about to close its work, and for this reason must necessarily very soon dispense with the services of the appointees who have served under it since its organization and during the life of the Louisiana Purchase Exposition, it is eminently fitting that we make record of the faithfulness and loyalty with which said appointees of every character whatsoever have discharged their respective duties; therefore, be it

"*Resolved*, that we take pleasure in certifying to the efficient manner in which our Secretary and Chief Executive Officer, Mr. Charles A. Ball, has discharged the important duties attached to his position. From the very inception of the work upon which this Commission entered, Mr. Ball has proven to be most loyal and faithful, and has ever been ready and willing to carry out the instructions of this Commission. His wide acquaintance with the people of New York State, and especially with her official representatives, has been of inestimable service to this Commission, not only while the various exhibits were being developed, but also during the Exposition period itself. That Mr. Ball has popularized the Commission's work at St. Louis is attested by the universal commendation which he has received from New York people who have come in contact with him during their visits to the Exposition and to the New York State building. Mr. Ball has shown himself to be most capable in directing the various appointees at the State building and in the several exhibit departments in the discharge of their various duties, and has not only carried an this work to the best interests of the State, but in such a manner as to greatly endear himself to this Commission and to all of its employees as well. His foresight in providing for the necessary vigilance during the hours of the night in the protection of the lives of those in the State building, once seriously jeopardized by fire, as well as the property of the State from loss by fire, is especially entitled to the sincere thanks and gratitude of this Commission;

"*Resolved*, that in Chief Clerk Anthony Pfau, Stenographer Seward H. French, Clerks Herman W. Kandt and Harry A. Sylvester, the experience of this Commission has demonstrated that it made most worthy selections. They have been faithful assistants to Mr. Ball in the discharge of his duties and this Commission gladly records its commendation of the ability with which they have discharged their duties;

"*Resolved*, that we extend to the Honorable Frank J. Le Fevre, the Superintendent, and Mr. George B. Cowper, the Assistant Superintendent, our sincere appreciation for the most praiseworthy manner in which they have discharged the difficult duties falling to them, and our very pleasant relations with them shall be ever held in grateful remembrance;

"*Resolved*, that we have been especially gratified with the highly satisfactory manner in which Mrs. Dore Lyon, the hostess, Mrs. F. B. Applebee, the assistant hostess, and Miss Laura C. MacMartin, the matron at the State building, have acquitted themselves of the duties assigned to them. We especially accord them our highest appreciation;

"*Resolved*, that this Commission especially commends the faithful and efficient services rendered by Mr. DeLancey M. Ellis, Mr. J. H. Durkee, Mr. Charles H. Vick, Mr. A. B. Strough, Mr. H. H. Hindshaw, Mr. Harry Watrous and Mr. Charles M. Kurtz, and all their assistants in the various exhibit departments, in which our State has signalized her pre-eminence as shown by the large number of awards received. These gentlemen have always proven loyal to the interests of the State and to this Commission and they are entitled to the highest regard by this Commission;

"*Resolved*, that for all the subordinate employees of this Commission throughout the State building and all the departments working under this Commission, this Commission desires at this time to make complete record of their efficient loyalty and faithfulness in the discharge of the various duties assigned to them, and we especially attest our full appreciation for their efforts at all times to make the work of this Commission in enhancing the interests of the State a complete success;

"*Resolved*, that we cannot forget the efficiency of Mr. Hugh J. Baldwin, who, we believe, by his watchfulness at the time of the fire in the State building, saved the lives of many of the occupants of the building as well as the property of the State; for Mr. Hugh W. Bingham, also on duty during that night, who so efficiently aided Mr. Baldwin in protecting life and property, we here record our sincerest gratitude; and be it further

"*Resolved*, that these resolutions be spread upon the minutes of the proceedings of this Commission and the Secretary is hereby authorized to transmit a copy of these resolutions to each of the employees of this Commission."

[Illustration: VARIED INDUSTRIES BUILDING]

CHAPTER III

New York State Building

The New York State building was admirably located upon one of the most attractive sites within the gift of the Exposition Company, to whom the Commission, in behalf of the State of New York, desire to make grateful acknowledgment.

THE SITE

The building stood on the brow of a hill, the land sloping off gently to the north, and faced upon a broad plaza, through which ran one of the most frequented highways within the grounds, known as Commonwealth avenue. For its neighbors were the buildings of Kansas, Iowa, Massachusetts, Ohio, Wisconsin and Oklahoma, while westward, at the foot of the hill, was located the great cage erected by the United States government, which held the exhibit of live birds from the Smithsonian Institute.

To no state, with the possible exception of Missouri, the home state, was so large a site assigned as to New York. Its extent, the undulating character of the grounds, and the presence of many beautiful, stately trees, afforded countless opportunities for landscape effects. From the opening day the grounds presented a charming appearance, the well-kept lawns giving place here and there to large beds of nasturtiums, poppies, cannae, and rhododendrons, while at the lowest point on the grounds, near the northeast corner, was located a lily pond. It was filled with the choicest aquatic plants of every variety, which were furnished through the courtesy of Shaw's Gardens and the Missouri Botanical Society. During the season many beautiful bouquets of varicolored blossoms were gathered and its surface was almost entirely covered by odd shaped leaves from which peeped here and there the buds of pond lilies.

TRANSFER OF SITE TO THE STATE

The site was formally turned over to the Commission on October 1, 1902, and was received by a committee appointed by the president, consisting, of Commissioners John K. Stewart, John C. Woodbury and James H. Callanan. The ceremony took place in the presence of Honorable David R. Francis, president of the Exposition Company, the Director of Works, and other Exposition officials, the committee of the New York State Commission and invited guests.

The exercises were brief but impressive. President Francis spoke as follows:

REMARKS OF PRESIDENT FRANCIS

"A universal exposition, either in the United States or elsewhere, would be incomplete if the Empire State of the American Union were not represented. This site has been selected for the great State of New York, and upon this location we trust there will be erected a structure which will be in keeping with the glorious record New York and her sons have made from the beginning of this country. New York needs no encomium from me, none in fact from her sons. She speaks for herself. The Director of Works will present to the chairman of the New York Commission the site for the building of the State of New York."

Honorable Isaac S. Taylor, Director of Works, then formally presented the site to the Commission, handing to Commissioner John K. Stewart a handsome banner of purple silk, upon which was painted the coat of arms of the State of New York. Driving the staff in the ground, thus marking the site, Commissioner Stewart said:

REMARKS OF COMMISSIONER STEWART

"Mr. President and Gentlemen of the Commission: In behalf of New York
State I receive this emblem. We shall erect here a building suitable for the great Empire State of New York. I wish to introduce to you Honorable James H. Callanan, of Schenectady, who will respond in behalf of the Commission."

Commissioner James H. Callanan then made the following address:

ADDRESS OF COMMISSIONER CALLANAN

"In behalf of the Commission representing the Commonwealth of New York, I take pleasure in accepting the site allotted for the Empire State's building at the Louisiana Purchase Exposition. With this acceptance I beg you to receive the assurance from our Commission that New York will do her share to make the Exposition an unquestioned success. Upon this site we expect to erect a handsome and commodious structure where New Yorkers may meet one another during the Exposition, and where they may welcome their fellow citizens from every section of our common country. New York is also desirous of having exhibited here upon these spacious grounds the evidences of her prestige in the domain of manufacture, of commerce, of agriculture, of science and of art.

"The American people are progressive. The indomitable courage and ambition of the American knows no cessation of effort, no lagging behind. The expositions held in our country have celebrated great epochs of our advancement, and they will be pointed out to future generations as evidences of the onward march of a people unparalleled in the history of the human race.

"To these great achievements of a mighty people it is impossible to estimate the share contributed by the sturdy pioneers and their descendants of this vast tract of country, the cession of which more than doubled the area of our country a century ago. What great states have been carved out of this territory! What wonderful wealth of resources have been brought forth here! What a splendid citizenship has been established in this vast region! New York rejoices with you in the giant strides made by this newer section of our country.

"It certainly is most appropriate at this time when the republic is reaching out as a world power that we should celebrate the anniversary of the first great chapter in the history of our national expansion. Time has proven that Jefferson and his compeers built greater than they knew, for by that acquisition of territory there was developed a spirit of national progress that did not cease even when we first learned to know no superior among the nations of the earth.

"Representatives of half a dozen different nations met in the smoking room of an ocean liner sometime ago. It was suggested that each nation be toasted. An Englishman paid a glowing tribute to his country. A Frenchman lauded his nation and a Russian eulogized the land of the Czar.

Then an American arose and said: 'Here is to the United States, bounded on the north by the North Pole, on the east by the rising sun, on the south by the South Pole, and on the west by the setting sun.' As he finished another American present requested that he be permitted to attempt an improvement on the toast given by his countryman, which request was granted. He then toasted the United States in this fashion: 'Here's to the United States, bounded on the north by the Aurora Borealis, on the east by infinite chaos, on the south by the procession of the Equinoxes, and on the west by the day of judgment.' This indeed is extravagant language, but that fellow possessed the American spirit which recognizes no limit to the possibilities of our future.

"I recognize that this is no occasion for state boasting. Each state, territory and American possession is unselfishly interested in the success of this Exposition. However, in connection with what New York is expected to do for this grand enterprise, you will pardon, I know, this very brief reference I make to New York's supremacy in population, in wealth, in manufactures and in commerce. I think it less than twenty years ago that New York was ahead in agricultural productions, too. Agricultural supremacy has been tending westward for nearly a half century, however, and we cheerfully surrender to your broad prairies. Iowa, Ohio and Illinois now outrank us in farm industry, the first once a part of the Louisiana tract and the other two cut from the Northwest Territory.

"An Eastern farmer on his first visit to the west asked his Western brother how it was that 'he could plow such straight furrows over such enormous fields.' 'That's easy,' said the native, 'we follow the parallels of latitude and the meridians of longitude.' That reply was significant. It demonstrates quite fully where agriculture is king in the United States.

"The end of the great strides that you are making here in the west is not in sight. Some day your population will be as dense as ours. Slowly, but steadily, the center of population is creeping westward and by another decade or so it will most likely cross the great Father of Waters and move across the land which Jefferson's genius gave to the republic. New York will be more powerful by reason of your greatness. Your increasing productions will contribute to our commercial prestige more and more as the years roll on to make our metropolis continue to be the greatest seaport on this continent for all time.

"We share your glory in more ways than this, too. Many of the sturdy men and women who have settled within the confines of this great region were native New Yorkers. Our blood has been mingled with yours and our children are first cousins of yours. New York gave to you because she could spare and you accepted of us because you wanted the best you could find.

"New York then bids the people of this section All Hail! We are with you heart and soul to make the Exposition a magnificent success. New York has never failed when a patriotic effort was demanded and as ever before she will now respond with enthusiasm and will do everything possible here to sustain her imperial position.

"Let us hope that the Exposition will accomplish all that is intended. Let our prayer be that all Americans who pass within the gates when all shall be made ready for the opening of this Exposition in 1904, will cherish a higher ambition and a greater love of country and be impelled to declare with the poet, that

"'There is a land of every land the pride,
Beloved of Heaven, o'er all the world beside,
where brighter suns dispense serener light,
And milder moons imparadise the night.
Oh, thou shalt find howe'er thy footsteps roam,
That land thy country and that spot thy home.'"

At the conclusion of Commissioner Callanan's remarks the assemblage dispersed.

DEDICATION OF THE SITE

The site was formally dedicated at the time of the formal dedication ceremonies of the Exposition, the special ceremonies being held directly after the general exercises held in observance of State Day, on May 2, 1903. There were present Governor and Mrs. Odell, the Governor's staff, a joint committee of the Legislature, Exposition officials, members of the State Commission and invited guests.

Having assembled upon the site, William Berri, Vice-President of the Commission, addressed Governor Odell as follows:

ADDRESS BY VICE-PRESIDENT BERRI

"*Governor Odell*: It gives the New York State Commission to the Louisiana Purchase Exposition very great pleasure to have you present here to-day to participate in the simple exercises authorized by the Commission connected with the beginning of the work of construction of the New York State building which is to be erected upon this site. A more desirable grant of space on the Plateau of States could not have been made for us by the management of this Exposition, and we hope to place here a building that will add dignity to the location and worthily represent the State of New York in architectural beauty and practical usefulness. Your commission has been fortunate in securing for the architect Mr. Clarence Luce, and the plans and drawings which we have decided upon from his hand give promise of a structure that the State we represent will be proud of, and we shall also endeavor to so furnish it and utilize its facilities as to make it a serviceable and attractive addition to the large number of State buildings that are to be erected in its vicinity.

"Everything has to have a beginning, so we are here to-day to begin our work of actual construction, and it is specially fitting that we should have present the Governor of New York to assist in the ceremonies attendant therewith, for he has always heartily supported the project of the St. Louis Exposition and has furthered its interests on every occasion. Therefore, on behalf of the New York State Commission, I ask you, Governor Odell, to honor the great World's Fair of 1904 by performing the first actual work upon the structure we propose to erect by turning the first spadeful of earth for the State of New York and the New York State building."

The Governor responded briefly, commending the Commission for its work, predicting wonderful benefits to accrue from the Exposition and prophesying that New York would be at the forefront in all of its departments, after which he lifted the first spadeful of earth upon the site. He then handed the spade to Mrs. Odell, who lifted another sod; after which various ladies in the party performed the same act; at the conclusion of which the assemblage adjourned.

OPENING OF THE BUILDING

The building of the State of New York was the only building on the Terrace of States entirely ready for the reception of guests on the opening day of the Exposition. It was a structure thoroughly in keeping with the dignity and prestige of the great Empire State. Of marked simplicity in design, there was in its every line and appointment evidence of the utmost refinement and culture.

The building was planned primarily for the comfort, accommodation and convenience of visitors from the Empire State, for the holding of such functions as the Commission were required to give in the name of the State, and for the meetings of any associations or delegations from New York attending the Exposition. It contained no exhibits of any kind, all of the exhibits being placed in the main exhibit palaces under the proper subdivision of the official classification.

THE ARCHITECTURE

The building was pure Italian in style, surmounted by a low dome and surrounded by verandas and terraces. Through the main approach one entered a large hall sixty feet square, running the full height of the building, arched and domed in the Roman manner, with galleries around the second story. From this hall ascended the grand staircase, both to the left and to the right.

MURAL DECORATIONS

Under the four arches were handsome mural paintings, the work of Florian Peixotto, illustrating "De Soto Discovering the Mississippi," "The French and Indian Occupation," "New York in 1803," and "New York in 1903." The four pendentives which supported the dome contained emblematic pictures representing the four States most benefited by the Louisiana Purchase, Missouri, Louisiana, Mississippi and Alabama. The lower hall was of the simple Doric order, and the staircase was augmented by two memorial columns surrounded by dancing groups beautifully modeled, each column surmounted by a light. To the right of the entrance hall, and separated from it only by huge pillars, was a large assembly hall fifty by sixty feet, which was used for receptions, dinners and other State functions given by the Commission. This hall was most richly decorated in old golds, Antwerp blues and siennas and, with its crystal chandeliers and barrel vaulted ceiling running up through the second story, was one of the most attractive features of the building. Beyond the grand hall were small dining rooms and serving rooms connected with the culinary department. To the left of the entrance hall were waiting rooms, writing rooms and retiring rooms for the accommodation of guests, while at the extreme south end of the building were two reading rooms, in which were on file the various daily papers of the State. But seldom were the reading rooms without visitors eagerly familiarizing themselves with what had happened at home subsequent to their departure. Also, on the first floor were coat rooms, a bureau of information, postoffice, telegraph and telephone offices.

OFFICES OF THE COMMISSION

The second floor contained the offices of the Commission, which were occupied by the Secretary and the clerical force, and also eight suites of rooms, consisting of parlor, bedroom and bath, for the accommodation of the members of the Commission and their guests. One of these suites, more handsomely furnished than the others, was called the "Governor's suite," and was reserved for his exclusive use. While not originally contemplated, the third floor in both the north and south ends of the building were finished and partitioned into rooms for the use of the attaches of the Commission. This increased the capacity of the building by eight rooms.

THE SCULPTURE

Eminent sculptors were employed to prepare the statuary for the building which was generally conceded to be as fine as any upon the Exposition grounds, being most admirably adapted to the building as to scale. There were two massive quadrigae flanking the dome typifying the "Progress of Art" and the "Progress of Commerce," which were the work of Phillip Martiny, to whom was also intrusted the work of preparing the elaborate group, crowding the main entrance to Festival Hall and entitled "Apollo and the Muses." About the huge columns flanking the steps which formed the approach and again about the columns at the foot of the grand staircase were dancing groups most gracefully modeled by Oscar L. Lenz. The same sculptor was also responsible for the figure of "Greeting" which stood in the lower niche at the north end of the building. The coat of arms of the State which appeared frequently in the scheme of decoration was by Allen G. Newman. The work of reproduction in staff of the models prepared by the artists was performed by Messrs. Barth & Staak.

THE LIGHTING

The lighting of the building throughout was by electricity, and was particularly effective in the main entrance hallway, in that the lights, for the most part, were concealed behind cornices giving a very soft effect, and displaying to the best advantage the mural paintings. Throughout the building electroliers of special design were used. In the main hallway they took the form of quaint Florentine lanterns which were particularly rich in modeling and were an important factor in the scheme of decoration.

THE FURNISHINGS

The furnishings were most appropriate and harmonious throughout, much of the furniture having been especially built for the place in which it was to stand. In the main hallway stood massive Florentine chairs and settees, with high backs, upholstered in mottled embossed leather, each bearing the coat of arms of the State. The waiting and writing rooms were appointed and finished in the same simple design which prevailed in the main hallway, light green being the dominating color, the furniture being of mahogany, upholstered in Bedford cord. The effect was most restful to the tired visitor who entered the rooms upon a warm summer day, and their popularity was attested by the number of Exposition visitors, both from New York and elsewhere, who sought their quiet and refreshing atmosphere to recover from the fatigue of Exposition sight seeing.

THE ARCHITECT

The entire work of designing the building, sculpture, decorations and furniture was intrusted to Mr. Clarence Luce, of 246 Fourth avenue, New York city. Thoroughly familiar with the traditions of the great Empire State, Mr. Luce made the work committed to him a matter of State as well as professional pride, and the result of his long experience, coupled with his artistic temperament and sound judgment, was a building to which each New Yorker pointed with the utmost pride and which each stranger praised unstintingly. The prompt completion of the work so thoroughly and satisfactorily done was a source of gratification to the Commission, who at the first meeting held in the building passed commendatory resolutions concerning Mr. Luce.

There were State buildings which represented an outlay of considerably more money, but none which typified the commonwealth for which it stood more thoroughly than did the New York State building.

THE RESTAURANT

A pleasant feature was a private restaurant, conducted by Messrs. Bayno & Pindat, of New York city, the former being the inventor of an electric range which was used in the preparation of food. The kitchen and commissary department was in the basement at the north end of the building. The privileges of the restaurant were by card only, and were extended to New Yorkers, Exposition officials and prominent Exposition visitors. The cuisine was most excellent, and throughout the season appetizing meals were served on the spacious verandas at the north end of the building, over which canopies had been erected, the illumination being furnished in the evening by electric lights, contained in Japanese lanterns. No restaurant upon the grounds enjoyed a greater popularity among those who were privileged to use it than did that of the New York State building.

THE ORGAN

To the Aeolian Company, of New York city, the Commission is indebted for one of the features of the building. This company placed a magnificent pipe organ in the east balcony of the rotunda, and in the gallery north of the grand hall, nearly 100 feet away, was installed an echo organ, while a set of cathedral chimes sounded softly from still another distant part of the building. All three instruments were under control of the organist at the console located upon the main floor of the entrance hall, and could be played either by hand or by music rolls manufactured by the Aeolian Company. The organ was equipped with an electric keyboard which permitted the playing of all three instruments or any single one, as the operator desired. The main instrument was contained in an artistic case, which, with its decorative ornament, was built by Charles and Jacob Blum, of New York city, and was an important enrichment of the hall.

Mr. S. H. Grover, a representative of the company, was in attendance throughout the summer and gave a recital each day at three o'clock in the afternoon. These recitals soon came to be a feature of the Exposition, and were largely attended by music lovers.

The program played on New York State day is given below, and is a fair specimen of the programs rendered throughout the season.

Overture, "Oberon" Von Weber
Serenade Schubert
The Nightingale Delibes
Overture, "Stradella" Flotow
Berceuse, "Jocelyn" Godard
Selections, No. 11, "La Boheme" Puccini
Am Meer Schubert
Introduction, Act III, "Lohengrin" Wagner

THE PIANO

The Commission also acknowledges the courtesy of Steinway & Co. in placing in the State building one of the finest instruments ever turned out by this famous firm of piano builders. Its purity of tone and singing qualities were remarkable, and during the season several recitals were given upon it by eminent musicians. The piano was appropriately named "The Wave," illustrating as it did the wonderful waterways of the Empire State. The case was made of white hard maple, admirably adapted for fine carving. Some distance from the edge of the top the smooth surface commenced to take the undulations of the surface of water, gradually increasing in volume until the edge was reached, where the waves seemed to flow over in an irregular line down the sides, here and there forming panels. The three supports were composed of female figures sculptured in wood; one supported by a dolphin suggested the mythical origin of the harp, another was poised upon a dolphin's back, and the third was a water nymph nestled among the rocks and spray. The music desk contained a picture of sunrise on Lake Erie. All of the carving was colored with translucent greens and blues enhancing the graceful undulations and wave movements. The panels were all designed to illustrate some of the most important views of the waterways of New York State. The first represented New York harbor, the next East river spanned by Brooklyn bridge, another the Hudson, with its palisades. The panel over the rear support was a view of Albany, showing the Capitol on the hill at sunset; another showed Cohoes Falls and the Erie canal; the next contained a picture of Little Falls; the last being a picture of Buffalo harbor. On the top, as a fitting finale, was a large picture representing the American Falls at Niagara. Underneath the front half of the top was painted the coat of arms of the State.

THE STAFF

The State building was at all times in charge of a competent and obliging staff, which always stood ready to minister to the comfort and pleasure of the guests of the Empire State. Honorable Frank J. LeFevre, of New Paltz, was Superintendent. He performed the arduous duties of directing the actions of the force and attending to a multitude of details with cheerfulness and efficiency. He was ably assisted by George E. Cowper, of Olean, the Assistant Superintendent.

The social functions given in the name of the State Commission were directed by Mrs. Norman E. Mack, the lady member of the Commission, whenever she was present. In her absence the social duties fell upon Mrs. Dore Lyon, who invariably extended the State's hospitality with grace and tact. The assistant hostess, Mrs. F. P. Applebee, won many friends in the course of the season through her courteous treatment toward all guests. The comfort of the Commission and their house guests was admirably provided for by Miss Laura MacMartin, the matron.

Acknowledgment is also due to those who faithfully served the Commission in the State building in various capacities throughout the Exposition period.

[Illustration: LIVINGSTON MEMORIAL TABLET]

CHAPTER IV

Functions Held at the New York State Building

[Illustration]

The State building was generally recognized as the social center of the Exposition. Many functions were given throughout the season by the Commission in the name of the State, and the building was constantly in demand for private entertainments. The use of the building was freely granted by the Commission so long as the date did not conflict with that of an official function. To enumerate all of the social events taking place in the State building is not within the province of this Commission.

A list of the official and the more important unofficial functions is given below:

Saturday, April 30. Opening day. A luncheon was given to members of the Commission and distinguished guests.

Wednesday, May 4. Luncheon given by the State Commission for Mrs. Martin H. Glynn, of Albany, wife of National Commissioner Glynn, and for Mrs. John K. Stewart, wife of Commissioner Stewart. Ladies only were present. The guests were received by Mrs. Norman E. Mack, assisted by Mrs. Glynn, Mrs. Stewart and Mrs. Dore Lyon.

Friday, May 20. Reception given by the State Commission to the New York State delegation to the National Editorial Association, 9 to 11 P. M. The guests were received in behalf of the Commission by Commissioner and, Mrs. James H. Callanan, of Schenectady, and by Commissioner and Mrs. John C. Woodbury of Rochester, assisted by Mrs. Dore Lyon.

Monday, May 23. Reception given by the National Society of New England Women. The guests were received by Mrs. Swinburn, of New York, the President of the Society, Mrs. John C. Woodbury and Mrs. James H. Callanan.

Tuesday, May 24. Reception given by the State Commission to the Federation of Women's Clubs, 4 to 6 P. M.

Wednesday, June 1. Breakfast at 12 M. given by the State Commission to Miss Alice Roosevelt. Only ladies were present. The guests were received by Commissioner Mrs. Norman E. Mack, Mrs. James H. Callanan, Mrs. John Young and Mrs. Dore Lyon. There were about 200 ladies present.

Tuesday, June 7. Ball given by President David R. Francis and Mrs. Francis in behalf of the Louisiana Purchase Exposition Company to the West Point cadets, 9 to 12 P. M. Music was furnished by two bands stationed in the north and south galleries of the entrance hall. Refreshments were served upon the verandas. Among the distinguished guests were General Nelson A. Miles and General H. C. Corbin.

Saturday, June 11. Reception tendered by the Executive Commissioners' Association to the State Commissioners and World's Fair officials. This was an informal affair for the purpose of bringing the States' representatives into closer relations. The receiving line consisted of Honorable J. A. Yerrington, President of the Association; Mr. Charles A. Ball, President of the Executive Committee of the Association; Mrs. F. B. Applebee; Mr. and Mrs. F. R. Conaway and Mr. Stacey B. Rankin.

Wednesday, June 15. Luncheon by the State Commission in honor of Mrs. William Berri, wife of Vice-President Berri, and Miss Stern, of New York city. The guests were received by Commissioner Mrs. Norman E. Mack,
Mrs. Berri and Miss Stern.

Friday, June 18. Dinner given at 7 P. M. by Mr. Louis Stern,
Chairman of the Executive Committee of the Commission, in honor of President and Mrs. Francis. Mr. Stern was assisted in receiving by Miss Stern and Mrs. Norman E. Mack.

Saturday, June 25. Dedication of the New York State building. Exercises described in Chapter V.

Thursday, June 30. Reception given by the State Commission to officers and members of the Council of the National Educational Association and to New York State teachers. The guests were received by Vice-President and Mrs. William Berri; Commissioner and Mrs. John K. Stewart; Mrs. Dore Lyon; Honorable Howard J. Rogers, Chief of the Department of Education of the Exposition, and Mrs. Rogers; John W. Cooke, president of the National Educational Association; and Mrs. DeLancey M. Ellis. An organ recital was played by S. H. Grover and refreshments were served in the grand hall.

Monday, August 1. Reception given by the Executive Commissioners' Association.

Thursday, September 1. Reception given by the Executive Commissioners' Association.

Thursday, September 8. Reception given by Mrs. Dore Lyon to the Hostesses' Association.

Monday, September 12. Electrical engineers tendered a reception to the visiting engineers assembled in convention on the Exposition grounds.

Monday to Wednesday, October 3 to 5. New York State week. Exercises described in Chapter VI.

Tuesday, October 11. Reception given by the Liberal Arts Club.

Friday, October 28. Dinner given by Commissioner Frederick R. Green, who was assisted in receiving by Commissioner Mrs. Norman E. Mack.

Tuesday, November 15. Brooklyn day. Exercises described in Chapter VII.

Saturday, November 19. Luncheon given by the Michigan Commission to the Governor-elect of Michigan. The invited guests included Vice-President William Berri and Secretary Charles A. Ball, of the New York State Commission.

Monday, November 21. Reception and ball given by the Beta Sigma Chapter of the Kappa Sigma Fraternity. (This function was to have been held in the Missouri building. The use of the State building was extended on account of the destruction of the Missouri building by fire on Saturday, November 19th).

Tuesday, November 22. Young people's dance. Courtesy to Missouri Commission on account of fire.

Thursday, November 24. Thanksgiving day. Exercises described in Chapter VIII.

Friday, November 25. Charity ball and Kirmess given by the ladies of St. Louis for the benefit of the Martha Parsons Free Hospital for Children of St. Louis, and for the fund for the Trades School for Girls of New York. The majority of the guests were in fancy costume. In addition to the regular dancing program there were special fancy dances.

Monday, November 28. Dinner given by the State Commission in honor of Honorable Oscar S. Straus and Mrs. Straus, and Honorable St. Clair McKelway and Mrs. McKelway. Vice-President Berri of the Commission presided, and the guests were received by Vice-President and Mrs. Berri and Mrs. Norman E. Mack, assisted by the guests of honor.

In addition to the above entertainments two musicales were given under the auspices of Boellman Brothers; and the Pikers' Club, an organization composed of attaches of the State building, gave a minstrel performance at the Inside Inn on Monday evening, September nineteenth, for the benefit of the Model Playground and Day Nursery.

[Illustration: ON THE LAGOON]

CHAPTER V

Dedication Day

The New York State building was dedicated with appropriate ceremonies on
Saturday, June twenty-fifth. The exercises were attended by Governor Odell and invited guests, members of the State Commission, Exposition officials, State and foreign representatives and many others.

PROGRAM FOR DEDICATION DAY

The program for the day was as follows:

10:30 A. M. Concert on Plaza in front of State building by Weil's band of St. Louis

11:30 A. M. Exercises in grand hallway, William Berri, Vice-President of the Commission, presiding

Invocation by the Rev. Carroll N. Davis, Dean of Christ Church Cathedral

Address of welcome by President David R. Francis

Address transferring State building to Governor Odell by Vice-President
William Berri

Acceptance by Governor Odell

Organ recital by S. H. Grover

8 to 11 P. M. Reception given to Governor and Mrs. Odell by the State Commission

Music by the Haskell Indian band

The day opened bright and clear, the warm rays of the sun being tempered by a cool breeze. The building was not opened to the public until the conclusion of the band concert, which was held between 10:30 and 11:30. As soon as the doors were opened a large audience quickly gathered to take part in the formal exercises of the day. In the assemblage was an interesting couple, Mr. Horace Stowell, aged 93 years, and wife, who had journeyed from Madison, N. Y., a distance of over a thousand miles, to be present at the dedication ceremonies and to visit the Fair.

THE FORMAL EXERCISES

Promptly at 11:30 William Berri, Vice-President of the Commission, called the assemblage to order and introduced Rev. Carroll N. Davis, who offered the invocation. At its conclusion Mr. Berri delivered his address. The slight change in program was due to the fact that President Francis was necessarily detained for a short time.

Vice-President Berri said:

"Governor Odell, it is with very great pleasure your New York State Commission to the Louisiana Purchase Exposition welcomes you in the New York State building here erected upon the spot where a little over one year ago you honored us by turning the first spadeful of earth for the foundation.

"Your Commission has endeavored to carry out your expressed wishes to provide for the people of New York who may visit this wonderful World's Fair, a building that shall fittingly represent the State of New York and add its share with the other state buildings to beautifying the grounds.

"We are much pleased that it is a matter of record that not only was this building complete in every detail and its doors thrown open for inspection on the opening day of the Exposition, but also that all exhibits under the control of your Commission, in the various departments, most of which are very much larger than ever before shown by New York State, were ready and in place at the moment President Francis officially declared that the great St. Louis Exposition was open to receive the world.

"We wish to thank President Francis and all officials connected with him in this great undertaking, for the uniform courtesy with which we have been treated, and for the valuable assistance that has been so generously given to us in carrying out our plans.

"It has been a most pleasurable task. We have fully accomplished what we have sought to attain. There is nothing lacking in the realization of our anticipations. As to whether we have acted wisely it is for you to judge. If, as the executive head of our State, it shall please you to commend the results we submit for your approval, this will be the proudest day in the history of the Commission."

As Governor Odell rose to respond to the remarks of Mr. Berri, he received an ovation, for which he bowed acknowledgment several times and finally raised his hand for silence. He spoke as follows:

ADDRESS OF GOVERNOR ODELL

"Mr. President, Ladies and Gentlemen"

"We are here to-day to dedicate a building which represents the interest of New York State in this great Exposition. Here, during the period when thousands shall visit these grounds, those who owe allegiance to the Empire State will find a place which will typify to them their home and impress them, let us hope, to a greater degree with the vastness of our State and of the position which it occupies in our commonwealth of nations. To those who have been intrusted with the work we owe thanks for the conception of their duty and for this magnificent edifice which, in its strength and beauty of architecture, is symbolical of the Empire State. In every phase of our nation's history, in all that has made it great and powerful and respected, New York has been both conservative and wise in the aid which it offered, powerful in the resources which it furnished in the building up of our republic. From the time when the courage and patriotism of our forefathers wrought out the nation down to the latest acquisition of our territory there is no page of history which does not tell of the devotion and statesmanship of New York's citizens.

"It is always a remarkable event in the history of the world when one nation disposes of any part of its domain to another through peaceful methods. War has almost always been the means through which nations have expanded and pushed forward their boundary lines. Trade requiring an outlet has more frequently been the cause of bloodshed than almost any other national or international question. That our country, therefore, at an early period in its history, should have been able, through peaceful means, to secure the vast domain beyond the Mississippi is a tribute to the statesmanlike policies of those who conceived its purchase. True it may be that the wars of other nations aided in its consummation, but it is also equally true that the man who was most directly responsible for the purchase was a son of the Empire State. Nor did the results of this early diplomatic victory stop here. The principle thus established has frequently led to more peaceful methods of adjusting questions of territorial boundary, both in our own and other countries. It may be that much that has since been accomplished through arbitration is but the evolution of this idea, and it may lead, let us hope, to the time when such questions will no longer render necessary the arbitrament of the sword.

"It was proper, therefore, that our State, in its dignity, with its conservatism and with its intense patriotism, should be among the first to contribute of its means to make of this Exposition the grand success which it promises. With each succeeding international exposition the world becomes wiser, artisans more skillful, the contributions to science and art more valuable; in a word, they raise the standard of civilization and hasten the time when all men shall pay homage to the ruler of the universe. As inventions are developed which make the worker more effective, which broaden the field of usefulness, there come responsibilities and problems which require education and discernment to meet and solve. Under the softened touch of Christianity, religion and education there should come about a universal brotherhood of man broad enough in scope to embrace all humanity. In all the work of the world, in all that is for the development of man, in everything that holds out promise to the future, New York State we may justly say, if not the leader, is at least in the fore ranks. Its broad acres are rich and fertile, and the commerce of the world enters at its ports. The manufacturer finds willing hands with remunerative wages striving to produce that which is necessary for our comfort and which adds so much to the wealth of the nation. Its laws are broad and ample in their scope, with no distinction as between man and man, and beneficent in their operation, while our citizens evince impulses which are worthy of emulation by all those who believe in the future of our republic. We have more of wealth and a greater population than any other State within the Union. Our cities are cosmopolitan in character, made up of representatives of all nations, but so nicely adjusted are our laws that they are assimilated into our population and become Americans among Americans, actuated by a common patriotism and a common desire for the continued development of our land.

"In these great halls, in these magnificent buildings devoted to art, to education, to mechanics and to agriculture, exhibits are to be found which are on a par if they do not excel, those of other nations. The advancement of New York, however, is but typical of every other State in the Union, in the continued prosperity of which all are equally interested. A nation of separate States, there is no dividing line of envy between them, no wish except for the prosperity and development of each, a common hope for a common country. How necessary it is, therefore, that in all that has to do with society a broad catholic spirit should dominate and control. Ours is not a country of classes, but one of equality—a country whose aim is the education of its citizens. It is our common object to perpetuate the principles of American independence. Anything that retards human progress, or that would make of a man a mere machine without brains, is to be deprecated. Our object should be to encourage and to promote thrift, and to instill into the mind of every citizen a desire for advancement. In this direction our State will be found always in the forefront and the evidence of her greatness will be measured rather by the intelligence of her citizens than by mere accumulation of wealth. Therefore, that which protects labor, which encourages capital, should be the aim of modern legislation. While we participate in the celebration of this great national event, as we mark our progress along every line, we feel a natural pride in all that has been done in other States, in all that has been accomplished by other people. As we look into the future, as we consider its possibilities, let us hope that our nation will never forget that this government is one by the people, and that its power and influence among the nations of the world will continue only so long as due weight and consideration is given to the rights of individuals. While rejoicing as citizens of New York, let us hope for the continuance of those policies and principles which have made our nation prosperous, and let us not forget that moderation and conservatism should be the measure of our efforts, and all that we do shall be for the advancement of all the people.

"The citizens of New York extend their congratulations to the people of the west and northwest. We hope that from this great Exposition there shall come a closer communication between all the people of the earth, a broadening of human effort, the advancement of civilization and a growing respect for our country and our flag which will make us a power for the good and peace of the world.

"It is a great pleasure for me to accept on behalf of the State of New York this magnificent building, and again to congratulate you as the President of the Commission, and the architect who has wrought this wonderful work, for the painstaking care that you have exercised in the development of New York's interests in this great Exposition."

During the address of the Governor, President Francis quietly entered and was introduced at its conclusion. He was warmly received and made a characteristic address. He paid a warm tribute to the Empire State and her Chief Executive, and complimented the State Commission upon the work it had performed and spoke of the New York State building as one of the social centers of the Exposition.

His remarks in part follow:

"Your distinguished son, Robert R. Livingston, was the man who first negotiated for the purchase of Louisiana. No exposition would be complete without a representation from the Empire State. The Exposition management has already pointed with pride to the New York building, the social functions of which have been among the marked attractions of the Exposition.

"I am here to thank New York not only for her material contribution to the World's Fair, but for the spirit her citizens have given to this Exposition.

"We of the West flatter ourselves that we have arrived at that stage of our progress when we can invite every people on the globe to come and see for themselves what a century of Western civilization has accomplished."

At the conclusion of the ceremonies Governor Odell held an informal reception, during which Mr. S. H. Grover, of New York, played an organ recital.

THE EVENING RECEPTION

The State building was appropriately decorated for the evening reception given in honor of Governor and Mrs. Odell, and many hundred guests called to pay their respects between the hours of eight and eleven. The receiving party consisted of Governor Benjamin B. Odell, Jr., Mrs. Odell, Mr. and Mrs. William Berri, Mrs. Norman E. Mack, Mr. and Mrs. John K. Stewart, Mr. and Mrs. John Young, Mrs. Daniel Manning, Mr. Frank S. McGraw, Mr. Frederick R. Green, Mr. John C. Woodbury, and Mr. William T. Van Brunt, representing President Harriman. The guests were presented to the receiving party by Major Harrison K. Bird, private secretary to the Governor. Two lines of United States marines guarded the approach to the receiving line and prevented crowding and confusion.

Music was furnished by the Haskell Indian band and later in the evening dancing was indulged in by many of the guests present. Supper was served at ten o'clock at small tables on the verandas, the following being the menu:

CELERY OLIVES RADIS AMANDES SALEES FEUILLES SUEDOISES BOUCHEES DE VOLAILLE A LA REINE CANAPES DE LUXE SANDWICHES ASSORTIS GLACE NEW YORK FRIANDISES CAFE LEMONADE EXPOSITION PUNCH

[Illustration: GRAND BASIN, FROM FESTIVAL HALL]

CHAPTER VI

New York State Week

The week beginning October third was set aside by the Exposition authorities as New York week; Monday, October third, being designated "New York City Day," and Tuesday, October fourth, "New York State Day."

NEW YORK CITY DAY

New York City Day was observed with exercises in the City Building on the Model street at eleven o'clock in the morning, which were presided over by Thomas W. Hynes, the Commissioner officially representing the city. Mayor McClellan was represented by Charles V. Fornes, President of the Board of Aldermen. There were also present an official delegation representing the city. Addresses were made by Archbishop J. J. Glennon, of St. Louis; Right Reverend Bishop McNamara, of New York city; Walter B. Stevens, Secretary, and F. J. V. Skiff, Director of Exhibits of the Exposition; Howard J. Rogers, Chief of Department of Education and Social Economy, and others. Luncheon was served at noon at the Tyrolean Alps, and from three to five in the afternoon a reception was held in the City Building, which was attended by exposition officials, national and state representatives, St. Louis society and many New Yorkers. In the evening a sumptuous banquet was served in the Town Hall of the Tyrolean Alps, which was presided over by Commissioner Hynes.

SERENADE TO GOVERNOR ODELL

Governor Odell and staff and invited guests reached St. Louis Monday morning, October third. At noon the Governor was tendered a serenade by the Philippine Constabulary band of 100 pieces. On Monday evening a dinner was given at the State building by the New York State Commission in honor of the Governor and Mrs. Odell, and President and Mrs. Francis. Owing to a death in the family, President and Mrs. Francis were unable to be present. Mr. D. M. Houser, of the Board of Directors, represented President Francis. There were no formal speeches, Governor Odell simply regretting that President Francis could not be present.

PROGRAM FOR NEW YORK STATE DAY

The program for New York State day was as follows:

11 A.M. Concert by the Garde Republicaine band, of Paris, France, on the Plaza in front of the State building

12 M. Formal exercises of the day in the grand entrance
    hall, Col. Edward Lyman Bill presiding
Invocation by Rev. Dr. William W. Boyd, of St.
    Louis, formerly of New York
Address of welcome by Col. Edward Lyman Bill.
Address of greeting in behalf of Exposition Company
    by Hon. Franklin Ferriss
Address by Governor Benjamin B. Odell, Jr.
Organ recital by S. H. Grover, of New York city

9 to 12 P. M. Reception and ball given by the New York
    State Commission in honor of Governor and Mrs.
    Odell. Dancing after ten o'clock

While not marked by the presence of militia and other spectacular features which generally accompany the celebration of a State Day, the exercises in the State building which were held at noon were most dignified and impressive. The day opened clear and cool, and the spacious verandas of the State building were well filled long before the time set for the concert.

THE GARDE REPUBLICAINE BAND

The Garde Republicaine band is composed of 100 skilled musicians and is considered by many to be the finest band in the world. No musical organization which visited the Exposition during the entire season received more compliments or more flattering press notices than those accorded this band. They played the following program:

1. March, "Lisbon"—L. Planel
2. Overture, "La Princesse Jaime"—C. Saint-Saens
3. Fantasie On the Opera "LeCompte Ory"—G. Rossini
   Soloists, MM. Paradis, Laforgue, Joseph Barthelemy,
   Morfaux, Couilland, Fournier
4. Three Celebrated Menuets—
   (a) Menuet—L. van Beethoven
   (b) "Ox" Menuet—J. Haydn
   (c) Menuet Favori—W. A. Mozart
5. March, "Egyptian"—J. Strauss

At the conclusion of the formal exercises they were entertained at luncheon by the State Commission. Through their leader, M. Gabriel Pares, they expressed hearty appreciation of the courteous treatment accorded them by the State of New York, and attested the same by playing a second concert in front of the State building between the hours of two and four in the afternoon. It was worthy of note that the building of the State of New York was the only State building at which this band played during its entire stay at the Exposition, their concerts being invariably given either in Festival Hall or in the grand bandstand in Machinery Gardens.

THE FORMAL EXERCISES

At twelve o'clock the assemblage was called to order by Colonel Edward Lyman Bill. There were present Governor and Mrs. Odell, the Governor's staff, a joint committee of the Legislature, members of the State Commission, invited guests, several representatives of the Exposition Company, representatives of State and foreign commissions, and a large audience, many of whom had journeyed all the way from New York State to be present at the ceremonies.

The personal party of the Governor consisted of Governor Benjamin B. Odell, Jr., Mrs. Odell, Mrs. William Kelly, Mrs. S.L. Dawes, Mrs. Hall and Miss Odell.

The Governor's staff comprised Brigadier-General Nelson H. Henry, Adjutant-General and Chief of Staff; Major Harrison K. Bird, Military Secretary; Lieutenant-Colonel Charles H. Sherrill, Aide-de-camp; Lieutenant-Commander Alfred Brooks Fry, Naval Militia, Aide-de-camp; Major Charles C. Davis, Thirteenth Regiment, Aide-de-camp; Major Richard
H. Laimbeer, Second Brigade Staff, Aide-de-camp; Major Amos E. McIntyre,
First Regiment, Aide-de-camp; Captain John T. Sadler, Thirtieth Separate Company, Aide-de-camp; Captain Edwin W. Dayton, Twenty-second Regiment,
Aide-de-camp; First Lieutenant William L. Thompson, Twelfth Separate Company, Aide-de-camp; First Lieutenant Chauncey Matlock, Third Battery,
Aide-de-camp; First Lieutenant Thomas Barron, Seventh Regiment, Aide-de-camp; First Lieutenant Augustus S. Chatfield, Eighth Regiment, Aide-de-camp; First Lieutenant Cornelius Vanderbilt, Twelfth Regiment, Aide-de-camp.

The joint committee of the Legislature comprised Hon. Jotham P. Allds, Norwich; Hon. S. Frederick Nixon, Westfield; Hon. James T. Rogers, Binghamton; Hon. Edwin A. Merritt, Potsdam; Hon. Robert Linn Cox, Buffalo; Hon. Thomas D. Lewis, Oswego.

Colonel Bill called upon the Rev. W. W. Boyd, of St. Louis, formerly of New York, to invoke the Divine blessing.

Dr. W. W. Boyd:

"Our Father, we thank Thee for this beautiful day and this assembly of the loyal sons and daughters of our native State. We rejoice that Thou hast gathered us into families, and so into communities, commonwealths and the perfect union of all the states.

"We bless Thee for the history of this great State, its part in the glorious Revolution, in the preservation of the Union, its development in every branch of human industry, its material prosperity, but above all, for its humanities, its growth in philanthropy, education and religion.

"Bless, we beseech Thee, His Excellency the Governor, and all associated with him in making, interpreting and executing the laws.

"Bless the President, Directors and all who have helped to create and develop this marvelous Exposition, especially the Commissioners of the State of New York, who have erected this splendid building, and by the varied exhibits in the palaces of the Exposition portrayed the wonderful progress of the Empire State.

"And grant, O most merciful Father, that the fruits of this great Exposition may be enlarged national prosperity, international comity and peace, and the strengthening of the ties of human brotherhood throughout the world.

"May Thy special blessing be upon the exercises of this hour; may the words of our mouth and the meditation of our hearts be acceptable in Thy sight, O Lord, our Strength and our Redeemer. Amen."

Colonel Bill then delivered the following address:

ADDRESS OF COLONEL BILL

"On behalf of the New York State Commission I extend greeting and hearty welcome to the official representative of President Francis, to Governor Odell, our distinguished guests, to the sons and daughters of New York, and to all who have honored us with their presence here to-day. It was on this site, upon May 2, 1903, Governor Odell lifted the first spadeful of earth where this beautiful structure has since been erected. Upon that occasion New York was represented by our Chief Executive, his staff, and troops numbering nearly fifteen hundred men from all branches of the military and naval service of the State. On last April thirtieth this building, sumptuously appointed, was formally opened to the public. I may say, with pardonable pride, that the report which the Commission made at that time showed that not only was our building complete in every detail, but all of the State exhibits as well were ready for inspection. The work of our Commission has been along pleasant lines, and we have been constantly stimulated by hearty support from the Exposition authorities. It is fitting that we should express our sincere appreciation to President Francis and the sterling coterie of men with whom he is surrounded for the aid and assistance which they have so willingly rendered this Commission in every way. Our Governor has taken a warm interest in New York's participation at this Fair, and on many occasions he has made manifest his desire that New York's representation should be ample and complete in every particular. In many of the magnificent places, such as Education, Agriculture, Horticulture, Forestry, Fish and Game, Mines and Metallurgy, our State has collective exhibits which show her varied resources. In this beautiful structure will be evidenced further proof of New York's generous participation in this great Exposition. The Louisiana Purchase Exposition has a deep interest for New York, for one of the principal figures instrumental in bringing about that purchase was Livingston, a distinguished son of the Empire State, and it was he who negotiated the treaty and was first to sign it. And yet the real authors of that great transaction on this side of the ocean were neither Jefferson, Madison nor Livingston, and I think historians will agree with me when I say it was more the influence of those hardy frontiersmen of Kentucky who demanded free navigation for the magnificent inland river which rolls by us in its eternal flow to the Gulf of Mexico. The influence of those men, the vanguard of civilization, could not be disregarded by those who were at the head of our governmental affairs more than a century ago. Then, the more we look at this transaction, the more evident it is that the outcome of it was due to that man whose shadow even now falls sharply athwart the whole continent of Europe—Napoleon Bonaparte. It was his ambition which threw into the grasp of the infant republic the splendid empire out of which have been carved twelve sovereign States and two Territories. At that time Napoleon uttered one of those far-seeing expressions which is important in its prophecy. 'Perhaps,' he said, 'it will be objected to me that the Americans of two or three centuries hence may be found too powerful for Europe, but my foresight does not embrace such remote fears. Besides, we may hereafter expect rivalries among members of the Union. Confederacies that are called perpetual last only until one of the contending parties finds it is to its interests to break them. It is to prevent the danger to which the colossal power of England subjects us that I would provide such a remedy.' No such vision of the future came to our American statesmen, many of whom bitterly opposed the purchase of the Louisiana Territory. When the bill came up for discussion on the floor of Congress, Josiah Quincy, afterwards mayor of Boston, and for many years president of Harvard College, said, speaking of the incorporation in the Union of the territory of Louisiana: 'It appears to me that this measure would justify revolution in this country. I am compelled to declare it as my deliberate opinion that if this bill passes, the bonds of this Union are virtually dissolved; that the States which compose it are free from their moral obligation, and that, as it will be the right of all, so it will be the duty of some to prepare definitely for a separation, amicably if they can, violently if they must.' He said further: 'If this bill passes, it is a death blow to the Constitution.' Strange words, indeed, in our ears at this time, and it shows that the American statesmen of those days had not the imagination of Napoleon.

"What has this purchase meant to New York to have in this Union this great empire? What has it meant to the Union itself to have this splendid territory incorporated in it? It has meant for New York prosperity and increased commerce to the people of all our land and furnished homes for the sons and daughters of New York. The States carved out of that great Empire have all borne their share in the heat of our national life and they have contributed immeasurably to the nation's growth and development, and we have come in this country, notwithstanding the immense separation and diversity of interests, to work together under one flag, with one interest for a common country, and this great Exposition should teach not only us of the East but of all other sections of the country that we should avoid the danger of finding ourselves separate in sentiment from one another. In this great western empire we all take a common interest, and the success of this Exposition redounds to the credit and honor, not only of the men who have carried it to such successful issue, but upon the whole country. We all shine in the reflected glory of the Louisiana Purchase Exposition, which shows the high-water mark of human progress. It is indeed the greatest of all international fairs and a lasting credit to the artistic skill of the men who planned and executed it. It is the culmination of all that has been done in the wide expanse of territory purchased from France in 1803, and the achievements of all nations in the world since that day. It is a far cry from the early oriental fairs in the East, which were perhaps the early ancestors of this great Exposition, and all honor and credit and glory is due the men who stood shoulder to shoulder in carrying this great enterprise to such a magnificent culmination. It represents American skill, American enterprise, American endeavor, and its influence will be felt upon this country long after those men who have played their successful part in this great moving drama have passed from earth. Words are inadequate to fittingly describe the beauties of this magnificent Exposition. It is individual effort as well as concerted effort which has brought about these splendid results. It is one of the brightest pages in American history, and what glorious memories a perusal of these pages arouse! We can turn the pages of recorded history from the time when the boats of the adventurous Genoese unfolded their white wings in the harbor of Palos and sped across the unknown seas to bring back upon their return evidence of the existence of a new world far across the wide waste of waters. In fancy we picture that sturdy band kneeling with Columbus, richly attired, upon the tropic sands, while over them floats the blood and gold banner of Spain, as the priest clothed in vestments of his office asks the blessings of Almighty God upon the land which Columbus claims in the name of the House of Castile. In the background we see waving palms and dark-skinned men who gaze with awe upon the white discoverers. In another scene we see the cold wintry waves surge and dash around the frail craft fighting its way across dark tempestuous seas from Plymouth, the little bark tossed like a feather here and there until she lands on that rock-bound coast known as New England. We see that little colony—Freedom's seed—germinate and thrive; first the grain, then the tender plant, ever exposed to severe conditions, then matured into the oak of a giant nation. We see those brave colonists who have planted the banner of human liberty upon the inhospitable shores push ever onward, ever extending the fringe of civilization, struggling against disheartening obstacles, fighting wild beasts and savage men, but pushing on with indomitable courage. We see the historical gathering at Philadelphia, resulting in that document embodying Jefferson's superb crystallization of popular opinion that 'all men are created free and equal and endowed with certain inalienable rights, that among these are life, liberty and the pursuit of happiness;' that American magna charta which swept away forever the will of kings in this land. The people became the rulers and the accident of birth carried no rank, conferred no privilege. We see the loosely joined colonies building a nation which contained these elements of greatness little dreamed of by those hardy pioneers who so generously gave up their offering of blood on Freedom's altar. The kaleidoscope still turns. We see those intrepid founders of the school of liberty pushing their lines ever onward across rivers, deserts, over mountains clad with eternal snow until the golden shores of California gladden the eye of our valiant explorers. Then a pause, and over land and sea hang dark clouds of fratricidal war. Four long years through the valleys and over the mountains of the Southland surges the red tide of battle. The days were dark and full of gloom, when lo! the clouds parted and the heavens again were blue. The nation had been born anew, and on the fair pages of her history appear no longer the dark stain of human slavery. The strong arm of enterprise quickly washed away the red stain of war. The word 'America' had a deeper and more sacred meaning than before, and the nation was re-established on the indestructible foundation of national unity; the blocks were laid in the cement of fraternal esteem. Still the picture which we see revolves. Across the waters of the Pacific America sweeps towards the fulfillment of her world wide destiny. The Stars and Stripes wave over the palace of the kings in Honolulu. Still again the nation's sword is unsheathed in the cause of human liberty, and the last vestige of Spanish power is swept from the new world. The thunder of Dewey's guns awakens us to the fact that the American banner is planted into the far Orient, there to stay forever, and under its protecting folds manifold blessings are carried to the people of those islands lying in the purple spheres of summer seas. While the drum of all American progress is heard around the world, it too may be truthfully said that the sun never sets upon the soil over which Freedom's banner proudly floats, for when the light of the dying day is fading from Porto Rican hills the golden rays of the morning sun are reflected upon the shimmering folds of Old Glory on the gray old battlements of Manila.

"It is indeed inspiring, the history of this great nation, guided to its ultimate issue as a stately ship is wafted over the seas to the harbor of its destination. I wonder if in this ceaseless struggle for gold and gain we pause long enough to study the true character of those men to whose valorous deeds we owe so much, those men who planted the tree of human liberty so deep that even the shock of revolution of succeeding wars could not uproot it, those men who demanded of Jefferson a free Mississippi and who made this Exposition possible. All honor to those heroes who stood shoulder to shoulder in the days which tried men's souls, who, in the gloom and suffering of Valley Forge, saw in the distance the rainbow of hope shining over the dark clouds of defeat. They saw the light of a great nation which would serve as a beacon in the world progress and a refuge for the persecuted of the nations of earth. All races contributed to the founding of this beloved country. The roster of the Revolution is filled with names which show that the liberty loving of all European nations gave up a generous offering of blood on Freedom's altar. In our veins courses blood of all nations, and it is the healthy commingling of that blood which has produced a race of world conquerors. It has produced the men who have made possible this great Exposition. We have been placed in the world's crucible, have been melted in the glowing heat of a nascent life, and have been forged into a weapon which shall carve the world. Our ideals are worthy, the hopes and aspirations of the nation devoted to justice and love; ideals which shall be the steadfast inspirer of nations and individuals to uprightness, to justice and to honor."

The presiding officer then expressed regret at the unavoidable absence of President Francis on account of bereavement in his family. He introduced judge Franklin Ferriss, General Counsel to the Louisiana Purchase Exposition Company, who delivered the following address:

ADDRESS OF JUDGE FERRISS

"I regret extremely, for your sake and his, that the brilliant man who stands at the head of this Exposition cannot be here to-day to greet you in person. Still I must admit that I am not unmindful of the fact that I owe to his misfortune and yours the very great privilege of appearing before you to extend a welcome to the people of my native State.

"The President of the Exposition bids me say to you that there has been no occasion on these grounds—that there will be none in the future—in which he would more gladly participate than this.

"The Exposition management feels under peculiar obligations to the State of New York. We are indebted largely to her prompt and liberal co-operation for the high stand which the Exposition has taken. We are indebted to the Governor, to the New York Commission, to the gracious hostesses of this building, to the splendid woman who has, with rare tact and dignity, co-operated with the Exposition as President of the Board of Lady Managers.

"In the building of this Exposition, science, invention, art, manufacture, the field, the forest, the mine, the air and the water have contributed their choicest treasures. How well we have succeeded in presenting them you must judge. But I wish to say to you that no matter how high a standard we have reached, still more important than all else is the representation upon these grounds of our splendid American man and womanhood. No man can walk about this Plateau of States, view these beautiful structures, see the people coming together from the north and the south, the east and the west, uniting in common loyalty and respect for our institutions, without feeling his heart swell with pride and gratitude.

"It is no disparagement to our sister States, for me, a loyal son of New York, to say that it is most fitting that the Empire State should be pre-eminent here also in the beauty of her building, the character of her exhibits and the magnificent representation of her people.

"I am proud of the State of New York—proud of her history, her scholars, her statesmen, her soldiers—proud of her material prosperity—proud of the great metropolis through whose gates thunders the commerce of the United States.

"I love the State of New York—her broad and fertile valleys, her stately rivers, the lakes which glisten like jewels on her bosom, her mountains which rear their tops to the clouds; but most of all I love the quiet life of the country home—the honesty and industry of the plain people.

"Our old home! Who can forget it? The great barn with its huge beams and fragrant mows of hay—the sparkling brook whose shining shallows bathed my naked feet—the broad meadow with its fence corners of luscious berries—the old schoolhouse, whose desks are impressed with generations of jack-knives! Was there ever so sweet a draught as that which we drew from the shining depths of the old well?

"And yet the country boy grew restless. With his ear to the ground, he heard the distant hum of industry. He heard the tramp of a million feet in the great cities. He felt that the battle of life was on, and, that he must take his place in the struggle. And so he turned his back upon the old home.

"Ah! how many grave faced fathers and tender, sweet faced mothers have watched their boys, one by one, go out into the world, and have turned back in solitude, cheered by an occasional visit, an occasional letter, to wait until their days should be fulfilled. And how many of us must now say that their days have been fulfilled, and that a simple stone marks their last resting place in the village churchyard.

"What have we gained by this? Contentment? They had it. Respect of our fellowmen? They had it. Success in life? They had it. True, their fortunes were small—and yet they had no clutching fear that speculation, fraud or treachery would rob them of the fruit of a life's toil. And they had an abiding faith that there would be provision for the years to come. Aye, that there would be provision for the last journey to that land, where, according to their simple faith: 'The wicked cease from troubling and the weary are at rest.'

"I will yield to no man in loyalty to the State of my adoption; but who can chide me if my heart clings to the home of my childhood, to the graves of my forefathers?

"If we, who have left the old home to build a new one in the West, can be faithful to the traditions of our childhood—if we can bequeath to our children the lessons of industry, honesty and economy which our fathers gave to us—we shall do more to honor the State of New York than we could do by rearing marble to the skies."

The presiding officer then introduced Honorable Benjamin B. Odell, Jr.; Governor of the State, who received a great ovation, it being some time before the Governor was able to proceed with his remarks. His speech was punctuated with liberal applause.

He said:

ADDRESS OF GOVERNOR ODELL

"The diplomacy which led up to the acquisition of the Louisiana territory furnishes one of the most interesting incidents in the world's history. The establishment of a republic devoted to the interests of, and affording liberty of conscience and freedom of action to its citizens, was an experiment in government which could not have succeeded if any restraint had been placed upon that liberty, or if its constitution had not been broad enough to meet the demands of a growing country. From the settlement of America down to the Revolutionary War sanguinary strife had been the lot of the American people. The thrifty Dutch and the stolid determined Anglo-Saxon sought not in this country a mere temporary home, for, unlike the Spaniards, their dream was not of gold, but rather their hope was for a liberty so broad and catholic in its character that it would grow with succeeding years and make certain that peace they had sought for in vain in the land of their birth.

"The earlier colonial and Indian wars had drawn upon the resources and heroism of our forefathers. Hardship and toil had imbued them with a consciousness of their strength and instilled into them that spirit of independence which enabled them, after long years of strife, to establish our republic. It was this people, after having gained their independence, in the belief that foreign complications were forever at an end, who, at the close of the Revolution, turned their attention to peaceful pursuits and endeavored to meet every requirement of a growing country. With characteristic skill and industry they began the development of those tremendous resources of our country, the measure of which is almost beyond human conception. Here, under liberal laws and wise administration, the people found that which had been heretofore lacking in the government of the world. Invention had not yet made possible the intercommunication facilities which we of the present enjoy. Upon water transit, therefore, they were obliged to depend for an outlet for the commerce of their western territory. The barriers which were sought to be interposed to communication over the mighty river which rises in the northwest brought forth vigorous protests from those who had just begun to cultivate its fertile fields. Angry passions were aroused, and the people of our country who had been so successful in carving out the republic demanded that this barrier should be removed. Livingston and Monroe, clothed only with power to effect a treaty which should insure this right of transit, with no possible opportunity of quick communication with their government, took upon themselves the responsibility which brought to a successful consummation the relinquishment of this vast territory.

"Thus was brought to the people of the United States a question which had never been contemplated by the framers of the constitution. That instrument had been the production of the wisest men of the times. They had successfully met the problem of drawing into an indissoluble union the thirteen states, many of which were acting under peculiar laws which were contrary to the Declaration of Independence, under which the battles for freedom had been fought and won. While there was authority for the admission of new states, there was no constitutional permission for the purchase of territory. The power of the Federal government to perform acts of sovereignty had not yet been passed upon, and there was grave doubt as to the wisdom of ratifying the treaty without a constitutional amendment. When we look over the results which have followed this expansion of our country, when we calculate our manifest growth in population, in wealth and in industry, all of these appear insignificant beside the result which was accomplished in showing to the world that we were living under a constitution broad enough in its provisions to be so interpreted as to insure success to popular government. That Jefferson and his advisers acted wisely in so construing their power at that time is undoubted. If there were no other achievements of that wonderful administration, then this alone would suffice to make it a memorable one.

"Doubt, lack of courage and insincere opposition are always the refuge of a coward. Here was a nation demanding that which was necessary for its trade, desirous of reaching a solution through peaceful means if possible, but determined to acquire it at all hazards if necessary. There was no question as to the consent of those whom we took over, and to whom we gave the protection of our flag, or as to nice points of constitutionality, when the greater object in view was the onward progress of civilization, the building up of hope and the fulfillment of our destiny as a nation, to perpetuate those principles which mean so much in the redeeming of the world. The exigencies of a later war found a precedent in the courage of Jefferson and enabled Lincoln to wipe from the escutcheon of state the blot of slavery which had too long tarnished it.

"That the acquisition of this territory was accomplished through peaceful means rather than by bloodshed was another triumph for civilization. While wars have come since, and may come in the future, the plan of arbitration which has been adopted so generally by this and other nations may perhaps have had its inception in this peaceful solution of a burning and important question to this country. Our Union now is one that is composed of commonwealths bound together by all that means common interest, the common weal and common protection of all the people. It leads to the hope that when the representatives of all of the states have decreed by a majority that which is for the best interest of the whole country, then these questions should no longer be the subject of partisanship or party differences, but the government should have the loyal support of all who believe in America and her future. The same laws govern us, the same protection should be and is accorded to every citizen, and there is no individual or isolated community that does not share in the prosperity of all others whose interests are on the same plane of equality. For a time natural advantages may unduly favor one section of the country, but the accumulation of wealth brings about the development of the natural resources by which other sections are built up, and their people share in the general prosperity. Our State perhaps has benefited more through the development of the west and the northwest territory than almost any other commonwealth. The natural valleys which permitted the building of the Erie canal and the connection of the Great Lakes with the harbor of New York brought this territory in close communication with the Atlantic seaboard. The growing demands of the world led to the cultivation of the fertile fields of the west, the development of the mines and the building up of cities and manufactures, until to-day we have other ports whose facilities have been increased by the improvement of waterways and the building of thousands and thousands of miles of railroad. While there may be an apparent decrease in some localities and a corresponding benefit in others, yet so intimate are our connections and associations that the prosperity of one, instead of being a menace to the growth of any other locality, really aids in building it up. So diversified are our interests, so skillful our people, that we may compare the whole Union to a great workshop, one vast cultivated field of industry, all laboring, not for the advancement of separate cities or localities, but for the continued growth of our common country.

"It is only through ignorance that people have a misconception of these truths. The development of the human mind is no less important than the development of the physical condition of man. His education, therefore, is a paramount duty of the state, and his protection against the weakening of his physical condition is equally important. That legislation has recognized these facts is shown in laws, not only of the nation, but of each individual state, which seek to guard and protect the youth against unwise labor, which seek to instill into his mind that intelligence which comes only from wise and broad educational facilities. Every able bodied citizen of our country is an asset, and those who through weakness, however painful the admission may be, are incapacitated from labor, must be entered upon the debit side of the national ledger. Therefore, the laws that guard against burdensome toil, too long hours of labor, and against ignorance, are not only humanitarian in their character, but are best calculated to promote the interest of all the people. In the division of society, those who labor and those who represent capital should always be in accord, and the demands of either should never trespass upon the rights of the other. It is too frequently the case that through misunderstanding of our laws and the higher economical conditions that friction does arise between these two great elements of society. The right of every man to sell his products or his labor in the best market is unquestioned, and any interference with this principle of sound government is a menace to the republic itself. We are reaching a point in our history when conservative and wise judgment must prevail, and the common sense of the people dictates such a solution of these problems as will meet every demand that is in harmony with sound government. Our own State has taken long steps in advance upon these questions, and to us with whom these differences more frequently occur the people will look for wise deliberations and conclusions.

"Every man should be a part of the government. He should feel it to be as much his duty to respond to civic responsibilities as do those living under a monarchy, whose early tuition instills in them the belief that they owe the best part of their lives to the military service of their government. As they are undeterred by fear of death or disaster, so should our young men be undeterred from entering public life by calumny, villification and abuse, which they see too frequently and too unjustly bestowed upon others.

"New York is here to-day by its official representatives to testify first to its loyalty to the purposes for which this Exposition was conceived; to show the people of the West that in their progress we are interested, and that to them we look for such returns in dividends upon the stock of patriotism as will give to our nation men of energy, of right impulses. To you we owe much, and from you we expect much. Our efforts will be to aid you in every laudable undertaking, to stand behind you in all that means the prosperity of our common country. You have here an Exposition of which you may be justly proud. Nothing like it has ever been known in the annals of the world. Skilled workmen from all parts of the earth are here to aid in its success. Here you witness not only the steady progress that has been made in the sciences, the arts, and agriculture, but you have before you also exhibits from some of the possessions which have recently come under our control. We may study here some of the problems which demand solution at the hands of the American people. Our flag has been planted in a far-off land, and we must face responsibilities which it would be cowardly to shirk. A message has come to us as to all other nations, to do the Master's bidding and to spread christianity and civilization into the remotest parts of the earth. To us have been intrusted duties that have cost us the blood of some of the bravest men of the north and of the south, of the east and west. Here we may see something of that which has been accomplished, as well as a presentation of those conditions which it is our duty to correct. It is our privilege to give to others the same liberty which we enjoy ourselves, to establish some form of government such as ours whenever these people are ready for it, and it is our duty to protect them in their weakness until they are prepared for it. It was the dream of our forefathers that our country should be confined between these two magnificent oceans, but despite these hopes in later years additional responsibilities have come, Which the American people are too proud to shirk and too courageous to abandon. There is no one who has seen the progress which is here represented who does not believe that the work for civilization which is ours to perform has already had such an impetus that the time will come when we shall bless those who had the courage to stand for it against those who demanded another solution of this important question. To our credit be it said, that no true American demands the surrender of these possessions, and that the only question of difference between the people of our country is whether they shall be given their independence now, or when they are in a condition to enjoy it.

"This Exposition stands, not only as a monument to our progress, but to our united and determined effort to take a prominent part in all that means the advancement of mankind and the prosperity of the whole world. We owe that which we are at present to the devotion and heroism of the men of the past, and to protect and guard the inheritance which has come to us should be our aim. To be broad and conservative in our conception of our duties and responsibilities should be our purpose. To instill into the minds of our youth a determination to meet every question with true American courage should be our object. Every effort that makes for the good of humanity is a fitting tribute to that national policy which has taught us that there is no responsibility too great for our citizens to bear, and that in the onward progress of civilization America recognizes her duty and will not fail in its performance."

At the conclusion of the Governor's address the benediction was pronounced by the Rev. W. W. Boyd, after which Governor Odell held a public reception, shaking hands with several hundred people, who pressed forward to greet him. During the progress of the reception Mr. S. H. Grover, of New York city, rendered an organ recital. Luncheon was served the Governor and party in the offices of the Commission, and the afternoon was devoted to sight seeing.

THE EVENING RECEPTION

In the evening was held the grand reception and ball in honor of Governor and Mrs. Odell. Six thousand invitations had been issued for the function, those invited including the President of the United States and his Cabinet, judges of the United States Supreme Court, United States army and navy officers, governors of all the states, New York State officers, members of the New York State Legislature, judges of the Court of Appeals and Appellate Division and Supreme Court, Exposition officials, members of the National Commission, members of State and Foreign Commissions, the Board of Lady Managers and many prominent citizens of the Empire State and St. Louis. In spite of the fact that the day assigned to the State of New York, a year before by the Exposition Company, fell upon the date of the greatest festival of all the year in St. Louis, viz., The Veiled Prophets' ball, which is similar to the Mardi Gras festival at New Orleans, it did not affect the attendance at the reception in the least, many people attending both functions. Throughout the evening the capacity of the building was taxed to the utmost by those who came to enjoy New York's proverbial hospitality.

The exterior of the building and the grounds were illuminated on a lavish scale by the Pain Pyrotechnic Company, of New York city. The entire building was outlined by means of thousands of fairy lamps, and many strings of Japanese lanterns were festooned from the roof line to the veranda balustrade. Fairy lamps were used in profusion about the grounds, forming unique figures, and at various points spelled the words "New York." At no other function during the entire Exposition were such elaborate illuminations attempted on the part of any state commission. The interior decorations consisted of the National and Exposition colors, gracefully wound here and there about the pillars, supplemented by festoons of smilax, which was used in profusion in the entrance hallway. Special music for the event was furnished by Fancuilli's band, of New York city, and Schoen's orchestra, of St. Louis, which were stationed respectively in the south and north galleries of the grand entrance hall.

THE RECEIVING PARTY

The receiving line was stationed at the foot of the grand staircase, the guests entering at the south portal of the building and approaching through the reception rooms.

Receiving with the Governor and Mrs. Odell were Mrs. Norman E. Mack, Colonel and Mrs. Edward Lyman Bill, Mr. and Mrs. John C. Woodbury, Mr. and Mrs. Frank S. McGraw, Mr. Frederick R. Green, Mrs. Daniel Manning, Hon. S. Frederick Nixon, Mrs. Doré Lyon and Hon. James T. Rogers. The guests were presented to the Governor by Major Harrison K. Bird, his military secretary, two lines of United States marines guarding the approach to the receiving party. The Governor's military staff, resplendent in vari-colored uniforms, formed a line directly in front of the receiving party, and, while adding eclat to the occasion, prevented any crowding about the receiving line.

Supper was served at eleven o'clock at small tables upon the verandas. The following was the menu:

RADISHES CELERY OLIVES SALTED ALMONDS BONBONS OYSTERS A LA PAULETTE CHICKEN SALAD ASSORTED SANDWICHES ICE CREAM PETIT FOURS LEMONADE COFFEE CLARET PUNCH

Dancing began at ten o'clock and continued until the wee sma' hours.

CONCLUDING FUNCTION

The final event of State week was a breakfast given by the State Commission on Wednesday noon in honor of Governor and Mrs. Odell, and
Mrs. Daniel Manning, President of the Board of Lady Managers. The breakfast was perfectly informal, no set addresses being delivered.

The functions of the entire period were voted by one and all to have been most successful in every respect, and New York again proved its right to the title of a most gracious and generous host.

[Illustration: COLONNADE OF STATES]

CHAPTER VII

Brooklyn Day

One of the last special days to be observed during the Exposition was Brooklyn Day, the exercises of which were held on November fifteenth. As one of the speakers on the occasion aptly said, it was the only day throughout the Exposition period which was formally set apart by the Exposition management in honor of a political division less than a municipality. A special train bearing a large delegation of representative Brooklynites arrived in St. Louis Monday, November fourteenth. Although the date was late in the season, the weather was ideal, and everything was done for the pleasure and comfort of the visitors. The ceremonies were divided between the New York State building and the New York City building, upon the Model street, and consisted of exercises at 11:30 A.M., followed by a luncheon at one o'clock at the New York State building, and a reception at the New York City building from eight to ten in the evening.

THE PROGRAM

The program for the formal exercises in the New York State building was as follows

Address of welcome, William Berri, Vice-President, New York State Commission

Address, Hon. J. Edward Swanstrom, on behalf of the Committee of One
Hundred

Permanent Chairman, Colonel William Hester, president of the Brooklyn
Eagle

Response, Major Peter J. Collins

Address, Hon. Rolla Wells, Mayor of St. Louis

Response, Hon. Charles A. Schieren, ex-mayor of Brooklyn

Oration, Hon. Thomas P. Peters, editor of the Brooklyn Times

Aeolian organ recital

Promptly at 11:30 A. M. the assemblage was called to order by Vice-President William Berri, who, in behalf of the State Commission, extended a cordial welcome to all present. He then called upon J. Edward Swanstrom, who made brief remarks in behalf of the Committee of One Hundred.

At the conclusion of Mr. Swanstrom's remarks, Colonel William Hester was installed as permanent chairman. Upon taking the chair Colonel Hester said:

COLONEL HESTER'S REMARKS

"I am very sensible of the honor conferred upon me, but will be unable to fulfill the duties, except in a most perfunctory way. It is very much to be regretted that the Honorable Martin W. Littleton is not able to be with us to-day. As the official head of the government of the borough, he was to have presided on this occasion. In his absence Major Peter J. Collins, who was at the head of an important department, will respond for his chief. I now introduce to you Major Collins."

SPEECH OF MAJOR COLLINS

"*Your Honor, Mr. Francis, and ladies and gentlemen:* In responding as the representative of the administration of the borough of Brooklyn, I feel that you must realize the unenviable position I occupy of appearing on such brief notice and of acting as the mouthpiece of our president, the Hon. Martin W. Littleton. Mr. Littleton instructs me to convey his most sincere regrets to your honor, to Mr. Francis and to the ladies and gentlemen constituting the Committee of One Hundred, on his enforced absence on this occasion. As some of you are aware, there has been an election in this land. Previous to this election there was carried on what some of us supposed was a political campaign. This campaign engaged the interest of every worthy citizen and public and private affairs of business have been neglected to some extent as a consequence. In the business of the borough Mr. Littleton is confronted with a vast accumulation of matters of greatest importance to Brooklyn, both in the local work and in the various boards and committee meetings in Manhattan, and he has reluctantly concluded that his absence from the city at this time would amount to an almost criminal neglect of his duty. He asks me to convey to you the congratulations and good wishes of the many thousands of our people who are unable to be with us to-day. Brooklyn has had a deep sympathy with your fair city in this tremendous enterprise, and has watched with keen interest and satisfaction your success in overcoming the many difficulties that lay in your way. Brooklyn herself has awakened from her sleep of almost ten years, and the sound of the hammer and the saw and the ring of the trowel are heard on every hand. Owing to the enterprise, energy and self-sacrificing efforts of many of the men who are with us to-day, she is astonishing the country by the wonderful increase in population. Brooklyn can no longer be regarded as the bedroom of Manhattan, for Manhattan is rapidly becoming only the workshop of Brooklyn; we can no longer be regarded as the little brother of Manhattan, for we are rapidly becoming a very big brother. Consequently, ladies and gentlemen of St. Louis, we feel qualified to appreciate the satisfaction and joy you may justly feel in this your hour of triumph, and we extend to you the right hand of fellowship and congratulate you on this wonderful creation of yours, that must go down in history as the greatest exposition in the history of mankind."

Mayor Wells was unavoidably detained by an important engagement. The Chairman then introduced Mr. Schieren, and in doing so said:

"This is no fairy story, yet I will commence it that way. Once upon a time we of Brooklyn had a city all to ourselves. We were proud of our city and very desirous that it should be well governed, and were careful in the selection of men to fill its highest office, and thus it came to pass that one of our most successful efforts in that direction was the choice for mayor of our city of the gentleman whom I shall now present to you, Ex-Mayor Charles A. Schieren."

Mr. Schieren was warmly received and spoke as follows:

ADDRESS OF EX-MAYOR SCHIEREN

"In the name of the Brooklyn delegation I thank you sincerely for your cordial greeting and the hearty welcome extended to us. We fully appreciate your kind hospitality. We have come here to enjoy this glorious Exposition which already has attained such a great fame. Its magnificence and grandeur, both as to the magnitude of its buildings and their exhibits, is a surprise to every visitor. You may be proud of your achievements.

"This Exposition seems to exceed all others held in this country, and in many respects those held in the world.

"The Centennial Exposition of Philadelphia, commemorating the foundation of our government, gave our people the first idea of the extent and scope of our labor-saving machinery and the advance made in the manufacture of our American goods. It stimulated the manufacturing interests in our country.

"The Columbian Exposition at Chicago commemorated the discovery of America. It was noted for its excellent foreign exhibits. It gave our people an opportunity to compare the products of America with those of other nations. The so-called White City had a peculiar charm and made a deep impression upon every one. It seemed a perfect dream, ever to be remembered. People declared that it could not be excelled, but hardly a decade has passed when the enterprising, energetic citizens of the commercial metropolis of the great southwest arranged another World's Fair to commemorate the historical events of the famous Louisiana purchase, even upon a larger scale and overshadowing all others in this country. We may exclaim justly—Will there ever be another Exposition greater and more important than the one just about to close?

"We seem to marvel at nothing in this progressive age. We always wonder what other marvellous inventions may be in store for us to necessitate another Exposition upon a gigantic scale, to be held somewhere in this country. Perhaps within another decade, when the Isthmian canal is finished, the golden stream which will connect the waters of the Pacific and Atlantic oceans, we may celebrate at the national capital city the greatest event of the twentieth century, bringing to the commerce of the world peace and plenty. At the same time we may hope to celebrate the establishment of our American merchant marine, the one thing needed to carry our American products and goods into the harbors of the world, floating the Stars and Stripes now so seldom witnessed upon the ocean vessels. This country seems to forge ahead at a rapid pace, not only in its material wealth, but in everything that tends to the happiness of our people, even the humblest citizens sharing in the general prosperity. Every section has cause to rejoice—the South with its cotton, the North with its financial resources, the West with its farm products, the East with its industries, all seem to participate in the general welfare of the country. In conclusion let me thank you again for the courtesy extended to our people, and we wish you great success in this stupendous enterprise."

At the conclusion of Mr. Schieren's remarks the presiding officer said: "For many years the *Brooklyn Times* was owned and edited by the late Mr. Bernard Peters. He was a man of strict integrity, high moral ideals, and a forceful writer. The editorial chair of the *Times* is now occupied by his son, Thomas P. Peters, a worthy son of a worthy sire. Ladies and gentlemen, I take pleasure in introducing to you the orator of the day, Mr. Thomas P. Peters."

Mr. Peters was greeted with hearty applause as he arose. His oration in part follows:

ORATION OF MR. PETERS

"To speak a word for Brooklyn at this time, I was not the first choice of the Committee of Arrangements. Unanimously that honor was assigned to one of Brooklyn's favorite sons. But sickness of a most serious nature overtook him only a few days ago, and after a brief illness, he was early last Wednesday morning called to his final rest. Although upon pleasure bent, our hearts are sorrowful because of this loss to Brooklyn.

"Joseph C. Hendrix had been prominent in Brooklyn life a quarter of a century, prominent enough to have been nominated at one time for mayor of the old city by one of the great parties. He served Brooklyn for many years as president of its board of education; was its postmaster, and also represented one of its districts in the halls of Congress. Of recent years he had withdrawn from public life and devoted himself to the financial world. There he soon assumed a commanding position as bank president, and his organizing abilities were constantly in demand. He was one of Brooklyn's great men, and I regret that he is not here to-day to fill the position for which he was so well fitted. Our borough is rightly in deep bereavement because of the taking off of this, a faithful servant.

"This party of Brooklynites has come over 1,000 miles to celebrate at this magnificent exposition a day set apart for itself. We come not from a sovereign State. Neither do we come from an independent city. We come from but part of a great city. I will venture to claim that Brooklyn Day at the St. Louis Exposition will be the only day set apart for any municipal body holding a place by law of less dignity than that of a city. Why, then, does Brooklyn send us out to make her name known here and to extend her greetings to St. Louis? Because for years Brooklyn was a city, and with more independent citizens to the total population than were to be found in any other part of the known world, and she is still true to her history. She had then a spirit that was the very personification of municipal patriotism. She could tear down a dishonest political rascal with greater celerity than any other city in the land. She kept her two great parties equally balanced; each a foil to the other, each a stimulant to the other for good government, and upon the average she enjoyed better service than American cities usually obtain.

"It is almost seven years since Brooklyn lost her cityhood. During that time she has been a dependent borough within the great city of New York. Many thought that when that transition took place Brooklyn would lose her old-time spirit, her pride would be humbled and she would sink into the slough of despair, but we are here to-day to make known to these United

States that Brooklyn's old-time courage is as high, her spirit is as heavily charged with municipal energy and her pride is the same pride as of old.

"Brooklyn is a peculiar community. She differs from all others. The wits have long fed upon her. General Horace Porter has called her a city of 4,000,000, 1,000,000 of whom are alive. Another has said that there are two places to which every dead New Yorker goes, either to heaven or to hades and to Brooklyn. He may escape one or the other of the two former. He cannot escape the latter. Simeon Ford has declared that Brooklyn lies midway between the quick and the dead, midway between reckless, extravagant and wicked old New York and sober, sombre and serene Greenwood. McKinley ran for President upon the issue of the full dinner pail. The students of Princeton College recently asserted that Roosevelt was running upon the issue of a full baby carriage. The President must have secured his inspiration from the manner in which the cartoonists always pictured the Brooklyn man, behind the perambulator. We ourselves recognize that Brooklyn is peculiar and unusual. Her like is not known to the world. That fact is proved to an extent by my former assertion, that Brooklyn is the only community without municipal rank that will have here a day of her own. The fact that we are here in body and that she is here in spirit clearly shows that the old courage is still in her heart. Brooklyn may be only a borough, she may be only an 'abutment for bridges,' as President Littlejohn once feared she would become, but she is to-day the same independent Brooklyn she was back in her cityhood, and she is as proud of the things that make her great as many of the cities of the things that make them merely flashy.

"Her former spirit lives; it lives because since consolidation Brooklyn has assumed a commanding place in the councils of the greater city. Brooklyn has chosen as her three borough presidents men of force, who have been recognized as leaders by all the boroughs. At first the borough government was a mockery of a government. It was only a government in name. Our first president, Edward M. Grout, chafed under its restraint. He demanded that the boroughs be allowed a voice in city affairs, and that local improvements be given into the charge of borough officials. To him the State Legislature listened, and his successor in that office found himself with something beside the shadow of power, and his administration was a marvel to Brooklyn in what it achieved. Other boroughs looked on in envy, while J. Edward Swanstrom set a pace so rapid that its like will be difficult to produce. Our first president, Mr. Grout, became the comptroller in the second administration of the greater city. The comptrollership of New York city is as important as that of Secretary of the United States Treasury. Brooklyn was then and is yet the dominant force in the life of the metropolis. The entire city recognized Mr. Grout to be a man acquainted with even the minutest details of the city's government. Brooklyn's place at the table of the board of estimate was a commanding one with Swanstrom and Grout in their seats, and to-day her representation there is equally good. Mr. Grout is still there. In the place of Mr. Swanstrom sits Mr. Martin W. Littleton, and by him the name of Brooklyn has been made famous from ocean to ocean, and throughout the entire South, for in him Brooklyn has a mouthpiece that thrills, and through him she speaks with a tongue of eloquence.

"Since consolidation Brooklyn has been the second borough in point of population and of wealth, but in statesmanship, in oratory and in achievement she has stood pre-eminent. And while many believed that after consolidation she would lose her independent spirit, she has rather increased her old pride in herself, and this pride has been fostered and strengthened because of the worthy sons who have represented her in the government of the great city of New York, two of whom we have brought with us, that St. Louis, at times herself deceived by those she trusted, may look upon their like for once at least. Loyal to Brooklyn have been Grout, Swanstrom and Littleton, and thus inspired, has Brooklyn proved loyal to herself and faithful to her traditions.

"Brooklyn is a gigantic borough. She is three times as large as Buffalo, the home of the Pan-American Exposition. She is twice as large as St. Louis, the home of the present Exposition. Brooklyn territorially is large enough and properly adapted to hold a population of 7,000,000, and still remain less congested than the present borough of Manhattan. Brooklyn is devoid of many of the characteristics that mark other great cities. She is almost totally lacking in hotel life. A city of one-tenth her population would have more hotels. But municipal greatness never rested upon hotel life. It breeds corpulence, not courage. It discourages the rearing of children, a thriving industry in Brooklyn. Brooklyn has not the wealth in proportion to her size that she should have. Brooklyn sat for long years under the shadow of old New York, contributing to the wealth of the metropolis, but obtaining nothing in return. Her population contributed to the real estate values upon Manhattan island. Her factories and forges made many of the fortunes that were spent across the East river. Only since consolidation have we received any dividends upon that ever increasing investment. We now pay $14,000,000 into the city treasury and take $17,000,000 out annually. Brooklyn has often been described as the bedroom of old New York. The description was apt, for Brooklyn has always been a city of homes, a city of those of moderate means, a city of respectability. Brooklyn has never been able to boast of her wealth, as other cities, nor has she had to blush for her poverty and depravity as some other cities have.

"She has, however, been able to vaunt herself in the matter of those things which by nature are companions of the home. She has always been noted for her great churches, and has had the finest pulpit orators of the day, and now she is as strong in that direction as she ever was in the past. Her private schools have been known far and wide, while so long as she controlled her public schools, they, too, stood extremely high. Since consolidation they have fallen somewhat behind the march. In dividing government among the boroughs, Mr. Grout achieved much. Where the greatest good was done was where centralization was left with the least sway. In school matters centralization rules absolutely, and to that extent the schools have been forcibly drawn away from the people, and the development has lain in the direction of complexity of educational system, rather than in that of perfecting the children in the rudiments of scholarship. Of late years we have taught our boys how to sew, even if we did neglect their spelling. This increases the number of special teachers, adds to the city's bills, but enables the school superintendents to read splendid reports of new and special courses when they attend pedagogic conventions. Your Exposition loaded New York's educational authorities with medals and prizes and honorable mentions. I would not censure you for this. No men ever worked harder for such honors. The trouble is they work too hard over frills and neglect the essentials. Were your judges to-day to hold an examination among our grammar scholars upon the three subjects, reading, writing and arithmetic, I am inclined to believe that you would send hurry orders for the return of many of those prizes.

"In school matters Brooklyn is at a loss no further than are the other boroughs of the greater city. She is at a loss because Mr. Grout's advice was not taken. In short, we so highly prize our sewers, our streets and our pavements that we directed that they be given directly into our own charge and under our own borough president, and then we held our children in such light esteem that we surrendered them into the keeping of a centralized board of education, which is in turn in the keeping of the board of superintendents, in which body Brooklyn has but a small voice. It has reminded me of those people who personally care for their own dogs and horses and leave their children to servants and hired tutors. The system has been wrong. The wrong system has been made top-heavy. The results have been poor.

"Brooklyn has developed the home life of America to a greater extent than any other city has done. She has few palaces. She has few hovels. She has a great army of American mothers and fathers that are bringing up the next generation of men and women, and she is rearing them in thousands of comfortable homes, where body develops with mind and where the spiritual welfare is an important factor.

"Brooklyn has a park system of which she is proud to-day, and of which she will grow prouder. In Prospect Park she has a jewel, in the very heart of the community. In Forest Park she has a promise of great future development. That new park lies upon high ground overlooking a vast section of the borough and exhibiting to the eye the bay of Jamaica and the ocean beyond. Forest Park is richly endowed by nature, and it will in the days to come be in beauty above either Prospect or Central. Brooklyn has great driveways leading to the ocean along her harbor front and out into Long Island, and she has laid out many small parks and is still engaged upon that work.

"In library matters Brooklyn to-day is well supplied. The system is most extensive and has been rapidly developed. It is another indication of what can be done when a department is decentralized. The Brooklyn Public Library is under the control of Brooklyn men. The board of estimate makes it an annual allowance. Andrew Carnegie gave to Brooklyn $1,600,000 for library construction. With that money twenty branch libraries are to be erected in time. Five are up; one is in operation. To-day there are over twenty branch libraries; most of them are in rented quarters, and they circulate over one million books a year among the people.

"As another indication of the life of Brooklyn brief reference should be made to the Institute of Arts and Sciences, the great college of those beyond school years. It has been referred to as the intellectual bargain counter of Brooklyn. It offers at very moderate prices literary, historical, musical instruction and entertainment and lectures in all the sciences. It is well supported, and the city is building it a central building that will be the Mecca of the ambitious and the cultured. No other city in the land supports such an institution, and it is a great credit to us.

"Brooklyn's spirit is due in a great measure to the nature of the press that caters to her. Her newspapers are intensely local in character. They give to her institutions such support as is not given to the institutions of any other city in the United States. It is this that has encouraged an intelligent and independent breadth of mind in Brooklyn. She keeps alive the old New England custom of a close watch over her government and of a constant discussion of all public questions. Englishmen are noted for their unremitting guard of their personal rights. They are not to be compared in this with Brooklynites who, in spite of a callous railroad system, still persist in demanding their rights.

"Her press has called into being all over Brooklyn numerous boards of trade and taxpayers' associations, and they, encouraged by the attention given to them, devote themselves to their neighborhoods. Edmund Burke referred to the journalists as a fourth estate. Aptly might we regard these trade boards as a second government. Highly are they respected. Many reforms, especially in transportation matters, have they achieved.

"I have outlined to you some of the features of Brooklyn life. She is in truth the place where the home life of Greater New York is developed, where it may be seen in its simple beauty adorned with its rugged virtue. I have not boasted of her rich men, but of her intellectual gifts; not of her social leaders, but of her clear-minded men and women; not of her wealth, but of her mental attainments. It is from such a community that we come to-day to write upon your visitors' book the name of Brooklyn. In our way we are as proud of our homes as was the old Roman matron of her two sons, although we may be as poorly decked with tawdry jewels as she was. We are as proud of our independence in politics as Philadelphia should be ashamed of her regularity. Boston is credited with being the Athens of America. Brooklyn deserves the title, but would leave to Boston her pedantic ways. We are sincere in our speech and simple in our faith, and when we say we rejoice in St. Louis' success, are glad to be here and are honored in having a day set aside for us, we but echo the sentiments that our hearts suggest."

At the conclusion of the oration the Chairman introduced Henry Sanger Snow, LL.D., who read the following original poem:

POEM OF DR. SNOW

I

Hail! city of the West, from ocean's strand
  Afar we bring thee greeting. At thy gate,
Wide-thrown in welcome, gathered nations stand
  And praise the deed ye grandly celebrate!
The imperial star that rose from eastern seas,
  Marking the new-born nation in the West,
Rides in *thy* zenith now—by slow degrees
  The march of Empire takes its westward quest—
  And over scene more fair, sure star could never rest!

II

Worthy thy festival of that high deed—
  Louisiana's treaty—greatest act
Of all that came from our great Jefferson:
  Nor king nor statesman sealed a nobler pact!
And worthy the *deed* of this fair festival,
  When the young land whose life had scarce begun,
With lofty courage doubt could ne'er appall,
  In the one act a finer victory won
  Than war in all her scarlet glory e'er hath done!

III

An hundred years have passed—what wonders wrought
  Along the Mississippi's mighty stream!
The changes time's transforming wand hath brought
  Seem but the unreal visions of a dream!
Where stretched in vast expanse to western sea
  The pathless forest and the trackless plain,
Great States and teeming millions soon should be,
  And orchards fair and fields of waving grain
  And every art of peace through that broad land should reign.

IV

Hail to the Statesman whose far-seeing eyes
  Saw in the germ the nation that should be,
Saw how a mighty empire should arise
  And span the continent from sea to sea,
And building for the future, led the way
  With prescience and high courage, daring fate,
An emperor's domain in a single day
  Bought for a purse of gold! a vast estate,
  From Europe's despot gained—to Freedom consecrate!

V

Conquest of Peace! on thy triumphal day
  No mourning captives, chained to victor's car,
Nor spoil of war, nor bloodshed marked thy way,
  Nor hate, nor wrong did thy escutcheon mar!
No throng of armed hosts thy mountains crossed.
  Thy forests echoed to no battle cry,
No glory gained with nation's honor lost,
  Nor victor's plaudit, echoed with a sigh.
  Louisiana won—nor any doomed to die!

VI

Conquest of Peace! No Alsace here doth kneel,
  And Lorraine, scarred with unforgotten scar;
No riven Poland, 'neath the warrior's heel,
  Spoil of the victor from the field of war.
The sun that shines thy boundless plains along
  Lights not the smallest hamlet but is free;
The winds that sweep thy mountains bear no song
  Save that the patriot sings—where Liberty
  And Peace and Law now are, and evermore shall be!

VII

So be it ever, through the coming age
 Our nation's destiny shall be fulfilled,
Not by the tears that greed or passion wage,
 Not by the blood of foes or brethren spilled!
But in the wiser and the nobler way
 The patriot Statesman taught us, when of yore
His victory of Peace in one brief day
 Won glory greater than a year of war!
 So may it be, dear land, with thee for evermore!

At the conclusion of the exercises the benediction was pronounced by the
Reverend Doctor Wintner, of Brooklyn, New York, in the following words:

"May the Lord our God, Creator of the universe and Father of mankind, bless all those in our home city afar off, and also those near here, and may He look down upon you in His kindness and grace, and grant you peace forevermore. Amen."

THE LUNCHEON

Immediately after the formal exercises, the delegation were guests of the State Commission at luncheon, at which Commissioner William Berri presided. Covers were laid for about 200. At the conclusion of the luncheon toasts were responded to by several. The program of remarks follows:

"A Welcome to the Fair,"
Honorable David R. Francis, President of the Louisiana
Purchase Exposition

"The Old Brooklynites,"
Ex-Senator Stephen M. Griswold
"'Tis the sunset of life gives us mystical lore."

"Brooklyn of the Future"
Dr. Henry Sanger Snow
"There is a fascination in recollections of the past and
hopes for the future."

"Brooklyn Women"
Judge Hiram R. Steele
"Woman! Blest partner of our joys and woes."

THE COMMITTEES

The local Brooklyn committee was as follows: President, Martin W. Littleton; Secretary, John B. Creighton.

Executive Committee: Herbert F. Gunnison, Robert W. Haff, Timothy L. Woodruff, Julian D. Fairchild, J. Edward Swanstrom, S.F. Rothschild, James J. McCabe, Frank E. O'Reilly, John N. Harman and Thomas P. Peters.

Entertainment Committee: Thomas P. Peters, James J. McCabe, James McLeer, Robert W. Haff and Timothy L. Woodruff.

Program Committee: J. Edward Swanstrom, Julian D. Fairchild and S.F. Rothschild.

Transportation Committee: Herbert F. Gunnison, Frank E. O'Reilly and William Berri.

THE EVENING RECEPTION

The New York City building on the Model street, in which the evening reception was held, was elaborately decorated with colored lights, the word "Brooklyn" appearing in fairy lamps over the main doorway. Within a wealth of palms and smilax was used.

The reception took place between eight and ten and was attended by the Brooklyn delegation, Exposition officials, State and national representatives and many invited guests. An orchestra furnished music and throughout the evening a buffet luncheon was served. The receiving line consisted of Thomas W. Hynes, Commissioner for New York city, and Mrs. Hynes; Vice-President Berri, of the State Commission, and Mrs. Berri; Colonel William Hester; Mr. and Mrs. J. Edward Swanstrom; Mr. and Mrs. R.W. Haff; Mr. and Mrs. Thomas P. Peters; Mr. John B. Creighton; Mr. and Mrs. Clarence W. Seamans; Dr. and Mrs. Henry Sanger Snow; Mr. and Mrs. Hiram R. Steele; Mr. and Mrs. Stephen M. Griswold; Mr. and Mrs. J. Adolph Mollenhauer; Mr. and Mrs. J. H. Raymond; Mr. Herbert F. Gunnison.

The exercises of the day were marked by an enthusiasm which invariably characterizes the undertakings of Brooklynites, and the large delegation which had journeyed all the way from home to spend four short days at the Fair felt more than repaid for the journey.

[Illustration: CYNGALESE STICK DANCERS]

CHAPTER VIII

Thanksgiving Day

[Illustration]

The fact that the Exposition did not close until December first compelled all employees to remain in St. Louis Thanksgiving Day; that day which, of all others, generally marks a family gathering. The Commission thoughtfully extended an invitation to all of its employees and their families in St. Louis to be their guests at Thanksgiving dinner in the State building. The number included about sixty-five people, every attache who was in town accepting the invitation.

The official colony of the Empire State at the great Exposition assembled at the State building at one o'clock. All were cordially greeted by Vice-President Berri, Mrs. Berri and Mrs. Norman E. Mack. Before sitting down to dinner a group picture was taken on the front steps of the building, a copy of which was subsequently presented by the Commission to each employee.

The table was set in the grand hall and was heavily laden with products of the State of New York. Owing to the approaching close of the Exposition, the agricultural and horticultural exhibits were heavily drawn upon. Great heaps of New York's superlative fruit and prize vegetables were used in decorating the table. Messrs. Bayno & Pindat served a tempting menu, features of which were those dishes always associated with Thanksgiving Day—roast turkey and pumpkin pie. A spirit of hearty good fellowship pervaded the entire occasion, and each one vied with his neighbor in adding to the total of the entertainment.

Remarks were made between the courses, and early in the event Vice-President Berri, who presided, arose and, after complimenting every one present on behalf of the Commission for the part they had taken in contributing to New York's success at the Fair, proceeded in a most happy vein and said in part, as follows:

REMARKS BY MR. BERRI

"We should be thankful way down deep in our hearts that we are citizens of such a great country—the United States of America. When you think of its wonderful struggle for years and know that to-day it is at the forefront of progress among the nations of the earth should we not be thankful that we are a part of it? We should be thankful that we have such a great President—a man respected by all nations. Republicans should be thankful that they won such a great victory at the polls, and Democrats should be thankful that the Republicans give them such good government.

"The married men here should be thankful that they have such good wives, and the wives that they have such good husbands; the unmarried men that they have in the future such a vista of happiness that is to come to them, and the young ladies should be thankful that there are so many young men around. There is no way to view this occasion but with a thanksgiving spirit, and nothing pleases me more than to be with you to-day. There has been no feature of our Fair at any time, in all of its various functions we have had, that gives me such great pleasure as to preside at this gathering. It is the first time we have been all brought together, and, while the hours of the Fair are numbered, I am sure that every one will go home never forgetting the pleasant days they have had at the great Exposition at St. Louis in the year nineteen hundred and four."

He then called upon Mrs. Norman E. Mack, the only other member of the
Commission present. Mrs. Mack was warmly applauded and said:

RESPONSE BY MRS. MACK

"It gives me great pleasure to be able to take my Thanksgiving dinner to-day with so many who have done so much for the glory of New York at this Exposition. I particularly wish to compliment those of our own building who have always been so courteous and nice to me, and by so doing have aided the New York Commission in making the New York State building the social center of the Exposition."

OTHER SPEAKERS

Brief remarks were also made by Mr. J. H. Durkee, Superintendent of Agriculture; Mr. DeLancey M. Ellis, Director of Education and Social Economy; Mr. James T. Patterson, Assistant Superintendent of Horticulture; Mr. A. B. Strough, in charge of the Forestry, Fish and Game exhibit; Dr. H. H. Hinshaw, in charge of the Scientific exhibit, and the following officials of the State building: Hon. Frank J. LeFevre, Superintendent; Mrs. Dore Lyon, Hostess; Mrs. F. P. Applebee, Assistant Hostess; Miss Laura C. MacMartin, Matron, and Mr. George B. Cowper, Assistant Superintendent. Others present were called upon and made appropriate remarks, and the Pikers' Club, an organization composed of attaches of the building, furnished the musical part of the entertainment.

PRESENTATION TO SECRETARY BALL

Vice-President Berri then presented Mr. Charles A. Ball, Secretary and Chief Executive Officer of the Commission, with a complete fishing outfit in behalf of all of the employees of the New York State Commission. Mr. Ball enjoys a wide reputation as an expert with the rod. In his remarks Mr. Berri said that it had never been demonstrated that the Secretary had ever returned with any fish, and expressed the hope that with such a perfect equipment some tangible results might be shown. He also humorously referred to the fact that in the fire which a short time before had threatened the destruction of the State building, Mr. Ball's first thought had been for the safety of his fishing reels. The presentation was a complete surprise to the Secretary, who feelingly expressed his deep appreciation of the thoughtfulness of his staff in making him a present which he should treasure as long as he lived. He also expressed his gratitude to all of the employees of the Commission for their loyal support, which had meant so much in the successful participation of New York at the greatest Fair the world ever knew. He closed with laudatory remarks concerning the Commission, and the wisdom and thoroughness which had characterized its work.

In the course of her remarks Mrs. Lyon read the following original poem:

POEM BY MRS. LYON

Like ships upon the changing sea of life,
  Unknowing and unknown until we met,
We've sailed awhile together, and no strife
  Has marred our joy, nor brought a faint regret.

O'er this composite family of ours,
  Begotten from each corner of our State,
Has breathed a peaceful spirit, and the hours
  Have sped on wings from early dawn till late.

'Tis something to have met each other here,
  And found in each some trait to be admired,
And felt the world replete with joy and cheer,
  And friendship still the thing to be desired.

The tiny corners that we once possessed
  By gentle contact have been rubbed away,
And words that might have hurt have been suppressed,
  And peacefully we hail this Festive Day.

The time when we must part comes on apace,
  And soon we'll wend along our various ways,
Then mem'ry's realm will crowded be for space
  To welcome friends of Exposition days.

To name each one and strive to pay the debt
  We owe, of deepest gratitude and praise
In words, would take me many hours yet,
  And possibly run over into days.

And—after all, when all is said and done,
  It only means we've met—to live—to part.
Then here's my wish—That we have just begun
  A friendship which may blossom in each heart.

LANTERN SLIDES

At the conclusion of the remarks a series of lantern slides illustrating some of the most attractive natural features of the Empire State were shown, the slides being a part of the exhibit in education. The entertainment concluded with informal dancing, music for the same being furnished by an orchestra which was in attendance. The assemblage dispersed with three rousing cheers for the Empire State and for the Louisiana Purchase Exposition Commission of the State of New York.

[Illustration: SIOUX CHIEF "BLUE HORSE" AND ARMY OFFICERS]

CHAPTER IX
Educational Exhibit and Schedule of Awards

THE EDUCATIONAL EXHIBIT

BY DELANCEY M. ELLIS

Director of Education and Social Economy

[Illustration]

The movement for an educational exhibit of the State of New York at St. Louis was inaugurated at a meeting of the State Teachers' Association, held at Saratoga in July, 1902, at which a resolution was offered inviting the various educational associations of the State to co-operate with the above association in promoting an exhibit commensurate with the State's educational importance. An immediate response was forthcoming.

THE CONFERENCE COMMITTEE

Ten powerful educational associations and the two State administrative departments (since merged into the Department of Education) each sent a delegate to a central committee, which took the name of "Conference Committee," and consisted of Chairman, Myron T. Scudder, principal State Normal School, New Paltz, representing the Normal Principals' Council; Secretary, Henry L. Taylor, representing the University of the State of New York; A. M. Wright, Second Deputy Superintendent of Public Instruction, representing the Department of Public Instruction; F. D. Boynton, superintendent of schools, Ithaca, representing the State Teachers' Association; Andrew W. Edson, associate superintendent of schools, city of New York, representing the Council of School Superintendents; Calvin W. Edwards, president Board of Education, Albany, representing the Association of School Boards; F. S. Fosdick, principal Masten Park High School, Buffalo, representing the Associated Academic Principals; George H. Walden, principal Grammar School No. 10,
Rochester, representing the Council of Grammar School Principals; H. J. Schmitz, acting principal State Normal School, Geneseo, representing the Science Teachers' Association; A. C. Hill, Department of Public Instruction, representing the Training Teachers' Conference; Erwin B. Whitney, school commissioner, first district, Broome county, representing the School Commissioners and Superintendents' Association.

This Committee organized as above in October, 1902, and appointed a subcommittee to appear before the Louisiana Purchase Exposition Commission and request an adequate appropriation and the appointment of a director to carry on the work.

APPOINTMENT OF DIRECTOR

At the Meeting of the Commission held June 10, 1903, DeLancey M. Ellis, of Rochester, was appointed director, and the sum of $20,000 was set aside for the preparation of the educational exhibit. Offices were immediately opened at 46 Elwood building, Rochester, N. Y., and the work of collecting and preparing the exhibit material was begun. As the schools were just about to close for the summer holidays but little could be accomplished, and none of the work of the school year 1902-1903 could be procured. It is to be regretted that time was not allowed to procure an exhibit of work covering an entire school year. That which covers a shorter period is of necessity fragmentary and hardly conveys clearly an idea of the quality or scope of the work being done in a given institution.

ADVISORY COMMITTEE

The Conference Committee was invited to retain its organization and to take the name of "Advisory Committee," to co-operate with and assist the director, the members of the committee to serve without compensation, but necessary expenses while in discharge of their duties to be paid from the appropriation for the exhibit.

It would be hard to overestimate the services performed by this committee. Each member took a hearty interest in the work in hand and freely gave of his time and advice in carrying the work forward to a successful conclusion. Any lack of interest or enthusiasm on the part of the members of a given association was quickly dispelled by a personal appeal to its members from its representative upon the committee. In this way the interest was most genuine and general throughout the State, and in no way could the sentiment of educational interests be more clearly crystallized than in a meeting of this committee, and to them is due the thanks of the Commission, as well as the thanks of the educational forces of the State of New York for their unselfish efforts and wise counsel, which in so large a way was responsible for the success of the educational exhibit.

PLANS PRESENTED BEFORE
EDUCATIONAL ASSOCIATIONS

The director was invited to present the plans for the exhibit at the following educational meetings during the year 1903: University Convocation, at Albany, in June; State Teachers' Association, at Cliff Haven, in July; School Commissioners and Superintendents, at Watkins, in September; Association of Superintendents, which met in conjunction with the Massachusetts Association of Superintendents, at Boston, in October, and Associated Academic Principals, at Syracuse in December. The subject was cordially received, and a general effort was made throughout the field of education in the Empire State to prepare an exhibit which would surpass any that had ever been gathered before. By means of circulars, several of which were sent broadcast throughout the State, full instructions were given to local authorities as to the preparation of the work, amount of material desired and the proposed plan of arrangement. Throughout the fall and winter the director visited many cities of the State, consulted with exhibitors as to the most attractive way of preparing material, and held himself in readiness to assist all who experienced any difficulty in the preparation of their exhibits. The exhibit material was collected, systematically arranged and mounted at the offices in Rochester, the entire expense of its preparation and transportation being borne by the State, with the exception of the binding of written work and small incidental expenses, which were borne by the local school authorities.

LOCATION OF THE EXHIBIT

The space assigned to the State of New York contained approximately 2,300 square feet and was most advantageously located. It was directly within and facing the main north entrance of the Palace of Education, and at the intersection of the main north and south aisle and transverse aisle "B." For its neighbors were the city of St. Louis and the State of Missouri, both of which prepared most meritorious exhibits; and the State of Massachusetts, which is always looked upon as standing in the front rank in educational progress.

The Exposition authorities announced that no unit smaller than the State in public school exhibits would be recognized, except in the case of four or five cities which had powerful, strongly centralized school systems, making them worthy of independent space and proper subjects for individual study.

EXHIBIT OF THE CITY OF NEW YORK

The city of New York was numbered among these exceptions, and approximately 1,500 square feet of space was assigned it adjoining the space assigned to the State of New York. The city government appropriated $10,000 for its exhibit and bore the entire expense of the same. Associate Superintendent Andrew W. Edson was named as committee in charge of the exhibit by Superintendent William H. Maxwell. The city authorities early expressed a willingness and desire to co-operate with the State authorities in the preparation of an exhibit and agreed to follow the same general style of installation and arrangement. Due acknowledgment is hereby made to Superintendent Maxwell, Associate Superintendent Edson and to committees in charge of minor details for the adoption of plans already inaugurated in the preparation of the State exhibit, and to C. B. J. Snyder, superintendent of school buildings in the city of New York, who prepared the plans for the booth for both the State and city exhibits at no expense to the State.

THE INSTALLATION

The booth was so planned that from the outside it was apparently a single inclosure, the State and city exhibits being separated on the interior by an appropriate screen nine feet high, through which an entranceway was cut. Mr. Snyder's plans provided for a scheme of installation which, while inexpensive, was both artistic and dignified and admirably adapted for the display of the material to be exhibited. In fact it was generally conceded that much more effective results had been obtained than by surrounding states which had expended considerably more money. The inclosure was massive, the woodwork being an effective imitation of Flemish oak, and the hanging surface a burlap of a neutral green tint; the facade, sixteen feet in height, being broken every few feet at fixed intervals by fluted pilasters with ornamental caps. On the outside a wainscoting extended three feet from the floor, above which were panels for hanging exhibit material, the whole being capped by an attractive dentulated cornice. The entranceway, which was thrown across the corner at the intersection of the aisles, was a massive arch, surmounted by the coat of arms of the State, tinted in old ivory, underneath which in gold letters was, "State of New York." The interior was cut by transverse walls, nine feet high and extending seven feet from the main wall, thus forming a series of alcoves convenient for study on the part of visitors and leaving in the center an open space for the display of models, apparatus and cabinet material. Directly facing the entranceway were general and private offices. Completely surrounding the interior of the booth, on the eye line, were 100 wall cabinets which have come to be so generally used for the display of exhibit material. The wall space above the cabinets was used for the display of especially meritorious and attractive material, while below was a countershelf upon which, here and there, rested a showcase for the display of sewing, clay modeling, botanical specimens, etc. Underneath the counters were shelves for bound books and cupboards for the storage of printed matter and supplies. All work was mounted uniformly upon a Scotch gray cardboard and neatly lettered in white ink.

SCOPE OF THE EXHIBIT

Instead of confining the exhibit to the work of the public schools, as was quite generally done by other States exhibiting, it was decided to show, so far as possible, work now being done in all forms and phases of education in the Empire State. Space was freely given to private institutions to demonstrate the place which they are filling in the educational work of the State. Every subdivision of the official classification found an exemplification within the New York State exhibit. The participation of twenty-four cities and numerous incorporated villages, both in elementary and high school work, made the exhibits of those departments thoroughly representative of the work of the State as a whole. It is unfair to pick the work of a few progressive school systems, and endeavor to make it stand for the work of the State at large.

PLAN OF ARRANGEMENT

The plan of arrangement was arrived at only after the most careful thought and discussion, the desire being to so arrange the material as to be most serviceable to the educator and to those seeking suggestions and helpful ideas. In arranging an educational exhibit, emphasis must be placed either upon political divisions, subjects or grades. It was early determined that no separate space should be assigned to any single locality, but that all of the work of the State in the grades should be exhibited grade by grade and that of the high schools by subjects, and arranged under various departments, such as science, classics, mathematics, etc., thus making it possible for a grade teacher to readily compare her work with that of New York's, and to profit by the comparison, no matter in whose favor it might be, and a high school instructor in charge of a department to readily find the work of that department. This method rendered it unnecessary to look over the exhibits from several cities to find the particular work desired. Moreover, a further subdivision was made, in that the work was arranged according to the population of the contributing cities and villages. That is, the work from the city of the largest population contributing was installed first, and so on in order. While it was not the purpose to invite comparison of work between rival cities of the State, but rather to present a united front to the world at large, still if it was the desire of some to make such comparison, the above indicated arrangement was the most equitable, as all cities of approximately the same resources and theoretically working under like conditions were placed side by side, and the work of the small village was not placed in juxtaposition with that of the large, strongly centralized city system with many times its resources. A complete catalogue of the exhibit was freely distributed, and cross-references made to work of the various localities, so there was no difficulty for those interested in a single place to locate the work it contributed.

It was generally conceded that, while the above arrangement made no concession to local pride, it was by all odds the wisest arrangement to follow in an exposition of international scope. The compliments which were bestowed upon the arrangement of the exhibit, and the readiness with which all visitors found the work in which they were particularly interested, demonstrated beyond a doubt the wisdom of the committee in pursuing the course above outlined. The entire exhibit was also carefully classified in harmony with the official classification of the Exposition under the several groups and subdivisions thereof, thereby rendering additional aid in promptly locating exhibits in any particular department.

EXHIBIT DIVISIONS

Entering the booth one found to the left of the entrance the exhibit of the former State Department of Public Instruction. (It should be stated here that the exhibits of the University of the State of New York and of the State Department of Public Instruction were prepared before unification was an accomplished fact. The two exhibits can be said to have formed the exhibit of the new Department of Education.)

Next was the exhibit of the kindergartens, filling three units. (The term "unit" is used to designate one of the wall cabinets containing thirty-three cards 22 x 28 inches.)

Adjoining the kindergarten section was the exhibit of the elementary grades, filling twenty-five units. All the subjects of the curriculum were shown, the work in the wall cabinets being "types" or "samples" of work, the great bulk of which was shown in bound volumes. Cross-reference was made on the margin of each card to the volume containing similar work, thus facilitating the search of the visitor for a number of class exercises of work of the same general nature, and relieving the visitor interested in a general way of looking over a vast repetition of material. Separating the elementary grades from the high schools was the exhibit of the rural schools of the State, those schools under the jurisdiction of the several school commissioners. It was most complete and interesting, and afforded a clear picture of the work done in the ungraded country schools. The exhibit of the high schools, filling fourteen units, was next in order, and, as stated above, was subdivided into subjects. Twenty-four cities of the State, to say nothing of the incorporated villages, private institutions, etc., contributed material in one or more of the foregoing departments.

Next was installed the exhibit covering the professional training of teachers, equally divided between the State Normal School system and the work of the training schools and classes in cities and villages, each occupying five units. Every Normal School of the State was represented, each making a special exhibit in the particular subject or subjects assigned it by a committee of Normal School principals, to whom was delegated the duty of preparing an exhibit. All of the city training schools in the State, save four, were represented, as well as the great majority of training classes, the whole exhibit having been arranged by the State Supervisor of Training Schools and Classes.

In the next section was installed the exhibit in higher education, exhibits being in place from Colgate University, Hobart College, Manhattan College, the College of Pharmacy—allied with Columbia University—and Syracuse

University, the latter institution making an exhibit both in applied sciences and in fine arts. Next were installed the exhibits of technical and trade schools, which contained interesting displays from the leading institutions in the State engaged in this line of work. Just beyond was the exhibit of the industrial schools, and then the display of special work in education which is being done by institutions not wholly educational in character. A unique unit was that devoted to the work of the Indian schools of the State, each of the several reservations being represented, and the whole exhibit being arranged by the State Inspector of Indian Schools.

The next alcove was devoted to the education of defectives. It contained concise exhibits from the institutions of the State devoted to the instruction of the deaf, dumb and blind, and was carefully studied by those engaged in this work.

The exhibit of summer schools and extension courses adjoined this and was designed to show the work which is best exemplified by the Chautauqua institution. In a manner allied with this work is that of the Education Department in visual instruction, which is carried on by lantern slides to aid in the teaching of geography, history and kindred subjects. It was, therefore, installed under this head. The exhibit received hearty commendation from educators generally, but particularly from foreign visitors. The scheme is thoroughly practicable, and nowhere else is it carried on with the same careful attention to detail, nor is the same perfection of slide making reached as in the State of New York.

The last exhibit before leaving the booth was that of the University of the State of New York.

SPECIAL FEATURES

There were many features of special interest. A series of thirty-two charts were prepared as the special exhibit of the New York State Teachers' Association, and will be reproduced in the forthcoming report of that body. To one interested in following the tremendous progress made in every branch of educational activity within our State during the past decade, these charts are invaluable. The two charts here reproduced and which formed a part of the exhibit of the Department of Public Instruction were the subject of much comment.

The model of the new State Normal and Training School at Fredonia, which was prepared by the manual training and art classes of the institution, came in for its share of attention. It was an accurate model of one of the State's finest educational structures.

The State Normal School at New Paltz sent a doll house made by the seventh grade boys for the first grade children in the practice department, the entire structure being completely furnished and appointed by the children.

A special feature was the exhibit of clay modeling from the State School of Clay Working and Ceramics at Alfred, the only school of its kind in the United States receiving State aid. Near by stood a cabinet full of home-made apparatus sent from various institutions, but a large part of which came from the physical laboratories of Pratt Institute, Brooklyn. The exhibit contained much of interest to a science teacher.

On the exterior of the facade was a huge educational map of the State, upon which was shown the location, grade, construction and normal capacity of every institution of learning within its borders. The superiority of New York's schoolhouses was shown by the large number constructed of brick and stone. The year 1904 marked the passing of the log schoolhouse, only four of which were shown upon the map as against approximately fifty ten years ago. The facade also contained an admirable exhibit of art work prepared by the students of the New York School of Applied Design for Women.

SIGNIFICANCE OF SOME CITY EXHIBITS

Various methods of instruction peculiar to certain cities or localities were fully set forth. Albany exhibited the work of one of the most complete systems of free kindergartens in the country, as well as the correlation of subjects in the elementary grades; also manual training and art courses in the high school. Batavia demonstrated the system of individual instruction as carried on in its schools, which involves the employment of two teachers in each classroom. Syracuse exemplified its courses in art, manual training and physical training in the elementary grades. Jamestown clearly set forth its course in manual training throughout the entire school course, while Ithaca, in addition to a well-rounded exhibit, by means of photographs, brought out the subject of high school athletics. The exhibit from Yonkers, which was general in character, portrayed the efficiency and superiority of the school equipment in that city.

EDITORIAL COMMENT

The exhibit from first to last demonstrated beyond peradventure the beneficial results accruing from a strongly centralized, and, at the same time, most liberal administration of educational interests.

A prominent morning daily paper, commenting editorially upon the exhibit, says: "It is worth your attention; it means more to every citizen of the Empire State than any other exhibit shown. The chief product of the Empire State is men; neither fields of grain or manufactures, invention or art are as important a product as men. In New York State are produced some of the greatest men of the country. A large part of the raw material comes into New York harbor past 'Liberty Enlightening the World,' and is gradually converted into citizenship. ... Some of the raw material imported is next to worthless; some of the domestic stuff is equally unpromising, but in the great bulk, year in and year out, there is the making of fine men. ... New York State men are scattered throughout the country. They found the cities of the west; they run the railroads; they manipulate the finances; they capitalize the new enterprises; they invest in the futures; they get into the public offices; they plan the political campaigns; they produce the new ideas; they center current history. Men are made in New York State in the schools. ... The better the schools the finer the quality of the men produced. Therefore, the school exhibit of New York State should interest every citizen, as the schools have been bettering year by year and the product increasing in value. ... The Commission in charge of this exhibit has spared no expense to make this educational showing a storehouse of novel ideas and suggestions dealing with the advance in pedagogy, and of the State's resources in the teaching of the young idea."

DISPOSITION OF MATERIAL

Many requests were received from the representatives of foreign governments, agents of pedagogical museums and individuals for portions of the exhibit, but the determination of the Lewis and Clark Exposition Commission of the State of New York to send the entire exhibit to the Exposition at Portland, Oregon, precluded the possibility of acceding to these requests and insures the holding intact of the entire exhibit throughout the Portland Exposition period, at the conclusion of which it is to be hoped that provision will be made for the establishment of a Pedagogical Museum at the Capitol in Albany, of which this exhibit may be made the nucleus.

ITEMS OF EXPENDITURE

The appropriation of $20,000 was expended approximately, as follows

Installation: Booth, wall cabinets, furniture, etc. $6,000 Salary of Director and assistants and maintenance at St. Louis ——————————— ——————— 8,500 Freight, express, cartage, telegrams, etc. ——————— 1,000 Material used in preparation and general supplies 2,700 Traveling expenses ————————————————— 1,250 Printing and stationery —— ——————————————— 350 Expenses of Advisory Committee ——— ————————— 200 ——————— Total ———————————————— ————————— $20,000 =======

THE STAFF

The Director acknowledges the loyalty and efficiency of those associated with him in the work of the department. To them belongs a large share of any credit which may be forthcoming for the value of the exhibit.

In an educational exhibit, probably more than any other, the necessity of a personal explanation to supplement the work exhibited is necessary. Miss Olive C. Kellogg, of New York city, and Miss Clara M. Paquet, of Cohoes, expert attendants, were always ready to explain the work exhibited, and to give full information concerning the distinctive features of the various city systems and institutions. They spoke the principal foreign languages, thus aiding visitors from abroad in more easily grasping the ideas set forth and the methods exemplified.

Miss Mary MacArthur, of Rochester, N.Y., served throughout the period of preparation and through the Exposition period as general assistant and stenographer; Hugh J. Kelly, of Albany, N.Y., as assistant and clerk, and E.J. Haddleton and H.B. Skinner, of Albany, as expert letterers and draftsmen.

Catalogue of Exhibitors in the Department of Education, Arranged by Groups, with the Awards, if Any, Received by Each

GROUP ONE

Kindergartens, Elementary Education, and Training of Teachers for Same

Albany, Board of Education, public schools. Gold medal
  Administrative blanks
  Forty-one volumes class exercises
  Photographs
  Course of study in drawing and drawings
Ballston, Board of Education, training class. Collective award,
    gold medal
  Students' written work
Batavia, Board of Education, public schools. Gold medal
  Eight volumes pupils' work
  Photographs
  Charts
  Pamphlets
Cambridge, Board of Education, training class
  Photographs
Canajoharie, Board of Education, public schools
  Pupils' selected work
Canajoharie, Board of Education, training class
  Students' written work
Canton, Board of Education
  Administrative blanks
  Photographs
Cape Vincent, Board of Education, public school
  Three volumes pupils' written work
Cato, Board of Education, public school
  One volume pupils' written work
Cattaraugus, Board of Education, training class. Collective award,
    gold medal
  Students' written work
Clayton, Board of Education, training class. Collective award,
    gold medal
  Students' written work
  Two volumes drawings
Clyde, Board of Education, training class. Collective award, gold
    medal
  Students' selected work
Cohoes, Board of Education, public schools
  Pupils' drawings

Colton, Board of Education, training class. Collective award, gold
   medal
   Students' selected work
Corinth, Board of Education, public schools
   Six volumes of pupils' written work
   Photographs
Corinth, Board of Education, training class. Collective award, gold
   medal
   Students' written work
Cortland, Board of Education, public schools
   Photographs
   Administrative blanks
   Pupils' selected work
   Annual report
Depew, Board of Education, public schools
   Six industrial charts
DeRuyter, Board of Education, teachers' training class. Collective
   award, gold medal
   Students' written work
East Aurora, Board of Education, public schools
   Six volumes pupils' written work.
   Catalogues
Education, State Department of. Grand prize
   Charts
   Statistics
   Administrative blanks
   Reports
   Maps
   Lantern slides
   Publications illustrating visual instruction system
Fairport, Board of Education, training class. Collective award, gold
   medal
   Students' written work
Freeport, Board of Education, public schools
   Three volumes pupils' written work
Froebel Normal Institute, New York city. Silver medal
   One volume catalogues
   Photographs
   Students' written work
   Administrative blanks
   Kindergarten songs
Glens Falls, Board of Education, training class. Collective award,
   gold medal

Students' written work
Gouverneur, Board of Education, training class. Collective award,
  gold medal
  Students' written work
Griffith Institute, Springville, Board of Education, training class.
  Collective award, gold medal
  Students' written work
Hamilton, Board of Education, training class. Collective award,
  gold medal
  Students' written work
Herkimer, Board of Education, public schools
  Pupils' selected work
Hornellsville, Board of Education, training class. Collective award,
  gold medal
  Students' work
Hudson, Board of Education, public schools
  One volume pupils' work in penmanship
Ithaca, Board of Education, public schools. Gold medal
  Sixteen volumes pupils' written work
  Sloyd work
  Administrative blanks
  Photographs
Jamestown, Board of Education, public schools. Silver medal
  Nineteen volumes pupils' written work
  Statistical charts
  Cabinet of manual training work
  Administrative blanks
  Photographs
Johnstown, Board of Education, public schools. Collective award,
  gold medal
  Six volumes pupils' written work
  Industrial charts
  Annual report
Johnstown, Board of Education, training class
  Students' written work
Kingston, Board of Education, public schools. Collective award,
  gold medal
  Seven volumes pupils' written work
  Drawings
  Photographs
Little Falls, Board of Education, public schools
  Pupils' selected work
Malone, Board of Education, training class. Collective award, gold

medal
Students' written work
Map, Educational map of New York State
(See award to Louisiana Purchase Exposition Commission)
Mechanicville, Board of Education, public schools
Six volumes pupils' written work
Medina, Board of Education, public schools
Six volumes pupils' written work
Map drawing and relief maps
Mexico, Board of Education, training class
Students' written work
Mohawk, Board of Education, public school
Four volumes pupils' written work
Newark, Board of Education, public schools
One volume pupils' written work
Catalogues and administrative blanks
New Rochelle, Board of Education, public schools. Collective
    award, gold medal
Eighteen volumes pupils' written work
Drawings
Photographs
North Collins, Board of Education, training class. Collective award,
    gold medal
Students' written work
Norwich, Board of Education, training class. Collective award,
    gold medal
Students' written work
Nunda, Board of Education, training class. Collective award, gold
    medal
Students' written work
Ogdensburg, Board of Education, public schools
Four volumes pupils' written work
Drawings
Administrative blanks
Ogdensburg, Board of Education, training class. Collective award,
    gold medal
Students' written work
Oneida, Board of Education, public schools
Seven volumes pupils' written work
One volume annual reports
Administrative blanks
Oneida, Board of Education, training class. Collective award, gold
    medal

Students' written work
Onondaga, Board of Education, academy
   Pupils' nature study work
Phelps, Board of Education, public schools
   Five volumes pupils' written work
Phoenix, Board of Education, training class. Collective award, gold
   medal
   Students' written work
Port Byron, Board of Education, public school
   One volume pupils' written work
Port Henry, Board of Education, public schools
   One volume pupils' written work
Port Henry, Board of Education, training class. Collective award,
   gold medal
   Students' written work
Port Jervis, Board of Education, union school
   Drawings
   Administrative blanks
Port Leyden, Board of Education, union school
   Two volumes pupils' written work
   Photographs
Public Instruction, State Department of
   (See award to Louisiana Purchase Exposition Commission)
   Administrative blanks
   Pamphlets
   Charts
   Statistics
   Publications
   Fifty-six volumes, report of superintendent
Pulaski, Board of Education, training class. Collective award, gold
   medal
   Students' work
Richfield Springs, Board of Education, training class. Collective
   award, gold medal
   Students' written work
Rochester, plan of Clifford street embellishment
Rural schools: Collective exhibit from following counties
   Broome county. Collective award, gold medal
     Pupils' written work
     Photographs
   Cattaraugus county. Collective award, gold medal
     Pupils' written work
     Photographs

Chautauqua county. Collective award, gold medal
  Pupils' written work
  Photographs
Chenango county. Collective award, gold medal
  Pupils' written work
  Photographs
Columbia county
  Pupils' industrial work
Cortland county. Collective award, gold medal
  Pupils' written work
Dutchess county. Collective award, gold medal
  Photographs
Genesee county
  Photograph
Herkimer county. Collective award, gold medal
  Pupils' written work
Lewis county. Collective award, gold medal
  Pupils' written work
Madison county. Collective award, gold medal
  Photographs
Monroe county. Collective award, gold medal
  Pupils' written work
Nassau county. Collective award, gold medal
  Pupils' written work
  Photographs
Niagara county. Collective award, gold medal
  Pupils' written work
  Photographs
Oneida county. Collective award, gold medal
  Pupils' written work
Onondaga county. Collective award, gold medal
  Pupils' written work
  Photographs
Ontario county. Collective award, gold medal
  Pupils' written work
Oswego county. Collective award, gold medal
  Pupils' written work
Rensselaer county. Collective award, gold medal
  Pupils' written work and industrial work
Schuyler county. Collective award, gold medal
  Pupils' written work
  Photographs
Ulster county. Collective award, gold medal

Photographs.
　Washington county. Collective award, gold medal
　　Pupils' written work
Rushford, Board of Education, training class. Collective award,
　　gold medal
　　Students' work
Sag Harbor, Board of Education, public schools
　　Seven volumes pupils' written work
St. Patrick's Academy, Catskill
　　Two volumes pupils' written work
　　Photographs
　　Drawings
Salamanca, Board of Education, union school
　　Eight volumes pupils' written work
　　Photographs
Salamanca, Board of Education, training class. Collective award,
　　gold medal
　　Students' written work
Sandy Hill, Board of Education, public school
　　Photograph
Sandy Hill, Board of Education, training class
　　Photograph
Schenectady, Board of Education, public schools. Collective award,
　　gold medal
　　Eight volumes pupils' written work
　　Administrative blanks
　　Photographs
South Byron, union school
　　Pupils' selected work
　　Photograph
Syracuse, Board of Education, public schools. Gold medal
　　Pupils' selected work in drawing
　　Photographs illustrating physical training course
　　Manual training work
Unadilla, Board of Education, training class
　　Photographs
Union, Board of Education, training class. Collective award, gold
　　medal
　　Photographs
Utica, Board of Education, public schools. Collective award, gold
　　medal
　　Nine volumes pupils' written work
　　Manual training and construction work

Graphic charts

Photographs

Warrensburg, Board of Education, public schools

Nine volumes pupils' written work

Waterloo, Board of Education, public schools

Pupils' selected work

Catalogues

Administrative blanks

Photographs

Home-made apparatus

Watertown, Board of Education, public schools. Collective award, gold medal

Thirteen volumes pupils' written work

Drawings

Annual reports

Watkins, Board of Education, public schools. Collective award, gold medal

Six volumes pupils' written work

Photographs

Administrative blanks

Watkins, Board of Education, training class

Students' written work

Wellsville, Board of Education, public schools. Collective award, gold medal

Seven volumes pupils' written work

White Plains, Board of Education, public schools

Nine volumes pupils' written work

Course of study in drawing and manual training

Drawings, manual training, and Venetian iron work

Photographs

Administrative blanks

Statistics

Whitney Point, Board of Education, training class. Collective award, gold medal

Students' written work

Yonkers, Board of Education, public schools. Gold medal

Nineteen volumes pupils' written work

Drawings

Photographs of buildings

Photographs illustrating physical training and school plans

The following awards were made in this group to exhibits not a part of the collective State exhibit:

New York city, Department of Education, collective exhibit. Grand
   prize
   a. School system
   b. Collective exhibit of elementary grades
   c. Collective exhibit of vacation schools and evening schools
   d. Collective exhibit of manual training, drawing, and
      domestic science
   e. Physical training and methods for atypical children
   f. Kindergartens
   g. Free lecture system
   h. Training schools
   i. Exhibit of school buildings
New York city, Department of Education, collective exhibit. Gold
   medal
   Manual training. Drawing. Domestic science
New York city, Department of Education, collective exhibit. Gold
   medal.
   Vacation schools. Evening schools
New York city, Department of Education, collective exhibit. Gold
   medal
   Physical training methods for atypical Children

The following awards were made to collaborators:

Andrew S. Draper, Albany. Grand prize
   Education Department
Charles R. Skinner, Albany. Gold medal
   Department of Public Instruction
DeLancey Al. Ellis, Rochester. Gold medal
   State exhibit
William A. Wadsworth, Geneseo. Gold medal
   Improvement of school grounds
Luther H. Gulick, New York city. Gold medal
   Physical training
Theodore C. Hailes, Albany. Silver medal
   Educational map
John Kennedy, Batavia. Silver medal
   Individual instruction
James P. Haney, New York city. Silver medal
   Manual training
Mrs. Anna L. Jessup, New York city. Silver medal
   Sewing
Mrs. Mary E. Williams, New York city. Silver medal
   Cooking

Evangeline E. Whitney, New York city. Silver medal
  Vacation schools
Matthew J. Elgas, New York city. Silver medal
  Evening schools
C. P. J. Snyder, New York city. Silver medal
  Facade of exhibit

A grand prize was also awarded to the Louisiana Purchase Exposition Commission of the State of New York for its collective exhibit in this group, with special mention of the Department of Education, administrative features; Department of Public Instruction, administrative features, visual instruction system, and the educational map.

GROUP TWO

Secondary Education. Training of Teachers for Same

Adelphi Academy and College, Brooklyn
    Catalogues
Albany, Board of Education, high school. Gold medal
    Fifteen volumes students' written work
    Photographs illustrating manual training course
    Drawings
Albany, Board of Education, training school
    One volume students' written work
    Photographs
Avon Club, Jamestown High School
    Administrative blanks
    Program of exercises
Batavia, Board of Education, high school. Gold medal
    One volume students' written work
    Photographs
    Drawings
Beck Literary Society, Albany Academy. Bronze medal
    Historical sketch
    Administrative blanks
    Programs
    List of members
Brockport, State Normal School. Collective award, gold medal
    Seventeen volumes students' work
    Photographs
Buffalo, Masten Park High School. Collective award, gold medal
    Administrative blanks
    Two volumes students' written work
    Four volumes student periodical and drawings
Buffalo, State Normal School. Collective award, gold medal
    Two volumes science note books
    Illustrated science work
    Ten volumes publications
    Photographs

Buffalo, Board of Education, Teachers' Training School. Collective
   award, gold medal
   Four volumes students' written work
   Lesson outlines
Canajoharie, Board of Education, high school
   One volume students' written work
Cape Vincent, Board of Education, high school
   Students' selected work
Cattaraugus, Board of Education, high school
   Photographs
   Catalogues
Cohoes, Board of Education, high school
   One volume students' written work and drawings
Cohoes, Board of Education, Teachers' Training School. Collective
   award, gold medal
   Students' written work
Corinth, Board of Education, high school
   Three volumes students' written work
   Photographs
Cortland, Board of Education, high school. Collective award, gold
   medal
   Administrative blanks
   Students' selected work
   Photographs
Cortland, State Normal School. Collective award, gold medal
   Six volumes students' written work
   Photographs
   Administrative blanks
   Catalogues
East Aurora, Board of Education, high school. Collective award,
   gold medal
   Two volumes students' written work
   Photographs
   Catalogues
Education, State Department of. Grand prize
   Charts
   Statistics
   Reports

Bulletins

Administrative blanks

Elmira, Board of Education, training school. Collective award,
   gold medal

Students' written work

Photographs

Fredonia, State Normal School. Gold medal

Model of building and floor plans

One volume lesson outlines

Freeport, Board of Education, high school

One volume students' written work

Genesee Wesleyan Seminary

Announcements

Photographs

Geneseo, State Normal School. Collective award, gold medal

Eleven volumes students' work

Photographs

Illustration of course in drawing

Goshen, Board of Education, high school

Weather maps

Hazen's School for Girls, Mrs., Pelham Manor

Science work

Herkimer, Board of Education, high school

One volume students' written work

Ithaca, Board of Education, high school. Gold medal

Four volumes students' written work

Administrative blanks

One volume catalogues

Drawings

Photographs

Jamaica, State Normal School. Collective award, gold medal

Four volumes lesson outlines and students' written work

Photographs

Jamestown, Board of Education, high school. Gold medal

Ten volumes students' written work

Administrative blanks

Photographs

Publications

Statistics

Jamestown, Board of Education, training school
Students' written work

Johnstown, Board of Education, high school
Two volumes students' written work
Annual report

Kingston, Board of Education, high school
Two volumes students' written work
Burnt leather work
Photographs

Kingston, Board of Education, training school. Collective award, gold medal
Students' written work

Little Falls, Board of Education, high school
Students' selected work.

Map, educational map of New York State. Gold medal
(Award to go to Louisiana Purchase Exposition Commission)

Mechanicville, Board of Education, high school
Students' selected work

Moravia, Board of Education, high school
Drawings

New Paltz, State Normal School. Gold medal
Ten volumes students' work in art
Photographs
One volume publications
Rope work
Doll house
Administrative blanks

New Rochelle, Board of Education, high school
Five volumes students' written work
Photographs

Ogdensburg, Board of Education, high school
Two volumes students' written work

Olean, Board of Education, high school
Home-made apparatus

Oneida, Board of Education, high school
Three volumes students' written work
Administrative blanks

Oneonta, State Normal School. Collective award, gold medal
   Eight volumes students' written work
   Drawings
   Science note books
   Photographs
Oswego, State Normal School. Collective award, gold medal
   Two volumes students' written work
   Cabinet of manual training work
   Relief maps
   Photographs
Palmyra, Board of Education, high school
   One volume students' work
Phelps, Board of Education, high school
   Students' selected work
Plattsburg, State Normal School. Collective award, gold medal
   Five volumes students' written work
   Photographs
Port Byron, Board of Education, high school
   One volume students' written work
Port Henry, Board of Education, high school
   One volume students' written work
   Photographs
Potsdam, State Normal School. Collective award, gold medal
   Four volumes publications and lesson outlines
   Photographs
Pratt Institute, physical laboratories, Brooklyn
   Home-made apparatus
   Photographs
Rochester, editors of "Clarion," East High School. Bronze medal
   Three volumes students' publication "Clarion"
Sag Harbor, Board of Education, high school
   One volume students' written work
St. Patrick's Academy, Catskill, academic department. Collective
   award, gold medal
   Students' selected work
   Photographs
Salarranca, Board of Education, union school, high school
   department. Collective award, gold medal

Two volumes students' written work
Photographs
Schenectady, Board of Education, high school
  Eight volumes students' written work
  Mechanical drawings
  Administrative blanks
  Photographs
Syracuse, Board of Education, High school. Collective award, gold
  medal
  Students' selected drawings
  Floor plans
  Photograph of building
Syracuse, Board of Education, training school. Collective award,
  gold medal
  Students' written work
  Photographs
Tappan Zee High School, Piermont
  Botany note book
Tarrytown, Washington Irving High School
  Home-made apparatus
Utica, Board of Education, high school. Collective award, gold
  medal
  Drawings
  Two volumes students' written work
  Photographs
Utica, Board of Education, training school. Collective award, gold
  medal
  Students' written work
Warrensburg, Board of Education, high school
  Administrative blanks
  Two volumes students' written work
Watertown, Board of Education, high school
  Six volumes students' written work
  Drawings
  Administrative blanks
Watertown, Board of Education, training school. Collective award,
  gold medal
  Students' written work

Watkins, Board of Education, high school
   One volume students' written work
   Photographs
   One volume students' publication
   Administrative blanks
White Plains, Board of Education, high school
   One volume students' written work
   Administrative blanks
   Photographs
Yonkers, Board of Education, high school. Gold medal
   Six volumes students' written work.
   Photographs

The following awards were made in this group to exhibits not a part of the Collective State Exhibit:

New York city, Department of Education. Grand prize
New York city, Department of Education, Commercial High School.
  Gold medal
New York city, Department of Education, training school. Gold medal
New York city, Department of Education, manual training. Gold medal

The following awards were made to collaborators:
J. Russell Parsons, Jr., Albany. Gold medal
DeLancey M. Ellis, Rochester. Gold medal
Myron T. Scudder, New Paltz. Gold medal
A.T. Marble, New York city. Gold medal
Frank D. Boynton, Ithaca. Gold medal
F.B. Palmer, Fredonia. Gold medal.
James P. Haney, New York city. Silver medal

A grand prize was also awarded to the Louisiana Purchase Exposition Commission of the State of New York for its collective exhibit in this group.

GROUP THREE

Higher Education. Colleges and Universities, Libraries, Museums, Technical Schools

Albany. State Normal College. Gold medal
  Statistics
  Publications
Clarkson Memorial School of Technology, Potsdam, N. Y. Bronze medal
  Nine volumes theses
  Three volumes students' written work
  One volume catalogue and addresses
  Photographs
  Mechanical drawings
Colgate University, Hamilton. Silver medal
  Thirty-seven publications
  Map of grounds
  Mechanical drawings
  Statistics
College of Pharmacy, Columbia University, New York city
  Drugs
  Pharmaceutical preparations
  Eight volumes text books
Education, State Department of. (See State Library.) Grand prize
  Reports
  Bulletins
  Administrative blanks
  Statistics
Hobart College, Geneva. Bronze medal
  Map of campus
  Eight volumes publications
  Photographs. Charts
Hobart College. Gold medal
  Astronomical department and discoveries
Manhattan College, department of civil engineering, New York city.
  Silver medal
  Theses
  Mechanical drawing illustrating construction of dams and
    embankments. Also bridge construction
  Annual catalogues
Map, educational map of New York State. Silver medal
  (Award to go to Louisiana Purchase Exposition Commission)
Post Graduate Medical School and Hospital, New York city

Photographs
Publications
Catalogues
Rochester Theological Seminary
Two volumes catalogues
State Library, Department of Education. Grand prize
Traveling libraries
Blanks
Statistics
Syracuse University, Syracuse. Gold medal
College of Fine Arts
Drawings, architectural and free hand
College of Applied Science
Metal work
Wood work
Model of steam engine
Home-made laboratory apparatus
University of the State of New York. Grand prize
Bulletins
Reports
Decimal classification
Traveling library for the blind
Photographs
Large pictures
Statistical charts
Specimens from Museum Department

The following awards were made in this group to exhibits not a part of the collective State exhibit:

Columbia University, New York city. Grand prize
General exhibit
Columbia University, New York city. Gold medal
Special exhibit of Teachers' College
Columbia University, New York city. Gold medal
Special exhibit of Department of Botany
Columbia University, New York city. Gold medal
Special exhibit of Mines and Metallurgy
Columbia University, New York city. Bronze medal
Special exhibit of Department of Indo-Iranian Languages
Cornell University, Ithaca. Grand prize
General exhibit
Cornell University, Ithaca. Silver medal
Special exhibit of water color sketches

Cornell University, Ithaca. Silver medal
    Special exhibit of Sibley College
Rensselaer Polytechnic Institute, Troy. Grand prize
    General exhibit
Vassar College, Poughkeepsie. Grand prize
    General exhibit
Rev. D. Stuart Dodge, New York city. Gold medal
    Relief map, Protestant College at Beirut, Syria
Pratt Institute, Brooklyn. Gold medal
    Special exhibit of Polytechnic Department
New York University, New York city. Gold medal
Kny-Scheerer Company, New York. city. Gold medal
    Operating tables
    Hospital appliances

The following awards were made to collaborators:

Andrew S. Draper. Gold medal
    Monograph
James Russell Parsons, Jr., Albany. Gold medal
    Monograph
James McKeen Cattell, Columbia University, New York. Gold medal
    Monograph
Edward Delevan Perry, Columbia University, New York. Gold medal
    Monograph
Melvil Dewey, Albany. Gold medal
    State librarian

GROUP FOUR

Education in Fine Arts

Clay Working and Ceramics, State School of. Silver medal
  Specimens of pottery and modeling tools
New York School of Applied Design for Women. Gold medal
  Framed designs and prospectus
Syracuse University, College of Fine Arts. Bronze medal
  Architectural and free hand drawing

The following awards were made in this group to exhibits not a part of the collective State exhibit:

Pratt Institute, Brooklyn, Art Department. Grand prize
Mademoiselle Veltin, New York city. Bronze medal
  School of Fine Arts for Young Ladies

GROUP FIVE

Education in Agriculture and Forestry

Education, State Department of, State Museum Division. Grand prize
Publications
Statistics
Charts
Scientific discoveries

The following awards were made in this group to exhibits not a part of the collective State exhibit

Cornell University, Ithaca. Gold medal
 Exhibit of root crops
Cornell University, Department of Botany, Ithaca. Gold medal
 Apparatus for photographing
Cornell University, Agricultural Experiment Station, Ithaca. Silver
 medal
 Poultry breeding
Cornell University, Ithaca. Bronze medal
 Insects
New York Agricultural Experiment Station. Gold medal
 Investigations on milk
New York Agricultural Experiment Station. Gold medal
 Curing and paraffining cheese
New York Agricultural Experiment Station. Gold medal
 Commercial feeding stuffs
New York Agricultural Experiment Station. Bronze medal
 Investigations on rusty spot in cheese
New York Agricultural Experiment Station. Bronze medal
 Wax model showing scale
Kny-Scheerer Company, New York city. Gold medal
 Biological preparations
 Biological and anatomical models

GROUP SIX

Industrial and Trade Schools

Business Education. Education of the Indian

Albany Business College, Albany. Gold medal
  Pen drawings
  Six volumes students' written work
  Photographs
Binghamton School of Business, Binghamton
  Photographs and prospectus
Clara de Hirsch Home for Working Girls, New York
  Photographs
  Industrial work
Education, State Department of
  (See Indian Schools)
Henley Business School, Syracuse
  Photographs
  Administrative blanks
  Students' written work
Indian schools. Silver medal
  [Footnote: Award to go to Education Department, State of New York]
  Collective exhibit, including material from the Allegany,
    Cattaraugus, Tonawanda, Onondaga, Shinnecock and
    Poospatuck Reservations
  Pupils' written work
  Photographs
  Drawings
  Industrial work
Industrial School, Rochester
  Two volumes pupils' written work
  Manual training and industrial work
Manhattan Trade School for Girls, New York city. Silver medal
  Pupils' written work
  Industrial work
  Photographs
  Statistics

New York Trade School, New York. Bronze medal
    Photographs.
    Courses of study

The following awards were made to collaborators:

S.E. Bartow, Albany Business College. Silver medal
    Pen drawings

GROUP SEVEN

Education for Defectives. The Blind, Deaf and Dumb, Feeble-Minded

New York Institution for the Improved Instruction of Deaf-Mutes,
New York city.
   Photographs
New York Institution for the Instruction of the Deaf and Dumb,
New York city. Gold medal
   Photographs
   Drawings
   Pupils' written work
   Pyrography
   Publications
   Eighteen volumes of reports
   Text-books
   Administrative blanks
Northern New York Institution for Deaf-Mutes, Malone
   Pupils' selected work in drawing
New York Institution for the Blind, New York city. Bronze medal
   Cord, rattan and raffia work
New York State School for the Blind, Batavia. Silver medal
   Three volumes pupils' work
   Basketry
   Broom making
   Mattress making
   Piano action repairing
   Sewing
   Photographs
   Administrative blanks
State Library, Home Education Division. Silver medal
   Traveling library for the blind
Western New York Institution for Deaf-Mutes, Rochester. Bronze
   medal
   Four volumes pupils' written work
   Five volumes reports and catalogues
   Twenty volumes publications
   Photographs,
   Administrative blanks
   Drawings
   Charts

The following awards were made in this group to exhibits not a part of the collective State exhibit:

American Association for Instructors of the Blind. Grand prize
New York State collaborators:
State School for the Blind, Batavia
New York School for the Blind, New York city
Association of Medical Officers of Institutions for Idiots and Feeble-Minded Persons. Grand prize
New York State collaborators:
State Custodial Asylum for Unteachable Idiots, Rome
State Institution for Feeble-Minded Children, Syracuse
Convention of American Instructors of the Deaf. Grand prize
New York State collaborator:
Wright Oral School for the Deaf, New York city
New York city, Department of Education. Gold medal
For the establishment of a special school for the education of atypical children
New York Institution for Feeble-Minded, Syracuse. Gold medal
Wright Oral School for the Deaf, New York city. Bronze medal

GROUP EIGHT

Summer Schools, Extension Schools, Popular Lectures, Educational Publications and Appliances

Adirondack Summer School, Saranac Lake
   Photographs and pamphlets
Chautauqua Institution, Chautauqua, N. Y. Grand prize
   Photographs
   Publications
   Administrative blanks
   Prospectus and syllibi
City History Club of New York. Bronze medal
   Six volumes pupils' written work
   Photographs
   Charts
   Statistics
People's Institute, New York city. Silver medal
   One volume, "Working with the People"
   Prospectus
   Photographs
Teachers' Association, New York State. Gold medal
   Statistical exhibit, 32 graphic charts
Training School for Deaconesses, New York city. Silver medal
   Administrative blanks
   Catalogues
   Photographs
Young Women's Christian Association, New York city. Silver
      medal
   One volume of reports
   Administrative blanks
   Clay modeling
   Pyrography
   Artistic design and art furniture

The following awards were made in this group to exhibits not a part of the collective State exhibit:

Funk & Wagnalls Company, New York city. Grand prize
Dodd, Mead & Company, New York city. Grand prize
Dr. Nicholas Murray Butler, New York city. Grand prize
American Book Company, school and college text-books. Grand
   prize

Silver, Burdett & Company, New York city. Grand prize
Prang Educational Company, New York city. Grand prize
Charles Beseler Company, New York city, stereopticons and appliances.
   Gold medal
Pitmanic Institute, Phonographic, New York city. Gold medal
C.W. Bardeen, Syracuse. Silver medal
S.S. Packard, New York city. Silver medal

The following awards were made to collaborators:

Henry L. Taylor, professional education in the United States. Gold medal

A grand prize Was also awarded to the Louisiana Purchase Exposition Commission of the State of New York for its collective exhibit in this group

* * * * *

A special Commemorative Diploma was conferred by the Department jury upon Andrew Sloan Draper, Commissioner of Education of the State of New York, "in recognition of his distinguished service to Education."

* * * * *

RECAPITULATION OF THE AWARDS MADE TO THE STATE OF NEW YORK IN THE
DEPARTMENT OF EDUCATION

Grand Prize Gold Medal

Group I............... 5	Group I............... 63
Group 2............... 3	Group I, collab........ 2
Group 3............... 7	Group 2............... 36
Group 4............... I	Group 2, collab........ 5
Group 5............... I	Group 3............... 14
Group 6...............	Group 4............... I
Group 7............... 3	Group 5............... 6
Group 8............... 8	Group 6............... I
Special............... I	Group 7............... 3
	Group 8............... 4
[**Total] 29	Special............... 4
	[**Total] 139

Silver Medal Bronze Medal

Group I............... 2	Group I............... ..
Group 1, collab........ 8	Group 2............... 2
Group 2............... I	Group 3............... 3
Group 3............... 5	Group 4............... 2
Group 4............... I	Group 5............... 3
Group 5............... I	Group 6............... I

Group 6................ 2 Group 7................ 3
Group 6, ... I Group 8................ I
Group 7................ 2
Group 8................ 5 [**Total] 15

    [**Total] 28
Grand prizes................. 29
Gold medals.................. 139
Silver medals................. 28
Bronze medals............... 15
Grand total............... 211

[Illustration: PALACE OF EDUCATION FROM FESTIVAL HALL]

CHAPTER X
Fine Arts Exhibit and Schedule of Awards

THE FINE ARTS EXHIBIT

By CHARLES M. KURTZ

Acting Secretary of the Executive Committee on Art

[Illustration]

Up to the time of the organization of the Committee on Art for the State of New York, appointed by the New York State Louisiana Purchase Exposition Commission, very little had been accomplished in the direction of securing a collection of representative works by the artists of New York for exhibition at the World's Fair at St. Louis. Professor Ives, Chief of the Department of Art of the Louisiana Purchase Exposition, and Assistant Chief Kurtz had visited New York at frequent intervals (the first time in January, 1902), had aroused considerable interest in the Exposition among the artists, and had secured the appointment of Advisory Committees of Painters, Sculptors, Architects, Mural Painters, Miniature Painters, Engravers, Wood Engravers, Illustrators and Workers in the Applied Arts to look after the organization of exhibits in their respective fields of expression and the interests of the Department of Art of the Louisiana Purchase Exposition in connection therewith.

WAYS AND MEANS

It was impossible, however, for the work to be carried on in an adequate and worthy manner without State co-operation and assistance, and a committee of artists, representing the various Advisory Committees, appeared before the Commission, asked that a committee of artists representing the State of New York be appointed to co-operate with the Advisory Committees in the organization of a creditable art exhibit, and that a suitable sum of money be appropriated from the funds placed at the disposal of the Commission to defray the cost of organizing the exhibit, packing, transporting it to and from St. Louis, and insuring it while in transit; the Exposition authorities having agreed to pay the cost of unpacking in St. Louis, installation, insurance while in the Art Palace, and repacking and forwarding at the close of the Exposition.

EXECUTIVE COMMITTEE ON ART

After several meetings at the offices of the Commission in New York city and a forceful presentation of the condition of affairs (and the urgent necessity of action by the Commission) by Mr. Watrous, of the Artists' Committee, the Commission formally resolved to appropriate the sum of $10,000 for the purpose indicated, and appointed the following "Executive Committee on Art for the State of New York" to assume general direction of the work within the limits of the appropriation: Herbert Adams (sculptor), Grosvenor Atterbury (architect), J. Carroll Beckwith (painter), Francis C. Jones (painter), Louis Loeb (painter and illustrator), Will H. Low (painter, illustrator and mural painter) and Harry W. Watrous (painter). These men variously represented membership in the National Academy of Design, the Society of American Artists, the National Sculpture Society, the Society of Mural Painters, the American Water Color Society, the Society of Illustrators, the New York Etching Club, the American Fine Art Society, the American Institute of Architects, the New York Architectural League, the Municipal Art Society of New York and the Fine Arts Federation of New York. The Committee formally organized by the election of Harry W. Watrous as Chairman. Charles M. Kurtz, Assistant Chief of the Department of Art of the Louisiana Purchase Exposition, was appointed Acting Secretary without salary.

At a general meeting of the members of all the Advisory Committees in New York city, called by Chairman Watrous at the National Academy of Design, for each committee representing a group of the classification a chairman and a secretary was elected and general plans were formulated for the carrying on of the work.

Thereafter, frequent meetings were held by the various committees, at nearly all of which the Chairman of the Executive Committee and the Acting Secretary were present and participated in the work.

CAREFUL SELECTION OF MATERIAL

The Juries of Selection for the different groups of the classification of the Department of Art, constituted from the membership of the Advisory Committees representing various sections of the country, met and acted during the last two weeks of March, 1904, in the city of New York, passing upon upwards of 4,000 works submitted for exhibition. Of this assemblage of works a comparatively small number represented artists of high reputation, and a small proportion was found to be of sufficient merit worthily to represent the artists of the State. The number of exhibits secured thus being very small, and many of the more prominent artists not having submitted works, the different group juries held meetings, prepared lists of representative works calculated to reflect credit upon the State, and specifically invited artists and owners to lend the same for the Exposition. By this means the larger and better portion of the exhibit was secured.

The State of New York, the Louisiana Purchase Exposition and the artists in general in the State of New York are under great obligations to the members of these juries who so freely, unselfishly and devotedly gave their valuable time and effort to the organization of the art exhibit which represented so comprehensively the best achievement of New York artists.

A REPRESENTATIVE EXHIBIT

Almost every New York painter of individuality and ability—in oil, water-color and miniature work—was represented adequately and creditably; the exhibit of sculpture was exceptionally fine; etching and engraving were exemplified by the ablest exponents of these branches of art, wood engraving by types of its highest expression; there was an excellent collection of works from the leading American illustrators, and noteworthy examples of the applied arts—of artistic handicrafts—by New York art workers were well in evidence. In architecture, while the exhibit was creditable, it might have been more comprehensive and representative; and the same might be said of the exhibit of mural painting. The latter, however, as readily may be understood, is extremely difficult of representation at an exposition—most of its examples having been executed in place, and only cartoons or photographs of achieved works usually being available for exhibition.

ADVISORY COMMITTEES

The members of the various Advisory Committees in charge of the organization of the group exhibits were as follows:

For Oil Paintings: Cecilia Beaux, J. Carroll Beckwith, J. G. Brown, Howard Russell Butler, William M. Chase, William A. Coffin, Frederick Dielman, R. Swain Gifford, H. Bolton Jones, John La Farge, Alexander T. Van Laer, Harry W. Watrous.

For Water Colors, Pastels and Lithographs: F.S. Church, Charles C. Curran, Francis C. Jones, Will H. Low, J.C. Nicoll, Will S. Robinson, Henry B. Snell.

For Miniature Painting: William J. Baer, Lucia Fairchild Fuller, Laura C. Hills.

For Sculpture: Daniel C. French, H.A. MacNeil, A. Phimister Proctor, Augustus Saint Gaudens, J.Q.A. Ward.

For Etchings and Engravings (other than wood engravings): Carlton T. Chapman, C.F. Mielatz, J.C. Nicoll, Alexander Schilling, James D. Smillie.

For Wood Engravings: George T. Andrew, Frank French, Henry Wolf.

For Drawings for Illustration: Henry S. Fleming, Charles Dana Gibson, Arthur I. Keller, Louis Loeb, Howard Pyle.

For Architecture: Grosvenor Atterbury, Arnold W. Brunner, Walter Cook,
H.J. Hardenberg, John Galen Howard, C. Grant La Farge, Charles F. McKim,
Henry Rutgers Marshall, George B. Post.

For Mural Painting: Will H. Low, George W. Maynard, Charles Y. Turner.

For Applied Arts: William Couper, John La Farge, Frederick S. Lamb, Louis C. Tiffany, Stanford White, Douglas Volk.

Harry W. Watrous, Chairman of Executive Committee, Ex-officio member of all committees.

Exhibits of New York Artists Arranged by Groups, Together with the Number of Works Contributed, and Award, if Any, Received by Each

GROUP NINE

Paintings and Drawings

Oil Paintings

Alexander, John W., 8. Gold medal
Anderson, Karl J., 1
Barse, George R., 1
Baylos, Zellna, 1
Beal, Gifford, 2. Bronze medal
Beaux, Cecilia, 3. Gold medal
Beckwith, Carroll, 3. Silver medal
Bell, Edward A., 1. Silver medal
Birney, W. V., 2. Bronze medal
Blakelock, R. A., 1
Blenner, Carle J., 2. Bronze medal
Blum, Robert F. (deceased), 1
Bogert, George H., 2. Silver medal
Borglum, Gutzon, 1
Brigham, W. Cole, 1
Bristol, J. B., 1
Brown, Ethelbert, 1
Brown, J. Francis, 1
Brown, J. G., 5
Brown, Matilda, 1
Bruce, Patrick Henry, 1
Brush, George de Forest. 1. Gold medal
Burroughs, Bryson, 2. Bronze medal
Butler, Howard Russell, 2. Bronze medal
Carlsen, Emil, 4. Gold medal
Carr, Lyell, 2. Bronze medal
Chapman, Carlton T., 2
Chase, William M., 7
Child, Edward B., 2
Church, Frederick S., 3. Silver medal
Clark, Walter, 2. Silver medal
Coffin, William A., 2. Silver medal
Collins, Alfred Q. (deceased), 2
Coman, Charlotte B., 2
Cooper, Colin C., 5
Cooper, Emma Lampert, 1. Bronze medal
Cotton, Mrs. Leslie, 1

Couse, E. Irving, 3. Bronze medal
Cox, Kenyon, 1. Gold medal
Cox, Louise, 1. Silver medal
Crane, Bruce, 6. Gold medal
Crane, Frederick, 2. Bronze medal
Curran, Charles C., 4. Silver medal
Curtis, Constance, 1
Curtis, Elizabeth, 1
Daingerfield, Elliott, 1
De Forest, Lockwood, 1
De Haven, Frank, 1. Silver medal
Denman, Herbert (deceased), 1
Dewey, Charles Melville, 2. Silver medal
Dodge, W. de Leftwich, 2
Dougherty, Paul, 1
Drake, W. H., 1
Dufner, Edward, 3. Silver medal
Du Mond, Frank V., 6. Silver medal
Dustin, Silas S., 1
Eaton, Charles Warren, 4. Silver medal
Emmett, Ellen, 2. Silver medal
Emmett, Lydia Field, 1. Silver medal
Ericson, David, 1. Silver medal
Field, Edward Loyal, 1
Flagg, Montague, 1. Silver medal
Florian, Walter, 3. Silver medal
Foote, Will Howe, 1. Bronze medal
Foster, Ben, 3. Silver medal
Fournier, Alexis J., 3
Fowler, Frank, 3
Fromkes, Maurice, 1
Gauley, Robert D., 3. Bronze medal
Gay, Edward, 2. Bronze medal
Gifford, R. Swain, 3
Glackens, W. J., 1. Silver medal
Green, Frank Russell, 2. Bronze medal
Groll, Albert L., 2. Silver medal
Guy, Seymour J., 4. Gold medal
Harrison, Birge, 5. Silver medal
Hart, Letitia B., 1
Hart, Mary T., 1
Hassam, Childe, 6. Gold medal
Havens, Belle, 1

Hawthorne, C. W., 1
Henri, Robert. 2. Silver medal
Henry, Edward L., 3. Bronze medal
Herzog, Louis, 2. Bronze medal
Hitchcock, Lucius W., 1. Bronze medal
Hoeber, Arthur, 1
Homer, Winslow, 2. Gold medal
Howe, W. H., 3
Humphreys, Albert, 1
Huntington, Daniel, 1
Hyde, William H., 1
Inness, George, Jr., 2
Isham, Samuel, 3. Silver medal
Johnson, Eastman, 2. Gold medal
Jones, Francis C., 2. Silver medal
Jones, H. Bolton, 3. Gold medal
Jongers, Alphonse, 2. Silver medal
Kaufman, John F., 1
Kendall, Margaret, 1. Bronze medal
Kendall, W. Sergeant, 5. Gold medal
Ketcham, Susan N., 1
Kline, William F., 2. Bronze medal
Kost, Frederick W., 2. Silver medal
Lang, Charles M., 1
Lathrop, W. L., 1. Bronze medal
Lawson, Ernest, 2. Silver medal
Lee, Henry C., 1
Lee, Homer, 1
Leigh, W. R., 1
Lie, Jonas, 3. Silver medal
Linson, Corwin K., 2
Lippincott, W. H., 2. Bronze medal
Lockman, De Witt M., 1
Loeb, Louis, 2. Silver medal
Low, Will H., 5
Lucas, Alfred P., 1
Lyman, Joseph, 1. Bronze medal
McChasney, Clara T., 1. Bronze medal
McCord, George H., 1. Bronze medal
McIlhenny, C. M. (deceased), 2
McLane, M. Jean, 2. Bronze medal
Marchand, J. N., 1
Marsh, Frederick Dana, 1. Bronze medal

Maynard, George W., 2
Metcalf, Willard L., 3. Silver medal
Miller, Charles H., 1
Millet, F. D., 1
Minor, Robert C. (deceased), 2
Mora, F. Luis, 1. Bronze medal
Moran, Thomas, 2
Moschowitz, Paul, 2. Silver medal
Mosler, Gustave H., 1. Bronze medal
Mosler, Henry, 1
Murphy, J. Francis, 2. Silver medal
Myers, Jerome, 2. Bronze medal
Mygatt, R. K., 1. Silver medal
Needham, C. Austin, 3. Bronze medal
Newell, G. Glenn, 1
Nicoll, J. C., 3
Norton, W. E., 1
Ochtman, Leonard, 5. Gold medal
Palmer, Walter L., 2. Silver medal
Parton, Arthur, 2. Bronze medal
Perrine, Van Deering, 3
Poore, Henry R., 3. Silver medal
Porter, Benjamin C., 3. Silver medal
Post, W. Merritt, 2
Potthast, Edward H., 3. Silver medal
Prellwitz, Henry, 1. Silver medal
Questgaard, W., 1
Raught, J. W., 2
Rehn, F. K. M. 3. Silver medal
Reid, Robert, 3. Silver medal
Remington, Frederic, 1
Rice, W. M. J., 1
Robinson, Theodore (deceased), 4
Robinson, Will S., 2
Rook, Edward F., 5. Silver medal
Rouland, Orlando, 1
Sartain, William, 1
Saxton, John Gordon, 1. Bronze medal
Schreyvogel, Charles, 1. Bronze medal
Schroeter, Alexander, 1
Schwill, William V., 3. Bronze medal
Sears, Taber, 1. Bronze medal
Sewell, Amanda B., 3. Bronze medal

Sewell, Robert V. V., 1. Silver medal
Sheppard, Warren, 1
Sherwood, M. C., 1
Shirlaw, Walter, 1. Silver medal
Shurtleff, R. M., 1. Bronze medal
Sieber, E. G., 1
Simmons, Edward E., 1
Smillie, George H., 1. Bronze medal
Smith, De Cost, 1
Smith, W. Granville, 1
Snell, Henry B., 3. Silver medal
Steichen, Eduard, 2
Stokes, Frank W., 1
Talcott, Allen B., 4. Silver medal
Thorne, William, 3
Todd, Henry S., 1. Bronze medal
Tryon, D. W., 4. Gold medal
Turcas, Jules, 1. Bronze medal
Twachtman, J. H. (deceased), 3
Van Boskerck, R. W., 3. Silver medal
Van der Veer, Mary, 1. Bronze medal
Van Laer, Alexander T., 3
Volk, Douglas, 3. Silver medal
Vonnoh, Robert W., 5
Voorhees, Clark G., 1. Bronze medal
Walcott, H.M., 2. Silver medal
Walker, Horatio, 4. Gold medal
Walker, Henry Oliver, 2. Silver medal
Watrous, Harry W., 2
Weber, F.W., 1
Weir, J. Alden, 2. Gold medal
Whittemore, W.J., 1
Whittredge, Worthington, 3. Silver medal
Weigand, Gustav, 1. Bronze medal
Wiggins, Carleton, 4
Wiles, Irving R., 5. Gold medal
Wiley, Frederick J., 5. Bronze medal
Woolf, S.J., 1
Wores, Theodore, 1
Wyant, A.H. (deceased), 3
Yates, Cullen, 1. Bronze medal
Total—Artists, 207; works, 423

Water Colors and Pastels

Annan, Alice H., 1
Barse, George R., 1
Beckwith, Carroll, 2. See "Oil Paintings"
Bicknell, E.M., 1
Birney, W.V., 1. See "Oil Paintings"
Blum, Robert F. (deceased), 2
Bridges, Fidelia, 1
Bristol, J.B., 1
Brown, J.G., 1
Budworth, W.S., 3
Butler, Howard Russell, 2. See "Oil Paintings"
Chapman, Carlton T., 1
Chase, William M., 1
Clements, George H., 1
Clinedinst, B.W., 2
Colby, Josephine W., 1
Colman, Samuel, 1
Coman, Charlotte B., 1
Cooper, Colin C., 1
Cooper, Emma Lampert, 4. See "Oil Paintings"
Crowninshield, Frederic, 1
Curran, Charles C., 1. See "Oil Paintings"
Curtis, Constance, 1
Daingerfield, Elliott, 2
De Luce, Percival, 1
Dewey, Charles Melville, 2. See "Oil Paintings"
Dewing, Thomas W., 8. Gold medal
Dielman, Frederick, 2
Drake, Will H., 1
Eaton, Charles Warren, 3. See "Oil Paintings"
Edwards, George Wharton, 2
Fenn, Harry, 1
Foss, H. Campbell, 2
Foster, Ben, 1. See "Oil Paintings"
Fry, G. T., 2
Gifford, R. Swain, 1
Gilbert, C. Allen, 3
Green, Frank Russell, 1. See "Oil Paintings"
Greene, F. Stewart, 1
Guerin, Jules, 2. Silver medal
Hardenbergh, Elizabeth R., 1
Hassam, Childe, 3. See "Oil Paintings"
Homer, Winslow, 1. See "Oil Paintings"

Hore, Ethel, 1
Isham, Samuel, 1. See "Oil Paintings"
Jones, H. Bolton, 1. See "Oil Paintings"
Keith, Dora Wheeler, 1
Keller, Arthur L., 3. Silver medal
Kinsella, James, 3
La Farge, John, 3. See "Commemorative Award"
Liebscher, Gustav, 1
Linson, Corwin K., 3
Lippincott, W. H., 1. See "Oil Paintings"
McCord, George H., 3. See "Oil Paintings"
McIlhenny, C. M. (deceased), 1
McLane, M. Jean, 2. See "Oil Paintings"
McChesney, Clara T., 1. See "Oil Paintings"
Mora, F. Luis, 1. See "Oil Paintings"
Moran, Percy, 2
Newell, G. Glenn, 2
Nicholls, Rhoda H., 2. Bronze medal
Nicoll, J. C., 2
O'Leary, Angela, 1
Ochtman, Leonard, 1. See "Oil Paintings"
Of, George F., Jr., 1
Palmer, Walter L., 4. See "Oil Paintings"
Platt, Alethea H., 2
Post, W. M., 1
Potthast, Edward H., 1. See "Oil Paintings"
Proctor, A. Phimister, 1. Bronze medal
Redmond, Frieda W., 1
Redmond, John J., 2
Rehn, F. K. M., 1. See "Oil Paintings"
Ritschel, William, 2
Robinson, Will S., 1. Bronze medal
Rockwood, Catherine C., 2
Rook, Edward F., 1
Rosenmeyer, B. J., 2
Sanders, Bertha D., 2
Schilling, Alexander, 2. Silver medal
Schneider, W. G., 1
Scott, Emily M., 2
Sherwood, Rosina E., 5. Silver medal
Shirlaw, Walter, 5. See "Oil Paintings"
Shurtleff, R. M., 2. See "Oil Paintings"
Smillie, George H., 1. See "Oil Paintings"

Smith, F. Hopkinson, 3
Smith, W. Granville, 1
Snell, Florence F., 1
Snell, Henry B., 4. See "Oil Paintings"
Soper, James H. Gardner, 1. Bronze medal
Spafard, Myra B., 1
Stowell, M. Louise, 1
Tryon, D. W., 15. See "Oil Paintings"
Twachtman, J. H. (deceased), 3
Van Laer, Alexander T., 1
Walker, Horatio, 3. See "Oil Paintings"
Weir, J. Alden, 3. See "Oil Paintings"
Weldon, C. D., 2
Whittemore, W. J., 2
Yates, Cullen, 2. See "Oil Paintings"
Zogbaum, Rufus F., 1
Total—Artists, 102; works, 194

Miniatures

Baer, W. J., 3
Baxter, Martha W., 2
Bayliss, Lillian, 1
Beckington, Alice, 4. Bronze medal
De Haas, Alice P. T., 1
Dix, Eulabee, 1
Emmett, Lydia Field, 1. See "Oil Paintings"
Holley, Caroline E., 3
Howard, Clara, 1
Kendall, Margaret, 3. See "Oil Paintings"
King, Paul, 1
Nicholls, Rhoda H., 3. See "Water Colors"
Searle, Alice A., 1
Shuttleworth, Claire, 1
Siboni, Emma B., 5
Strean, Maria J., 2
Thayer, Theodora W., 3
Turner, Helen M., 3
Underwood, Edith B., 1
Volk, Ellen S., 1
Weidner, Carl, 3
West, Anne Shaw, 1
Wing, Alice B., 1. Bronze medal

Worrall, R., 2
Total—Artists, 24; works, 48

Mural Paintings and Designs

Armstrong, Helen M.,
Blashfield, Edwin H., 14. Gold medal
Breck, George W., 2. Silver medal
Burgess, Ida J., 1
Burroughs, Bryson, 3. See "Oil Paintings"
Cowles, Maud Alice, 1
Cox, Kenyon, 2. See "Oil Paintings"
Crawford, Earl S., 1
Curtis, Constance, 1
Dielman, Frederick. 6
Deming, Edward W., 3. Bronze medal
Dodge, W. de Leftwich, 3
Kaufman, J. F., 1
Kline, William F., 1. See "Oil Paintings"
Lamb, Ella Condie, 1
Lauber, Joseph, 5
Lichtenauer, J. M., Jr., 2
Low, Will H., 6
Marsh, Frederic Dana, 4. See "Oil Paintings"
McLane, M. Jean, 1. See "Oil Paintings"
Mora, F. Luis, 1. See "Oil Paintings"
O'Brien, Madeleine, 1
Sears, Taber, 2
Sewell, Robert V. V., 2. See "Oil Paintings"
Shean, Charles M., 1. Bronze medal
Shirlaw, Walter, 3. See "Oil Paintings"
Turner, C. Y., 5. Silver medal
Vaillant, Louis D., 2
Walker, Henry Oliver, 10. See "Oil Paintings"
Wenzell, A. B., 2. Silver medal
Total—Artists, 30; works, 92

Drawings for Illustrations

Chapman, Carlton T., 1
Child, Edward B., 3
Clay, John Cecil, 3
Cowles, Genevieve, 1
Cowles, Maud A., 1. Bronze medal
Du Mond, Frank V., 5. See "Oil Paintings"

Edwards, George Wharton, 3
Fogarty, Thomas, 5
Gibson, Charles Dana, 3. Silver medal
Gillam, Victor, 3
Glackens, W. J., 8. Bronze medal
Hambidge, Jay, 1
Hinton, Charles L., 6
Hitchcock, Lucius W., 4. Silver medal
Hutt, Henry, 1
Keller, Arthur I., 6. Gold medal
Lawrence, William H., 1
Leigh, William H., 2
Leyendecker, F. X., 5
Linson, Corwin K., 2
Loeb, Louis, 5. Silver medal
Orson, Lowell, 6
McCarter, Henry, 3. Silver medal
McLane, M. Jean, 2. See "Oil Paintings"
Mora, F. Luis, 1. See "Oil Paintings"
Parrish, Maxfield, 2
Penfold, Edward, 5
Reuterdahl, H., 5
Rhead, Louis J., 3
Rosenmeyer, B. J., 1
Sherwood, Rosina E., 4
Shinn, Florence S., 2
Smith, W. Granville, 1
Steele, Frederic Door, 5. Bronze medal
Sterner, Albert, 2
Stevens, W. D., 3
Taylor, C. Jay, 3
Van der Veer, Mary, 1. See "Oil Paintings"
Walcott, H. M., 1. See "Oil Paintings"
Wenzell, A. B., 4. See "Mural Paintings and Designs"
White, C. H., 1
Winslow, Eleanor C., 1
Zogbaum, R. F., 2
Total—Artists, 43; works, 127

The following commemorative award was also conferred in this group:

La Farge, John, commemorating distinguished service in art. Medal of honor

GROUP TEN

Engravings and Lithographs

Etchings and Engravings

(Other than Wood Engravings)

Bacher, Otto H., 4. Silver medal
Beckwith, Carroll, 1
Bellows, A. F., 4
Bloodgood, R. F., 2
Blum, Robert F. (deceased), 3
Chapman, Carlton T., 8
Dielman, Frederick, 2
Farrar, Henry (deceased), 1
Guy, Seymour J., 1
Hale, Walter, 6
Hambidge, Jay, 1
Hovenden, Thomas (deceased), 2
Jones, H. Bolton, 1
King, James S., 1
Lathrop, W. L., 4
Laube, Joseph, 7
Lewis, Arthur Allen, 3. Bronze medal
Lippincott, W. H., 3
Loewenburg, N., 2
Mielatz, Charles F. W., 21
Moran, Mary Nimmo (deceased), 7
Nicoll, J. C., 9
Osgood, Harry H., 7
Reich, Jacques, 2
Robbins, Horace W. (deceased), 1
Roth, Ernest D., 4
Sandreczki, Otto W., 1
Schilling, Alexander, 10
Schneider, Otto J., 5
Scholl, E., 2
Senseney, George, 1
Shelton, W. H., 1
Smillie, James D., 12
Sterne, Maurice J., 13. Bronze medal
Trowbridge, Vaughan, 7

Vondrous, John C., 6
White, Charles H., 3. Bronze medal
Weir, J. Alden, 21. Silver medal
Wood, Thomas W. (deceased), 1
Yale, Leroy M., 7
Yewell, George H., 3
Total—Artists, 41; works, 200

Wood Engravings

Bernstrom, Victor, 2. Silver medal
Chadwick, C. W., 4. Bronze medal
Cole, Timothy, 10. Grand prize
Evans, John W., 5
French, Frank, 1. Gold medal
Heineman, E., 2
Klotz, H., 1. Bronze medal
Kruell, Gustav, 8. Gold medal
Merrill, Hiram C., 5. Bronze medal
Northcote, Stafford M., 1. Bronze medal
Watt, William G., 1
Wolf, Henry, 29. See "Commemorative Award"
Total—Artists, 12; works, 69

The following commemorative award was also conferred in this group:

Wolf, Henry, commemorating distinguished service in art. Medal of honor

GROUP ELEVEN

Sculpture

Adams, Herbert, 5. Gold medal
Alfano, Vincenzo, 2
Bissell, George E., 1. Silver medal
Bitter, Karl T. F., 4. Gold medal
Borglum, Gutzon, 8. Gold medal
Borglum, Solon, 9. Gold medal
Boyle, John J., 5. Silver medal
Brenner, Victor David, 28. Silver medal
Bush-Brown, H. K., 7
Carpenter, Margaret S.; 1. Bronze medal
Eberle, Mrs. A. V., 1. Bronze medal
Flanaghan, John, 4. Silver medal
French, Daniel Chester, 4
Glenny, Alice R., 1
Goodwin, Mrs. Frederick, 1
Harvey, Eli, 9. Bronze medal
Heber, C. A., 1. Bronze medal
Hyatt, Mrs. A. V., 2. Bronze medal
Jaegers, Albert, 1. Bronze medal
Konti, Isidore, 2. Gold medal
Linder, Henry, 1. Bronze medal
Longman, Evelyn B., 4. Silver medal
Lopez, Charles A., 6. Gold medal
Lukeman, Augustus, 1. Bronze medal
MacNeil, Hermon A., 3
Mears, Helen F., 1. Silver medal
Miranda, Fernando, 1
Niehaus, Charles H., 8. Gold medal
Piccirilli, Attilio, 4. Silver medal
Piccirilli, Furio, 1. Silver medal
Proctor, A. Phimister, 4. Gold medal
Rhind, J. Massey, 1. Bronze medal
Roth, Frederick G. R., 7. Silver medal
Saint Gaudens, Augustus, 1. See "Commemorative Award"
Salvatore, Victor, 1. Bronze medal
Schwarzott, Maximilian, 1. Bronze medal
Scudder, Janet, 1. Bronze medal
Stillman, Effie, 3. Bronze medal

Tonetti, F. M. L., 3. Bronze medal
Triebel, C. E., 1
Usher, Leila, 1
Vonnoh, Bessie Potter, 10. Gold medal
Ward, Elsie, 1. Bronze medal
Ward, John Quincy Adams, 1. See "Commemorative Award"
Warner, Olin L. (deceased), 2
Weinert, Albert, 1
Weinmann, Adolf A., 5. Silver medal
Yandell, Enid, 1. Bronze medal
Zolnay, George Julian, 2
Total—Artists, 49; works, 173

The following commemorative awards were also conferred in this group:
Augustus Saint Gaudens, commemorating distinguished service in
    art. Medal of honor
John Ouincy Adams Ward, commemorating distinguished service
    in art. Medal of honor

GROUP TWELVE

Architecture

Atterbury, Grosvenor, 3. Silver medal
Babb, Cook & Willard, 2
Boring & Tilton, 6. Silver medal
Brunner, Arnold W., 4. Gold medal
Carrere, Brunner & Burnham, 6
Carrere & Hastings, 7. Gold medal
Coulter, W. L., 2
Flagg, Ernest, 14
Friedlander, J. H., 3
Gilbert, Cass, 3. Gold medal
Green & Wicks, 1
Hardenbergh, H. J., 1
Heins & La Farge, 4. Silver medal
Langton, D. W., 1
Lord & Hewlett, 4
Total—Architects, 15; works, 61

The following commemorative award was also conferred:

John M. Carrere. Gold medal

GROUP FOURTEEN

Original Objects of Art Workmanship

Applied Arts

Adams, Ralph R., 2
Archer, Annie M., 1
Bell, Peter, 1
Binns, Charles F., 5. Silver medal
Burdick, Bessie, 2
Crosbee, Mrs. W. G., 2
Farnham, Paulding, 15. Gold medal
Foote, Florence, 4. Bronze medal
Fry, Marshall, 7
Hicks, Amy M., 2
Hoagland, Jane, 3
Lamb, Frederick S., 1
Lawrence, F. Walter, 27
Leonard, Anna B., 7. Silver medal
MacNeil, Mrs. Carol B., 5. Bronze medal
Perkins, Mrs. Annie F., 2
Perkins, Lucy F.4. Bronze medal
Pond, T. H., 1
Randolph, Isabella, 2
Robineau, Mrs. A. A., 7
Sanders, Bertha D., 1
Solon, L. M., 1
Tiffany, Louis C. (designer), 79. Silver medal
Volk, Mrs. Douglas, 2. Silver medal
Volk, Wendell D., 1
Volkmar, Charles, 9. Bronze medal
Von Rydingsvaard, Karl, 1
Wolrath, Frederic E., 2. Bronze medal
Yandell, Charles R., 9
  Total—Artists, 29; works, 205

The following special commemorative awards were also conferred in the Department of Art:

Harry W. Watrous, for valuable assistance in the formation of the exhibit of the United States section. Gold medal

Charles M. Kurtz, for service in connection with the Department of Art, direction of installation, etc. Gold medal

George Julian Zolnay, for service in connection with the Department of Art, direction of installation, etc. Gold medal

RECAPITULATION

Showing the Relative Importance of the Participation of the State of New York in the United States Section of the Department of Art of the Louisiana Purchase Exposition, St. Louis, 1904

New York's Participation compared with that of the entire United States including New York.

	Oil Paintings	Water Color and Pastel	Miniatures	Mural Paintings	Drawings for Illustration	Etchings and Engravings	Wood Engravings	Sculpture	Architecture	Applied Arts	Totals
[*]Total number of artists represented in the United States Section	472	185	52	41	54	59	14	92	74	200	1,243
[*]N. Y. artists represented	207	102	24	30	43	41	12	49	15	29	552
Total number of works in the United States Section	904	314	90	114	178	269	82	354	290	946	3,541
Works by New York artists	413	194	48	92	127	200	69	173	61	205	1,592

[Footnote *: Where an artist has exhibited in more than one class, his name has been counted more than once.]

1=Oil Painting
2=Water Color and Pastel
3=Miniatures
4=Mural Paintings
5=Drawings for Illustration
6=Etchings and engravings
7=Wood Engravings
8=Sculpture
9=Architecture
10=Applied Arts

New York's Participation compared with that

of the entire United States including New York 1 2 3 4 5 6 7 8 9 10 Totals

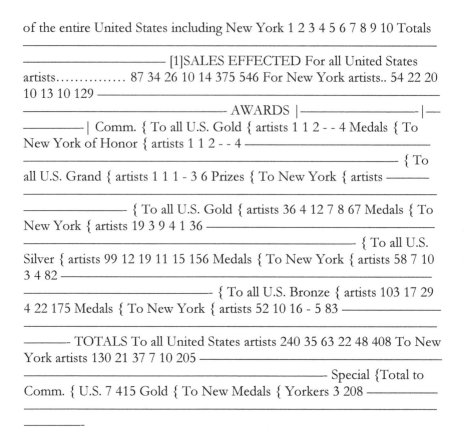

———————————————— [1]SALES EFFECTED For all United States artists............... 87 34 26 10 14 375 546 For New York artists.. 54 22 20 10 13 10 129 ——————————————————————————
——————————————————————— AWARDS |————————————|—
—————————| Comm. { To all U.S. Gold { artists 1 1 2 - - 4 Medals { To New York of Honor { artists 1 1 2 - - 4 ——————————————————
——————————————————————————————————————— { To all U.S. Grand { artists 1 1 1 - 3 6 Prizes { To New York { artists ————

—————————————— { To all U.S. Gold { artists 36 4 12 7 8 67 Medals { To New York { artists 19 3 9 4 1 36 ——————————————
——————————————————————————————————— { To all U.S. Silver { artists 99 12 19 11 15 156 Medals { To New York { artists 58 7 10 3 4 82 ——————————————
—————————————————————————— { To all U.S. Bronze { artists 103 17 29 4 22 175 Medals { To New York { artists 52 10 16 - 5 83 ——————————————

————— TOTALS To all United States artists 240 35 63 22 48 408 To New York artists 130 21 37 7 10 205 ——————————————
——————————————————————————————————— Special {Total to Comm. { U.S. 7 415 Gold { To New Medals { Yorkers 3 208 ————————

———————

[Footnote 1: In the report of the Superintendent of the Bureau of Sales, the Paintings sold approximated in value $70,000; the Engravings, $900; the Sculpture, $2,000, and the works of Applied Art, $7,500.

Out of the 904 oil paintings, 241 were owned by private parties (many being portraits) and were not for sale. Of the 662 works for sale, the 87 sold constituted nearly 13% of the whole number. The oil paintings contributed by New York artists which were not for sale numbered 138, leaving 281 for sale. The 54 works sold constituted approximately 20% of the New York pictures offered for sale.

Of the 314 water colors, 73 were not for sale. There were 241 for sale. The 34 works sold were approximately 13% of the entire number offered. Of the 194 water colors by New York artists, 46 were not for sale. Of the 148 works for sale, the 22 sold is nearly 15% of the number of works offered by New York artists in this medium.]

THE INTERNATIONAL JURY

The International Jury in the Department of Art was composed of the following members

United States.—Thomas Allen, E. A. Batchelder, S. S. Beman, Hugh H. Breckenridge, Richard E. Brooks, Carlton T. Chapman (New York), William M. Chase (New York), Ralph Clarkson, Walter Cook (New York), Conlin Campbell Cooper (New York), Charles Percy Davis, Frank Miles Day,
Lockwood de Forest (New York), Frederick Dielman (New York), Frank Duveneck, Daniel Chester French (New York), Mrs. Eugene Field, R. Swain
Gifford (New York), Charles Grafly, Will H. Low (New York), Hermon A. MacNeil (New York), Elizabeth St. John Mathews, J. L. Mauran, C. F. W. Mielatz (New York), James Craig Nicoll (New York), Joseph Pennell, Mary Solari, Theodore C. Steele, Alice Barber Stevens, Edmund C. Tarbell, S. Seymour Thomas, Alexander T. Van Laer (New York), Bessie Potter Vonnoh
(New York), Robert W. Vonnoh (New York), C. Howard Walker, H. Langford
Warren, Rose Weld, Frederic Allen Whiting, Carleton Wiggins (New York), Henry Wolf (New York), Edmund H. Wuerpel

Argentina.—Eduardo Schiaffino, George Julian Zolnay (New York)

Austria.—Dr. Paul Cohn, Adolph Kraus, Gustav Niederlein, Nicolaus Staits, William J. King

Belgium.—Guillaume de Groot, Ernest Verlant

Brazil.—J. Americo dos Santos

Bulgaria.—Charles M. Kurtz (New York)

Canada.—Paul Harney

Cuba.—Gonzalo de Quesada

Germany.—William J. Baer (New York), Erich Hoesel, Richard Müller, Hans von Petersen, Max Schlichting, Fr. von Thiersch

Holland.—William H. Howe (New York), Willy Martens, John C. Schüller, Herbert Vos

Hungary.—Bertelon Karlovsky, George Julian Zolnay (New York)

Italy.—Professor Pepoti Cantalamessa, Il Marchese Majnoni d'Itagnano, Ugo Ojetti

Japan.—Tooru Iwamura, Heromich Shugio

Mexico.—Isidoro Aldasoro

Portugal.—Marcel Horteloup

Russia.—William H. Fox, J. M. Godberg, Emil Vautier

Sweden.—Anshelm Schultzberg, Dr. Eugene Wagner

From the above jurors the juries for the several groups of the classification were made up—each group jury being international in character.

LOAN COLLECTION OF PAINTINGS

A prominent feature of the United States section of the Department of Art was a loan collection composed of especially noteworthy paintings from some of the most noted private collections of the United States. This collection was organized by Mr. Will H. Low, of New York. It contained 122 paintings representing many schools and periods. Of these works forty-three were lent by New York owners, as follows:

George J. Gould.—Domenico Ghirlandajo, Rembrandt van Ryn ("The Standard Bearer"), Frans Hals, Aert van der Neer, Gerard Don, Jean Marc Nattier, Sir Joshua Reynolds ("The Duchess of Marlborough"), Thomas Gainsborough; John Constable, J. M. W. Turner, Eugene Fromentin, Constant Troyon, Theodore Rosseau ("The Charcoal Burners' Hut" and "Le
Cure, Evening"), J.B.C. Corot ("Le Dance des Amours"), N.V. Diaz, Mariano Fortuny and J.L. Gerome

Helen Miller Gould.—Jean Francois Millet ("Washerwomen"), J. L. E. Meissonier ("The Smoker"), Rosa Bonheur, Alfred Stevens and Ludwig Knaus ("The Children's Party")

Estate of Jay Gould.—J.B.C. Corot ("Antique Dance") and Emile van Marcke

Duraud-Ruel.—Alexandre Gabriel Decamps, Eugene Delacroix, Gustave Courbet, Eugene Fromentin, Francois Bonvin (two examples), J.B.C. Corot, and Jules Dupre

Charles Fairchild.—William Morris Hunt and Elihu Vedder

Lockwood de Forest.—Frederick E. Church

National Academy of Design.—Octave Tassaert and R. Caton Woodville

Cottier & Co.—Sir John Everett Millais

Charles M. Kurtz.—Anton Mauve ("Sheep on the Dunes")

Julia Wilder Kurtz.—Thomas Couture

CHAPTER XI
Agriculture and Live Stock Exhibit and Schedule of Awards

AGRICULTURE AND LIVE STOCK EXHIBIT

By J. H. DURKEE

Superintendent

[Illustration]

The New York State Commission, in July, 1903, appointed J. H. Durkee, of Sandy Hill, N. Y., superintendent of agriculture, live stock and dairy products, with John McCann, of Elmira, Howard Moon, of Cobleskill, Theodore Horton, of Elmira, and W. A. Smith as assistants in the department of agriculture, W. W. Smallwood, of Warsaw, and W. A. McCoduck, of Sandy Hill, having direct supervision of live stock and dairy products respectively. George A. Smith, of Geneva, was superintendent for collecting dairy products. These gentlemen did the work assigned them faithfully and well, which is fully attested by the number of grand prizes and medals won in these departments.

SCOPE OF EXHIBIT

New York State has no distinctive agricultural product as has many of the other, especially some of the western, States but grows nearly everything in larger or smaller quantities that is grown in the north temperate zone.

In collecting and installing this exhibit, the aim was to gather these varied products and arrange them so as to show the real grain or vegetable to the best advantage rather than to show a fancifully arranged display of such products as would be of little or no value to those interested in practical agriculture. With this end in view, each section of the State was drawn upon for the best samples of the staple crops of that section. These samples were carefully inspected by competent judges, and only those of real merit were placed in the collection for exhibit. So thoroughly was this work of selection done that a large proportion of the samples received an award.

LABELING EACH SPECIMEN

That the exhibit might be of the greatest value to those most interested in agricultural pursuits, on each sample was placed a card giving the name and variety of the sample, also the name and post office address of the grower. Every day men could be seen with pencil and paper in hand taking names and addresses for future correspondence.

CONTINUOUS DISPLAY OF VEGETABLES

New York was one of the few States that had its exhibit complete at the opening of the Exposition, and was the only State that made a large and continuous display of fresh vegetables. Its display was greatly admired and favorably commented upon by the press, as well as by individuals. From the opening of the Exposition until the crop of 1904 was ready, the tables of the New York exhibit were kept filled with the standard vegetables of 1903, which had been placed in cold storage and were brought out as needed.

At the close of the Exposition, December 1, 1904, New York had over forty varieties of potatoes as well as many other vegetables on exhibition that were gathered in 1903, having been out of the ground over fifteen months. To the inexperienced eye, they could not be distinguished from the crop of 1904. In October and November, New York's vegetable display was unusually fine. The judges who passed upon it said it was the finest collection of vegetables they had ever seen.

AWARDS

The catalogue of exhibitors which follows shows conclusively that New York is truly the Empire State so far as agricultural products are concerned. It was the only State that was awarded a grand prize on fresh vegetables alone. J. M. Thorburn & Co., of New York, Glendale Stock Farm, Glens Falls, and Cornell University, Ithaca, also received grand prizes on vegetables.

Catalogue of the Exhibitors in the Department of Agriculture, with the Award, if Any, Received by Each

GROUP EIGHTY-FOUR

Vegetable Food Products—Agricultural Seeds

Alms House Farm, Varyburg
    Wheat
    Oats—White Michigan
J. B. Anderson, Kennedy. Bronze medal
    Barley—Six-Rowed
    Oats—Swedish
R. I. Anderson, Florida
    Corn—Eight-Rowed Red
C. S. Baldwin, Wellsville. Bronze medal
    Corn—Red Glazed, ears
W. H. Bellamy, Wellsville. Bronze medal
    Oats—Swede, White Russian
F. J. Bellinger, Hammond. Silver medal
    Oats—Clydesdale
E. A. Bentley, Wellsville. Bronze medal
    Corn—Eight-Rowed Yellow, ears
T. T. Blodgett, Fishkill. Silver medal
    Rye—Dark
    Oats—White Swede
L. G. Brainard, Ellington. Silver medal
    Rye—Winter
C. E. H. Breckon, Clarence. Bronze medal
    Beans—White Kidney
Charles Brian, Perry. Silver medal
    Wheat—Klondike
Briggs Bros., Rochester. Bronze medal
    Corn—Leaming, Golden Beauty
George Bronson & Son, Bath. Bronze medal
    Oats—New Lincoln
    Buckwheat—Gray
    Wheat—Gold Coin
    Corn—Dibbs' Ninety-Day-Eight-Rowed Yellow, ears
L. M. Bronson, Bath
    Wheat—White Winter
Brooks Bros., Painted Post. Silver medal
    Wheat—Gold Bullion
    Buckwheat—Silver Gray
    Corn—Red Beauty Pop

Oats—Russian, Lincoln, White Swede
George W. Brooks, Painted Post. Bronze medal
  Buckwheat—Silver Gray
  Beans—Coffee
  Mustard—Black
M. D. Bennett, Elmira, R. F. D. No. 1. Silver medal
  Buckwheat—Silver Hull, Japanese
Lewis J. Brundage, Starkey. Silver medal
  Wheat—Duck
  Buckwheat—Silver Gray
  Wheat—Gold Coin, Prosperity
  Barley—Two Rowed
  Beans—Red Kidney, White Kidney, Marrow
  Barley—Hulless
R. R. Buck, Warsaw. Gold medal
  Wheat
Isaac Budlong, Scottsville. Bronze medal
  Wheat—Prosperity
W. Carroll, LaGrangeville. Bronze medal
  Oats.—White
  Corn.—Early Mastadon, ears
Charles Caswell, Abbott. Bronze medal
  Corn.—White Red Glaze, ears
W. L. Chapin, Warsaw. Silver medal
  Wheat.—Malay Winter
Perry E. Chappel, Warsaw. Silver medal
  Wheat.—Fultz
D. E. Chase, Warsaw. Silver medal
  Wheat.-Red Clawson
  Oats.—Lincoln
C. W. Clark, Skaneateles. Silver medal
  Collection of Teasels
J. H. Clute, Painted Post. Bronze medal
  Corn.—Twelve-Rowed Yellow
  Wheat.-Long Medt
  Beans.—Burlingame's Prolific, Marrow
Miles Colburn, Ellington. Bronze medal
  Oats.—Early Siberian
Harry Cole, Caneadea
  Corn.—Yellow, ears
M. D. Corbett, Bath. Silver medal
  Rye.—White
Cornell University, Ithaca. Bronze medal

Wheat.—White Chall Medt, Reliable
F. H. Crowley, Painted Post. Bronze medal
Corn.—Eight-Rowed Yellow
Buckwheat.—Silver Hull, Small Silver Gray
E. Crippen, Horseheads. Bronze medal
Wheat.—Clawson
Crossman Bros., Rochester. Grand prize
Field, Garden, and Flower Seeds
Peas.—Crossman's First and Best, Crossman's Extra Early
True, Early Kent, Early June, Dan O'Rourke, Philadelphia
Extra Early, Alaska, Grandun, American Wonder, Nott's Excelsior,
Extra Early Premium Gem, McLean's Little Gem, Surprise
or Eclipse, Tom Thumb, Abundance, Advancers McLeans,
Dwarf Daisy, Dwarf Champion, Everbearing, Heroine, Horsford's
Market Garden, Pride of the Market, Stratagem Imp,
Shropshire Hero, Yorkshire Hero, Duke of Albany, Telephone,
Telegraph, Champion of England, Forty Fold, Long Island
Mammoth, Large White Marrowfat, Black-Eyed Marrowfat,
Canada Field, Mammoth Podded Sugar, Melting Sugar, Dwarf
Gray-Seeded Sugar, Tall Gray-Seeded Sugar, Laxton's Alpha
Beans.—Early Dwarf Prolific Black Wax or Butter, Early
Dwarf, Challenge Black Wax or Butter, Early Pencil Pod
Black Wax, Early Dwarf Improved Golden Wax, Early Dwarf
Black-Eyed Wax, Early Dwarf Golden-Eyed Wax, Early
Dwarf Red Flageolet Wax, Early Dwarf Refugee Wax, Early
Dwarf Wardwell's Kidney Wax, Early Dwarf Dair's White
Kidney Wax, Yosemite Mammoth Wax, Improved Early Red
Valentine, Early Mohawk, Early Yellow Six Weeks, Early
China Red-Eye, Early Refugee, Burpee's Stringless Green Pod,
Refugee or Thousand to One, Dwarf Horticultural, Broad
Windsor, Improved Red Kidney, Royal Dwarf or White
Kidney, White Marrowfat, White Medium, Boston Small Pea
Bean, Henderson's Dwarf Lima, Burpee's Bush Lima, Dreer's
Bush Lima, New Prolific Pickle, Coffee or Sofa Bean, New
Golden Cluster Wax, German Black Wax, Horticultural or
Speckled Cranberry, Kentucky Wonder, Lazy Wife's, Lima
Early Jersey, Lima King of the Garden, Lima Large White,
Lima Dreer's Improved, Lima Small or Sieve, Southern Prolific,
Scarlet Runners, White Dutch Runners, Dutch Case Knife,
Red Speckled cut Short or Corn Hill
Corn.—First of All, Adams' Extra Early, Early Red Cory,
Early White Cory, Early Mammoth White Cory, Early Marblehead,
Early Minnesota, Early Adams, Early Sweet or Sugar,

Shakers' Early, Perry's Hybrid or Ballard, Crosby's Early,
Moore's Early Concord, Early Mammoth, Black Mexican,
Crossman's Genesee Sweet, Stowell's Evergreen, Country Gentleman,
Large Late Mammoth, Clark's None Such, Egyptian
or Washington Mammoth, Hickox's Improved, Old Colony,
Parshing White Pearl, Parshing White Rice, Angel of Midnight
Yellow Dent, Extra Early Huron Yellow Dent, King
of the Earliest Yellow Dent, Golden Beauty Yellow Dent,
Golden Dent Yellow Dent, Longfellow Yellow Flint, Leaming
Improved Yellow Dent, Pride of the North Yellow Dent, Sanford
White Flint, Mastadon, Improved Hickory King White
Dent, Iowa Red Mine Yellow Dent, Golden Dew Drop, Southern
Sheep Tooth, Red Cob Ensilage, Sweet or Sugar

Cow Peas.—Black, Black Eyed, Clay, Whip-Poor-Will,
Wonderful

Buckwheat.—New Japanese, Silver Hull

Artichoke.—French Green Globe

Asparagus.—Conover's Colossal, Palmetto, Barr's Mammoth,
Columbian Mammoth White

Beets.—Eclipse, Dark Red Egyptian Turnip, Crosby's Dark
Red Egyptian, Crimson Globe, Detroit Dark Red Turnip, Edmand's
Blood Turnip, Extra Early Turnip Bassano, Early
Blood Turnip Bastians, Lentz's Early Blood Turnip, Dewing's
Early Blood Turnip, Long Dark Blood, Red Globe, Yellow,
Mammoth Long Red, Norbitian Giant Long Red, Yellow Ovoid,
Golden Tankard, French White Sugar, Lane's Improved White
Sugar, Vilmorin's Improved White Sugar, Klein Wanzleben

Broccoli.—Early Purple Cape, Early Large White

Brussells Sprouts.—Tall Extra, Dwarf Improved

Cabbage.—Early Jersey Wakefield, Early Large Charleston
Wakefield, Early Express, All Seasons, Premium Flat Dutch,
Louisville Drumhead, Danish Round Winter or Baldhead,
Stone Mason Marblehead, Hollander

Carrots.—Chantenay, Half Long Scarlet, Early Scarlet
Short Horn, Danvers Half Long Orange, Mastodon White
Intermediate, Large White Belgian

Cauliflower.—Early London or Dutch

Celery.—Golden Self-Blanching, French, Golden Heart or
Golden Dwarf, Sandringham Dwarf White, Golden Rose or
Rose-Ribbed Paris

Corn Salad.—Large Seeded, Improved Green Cabbaging

Cucumbers.—Cumberland, Early Russian, Green Cluster,
Green Prolific, Jersey Pickling, Early Frame, Early White

Spice, Livingston's Emerald, Nichol's Medium Green, Long
Green
Chicory.—Large Rooted
Collards.—True Georgia or Creole
Cress.—Curled or Peppergrass, True Water Cress
Egg Plant.—Improved New York Purple Spineless
Endive.—White Curled
Kale.—Semi-Dwarf Moss Curled
Kohl Rabi.—Early White Vienna
Leek.—Large Carentan Winter
Lettuce.—Crossman's New Improved, Early White Cabbage,
  Early Curled Simpson, Black-Seeded Simpson, Early Prize
  Head, Big Boston, Grand Rapids, All the Year Round, Yellow-Seeded
  Butter
  Musk Melons.—Extra Early Hackensack, Fine Large Green
  Nutmeg, Baltimore Acme Cantaloupe, Jenny Lind, Montreal
  Market, Bay View, Cosmopolitan, Long Island Beauty, Paul
  Rose or Petoskey, Delmonico, Early Christiana, Banana, Tip
  Top
Water Melons.—Cole's Early, Green Gold, Florida Favorite,
  Pride of Georgia, Hungarian Honey, Seminole, Black Spanish,
  Phinney's Early, Ice Cream White-Seeded, jumbo or Jones,
  Striped Gipsy, Georgia Rattle Snake, Mammoth Iron Clad,
  Kolba Gem, New Dixie, Volga, Kleckley's Sweet, Iceberg
Mustard.—White London or English, Giant Southern Curled
  Mushroom Spawn.—Best English
Okra.—White Velvet Pod
Parsley.—Champion Moss-Curled
Parsnips.—Long White Dutch, Imp. Hollow Crown, Guernsey or Cup
Pumpkins.—Imp. Cushaw, Mammoth Tours, King of Mammoth,
  Connecticut Field
Onions.—Early Red Globe, Large Red Wethersfield, Yellow
  Dutch or Strasburg, Yellow Danvers, Yellow Danvers Globe,
  Prize Taker, White Globe, White Portugal or Silver Skin,
  New White Queen, Bermuda White, Large Italian, Large Dark
  Red Bassano
Peppers.—Large Bell or Bull Nose
Radishes.—Early Scarlet Globe, White-Tipped Scarlet Turnip,
  Golden Globe Turnip-Rooted, French Breakfast, Early
  Deep Scarlet, White Strasburg or Hospital White Stuttgart,
  Large Scarlet Short Top, Long Brightest Scarlet, Long White
  Vienna or Lady Finger, New Chartier or Sheppard, Long
  White Naples, Chinese Rose Winter, California Mammoth

White Winter, Japanese Early Mammoth Sakura Jima

Rhubarb.—Lennaens, Victoria Myatts, St. Martins

Salsify.-Salsify or Vegetable Oyster, Mammoth Sandwich Island

Spinach.—New Giant, Prickley or Winter, Long Standing, Victoria Long Standing, New Zealand

Squash.—Early Yellow Bush Scallop, Early White Bush Scallop, Early Golden Crookneck, Early White Crookneck, Mammoth Golden Crookneck, Perfect Gem, Boston Marrow, Hubbard Improved, Warty Hubbard, Pike's Peak or Sibley, Turban or Turk's Cap, Butman

Tobacco.—Connecticut Seed Leaf, Conqueror, Little Dutch, Orinoco Yellow, Tuckahoe, White Burley

Sunflowers.-Mammoth Russian

Tomatoes.-Dwarf Monarch, Matchless, Dwarf Aristocrat, Long Keeper, Early Atlantic Prize, New Stone, Ignotum, Paragon, Scoville's Hubird, Trophy, Queen Red, Acme, Dwarf Champion, Imperial, Ponderosa, Golden Queen or Sunrise, Peach, Plum-Shaped Yellow, Red Cherry, Strawberry or Ground Cherry

Turnips.—Milan Extra Early, Purple Top, Early White Flat Dutch Strap Leaf, Early Six Weeks or Snowball, Purple Top Strap Leaf, Purple Top White Globe, Purple Top Scotch or Aberdeen, Amber Globe, Seven Top, Skirving's Imp. Purple Top, White Sweet or White Russian, Sweet German

Miscellaneous

Beggar Weed

Broom Corn.—Evergreen

Canary

Chafas

Hemp—Russian

Honey Locust

Kaffir Corn—White, Red

Osage—Orange

Rape—Dwarf Essex

Sugar Cane—Early Amber, Orange, Teosinte

Vetches—Spring

Wild Rice

Herbs—Anise, Balm, Borage, Caraway, Chervil Curled, Coriander, Dill, Horehound, Lavender, Rosemary, Rue, Sage (English Broadleaf), Summer Savory, Sweet Basil, Sweet Fennel, Sweet Marjoram, Tansy, Thyme (Broadleaf) Wormwood

Grasses—Red Top Fancy Clean, Kentucky Blue Fancy

Clean, Bermuda Grass, Fescue Meadow, Orchard Grass, Rye
Grass (Perennial), Sweet Vernal, Hungarian Grass, Millet
(German, Golden Japanese, Barnyard, Siberian), Lawn Grass
(Crossman's Park Mixture), Rye Grass (Italian)
Clovers.—White Dutch, Alsike or Swedish, Alfalfa or
Lucerne, Crimson, Medium Red, Timothy
Flower Seeds.—Abronia Umbellata, Ageratune Mexicanum
Blue, Alyssum Sweet, Amaranthus, Antirrhinum Majus Snap
Dragon, Asters (Branching Mixed), Balsam Double Mixed,
Bartonia Aurea, Calendula Prince of Orange, Calliopsis Mixed,
Canary Bird Flower, Candytuft (White, Mixed), Canna Mixed,
Carnation Mixed, Celosia Dwarf Mixed Cockscomb, Centanrea,
Cyanns Bachelor Button, Cobaea Scandens Purple, Cosmos
Mixed, Cypress Vine Mixed, Double Daisy Mixed, Eschscholtzia
Californica, Gaillardia Lorensiana, Gomphrena Globosa,
Gourd (Apple Shaped, Bottle Shaped, Dipper Shaped, Egg
White, Hercules Club, Mock Orange, Pear Shape, Sugar
Trough), Helichrysum, Hollyhock Double Mixed Chaters, Ice
Plant, Larkspur (Perennial Mixed), Lobelia Speciosa Crystal
Palace, Lupinus Mixed Colors, Marigold French Dwarf, Martynia
Probosidea, Marvel of Peru, Mixed Four O'Clock, Moon
Flower Cross-bred or Hybrid, Mignonette Sweet Large-
Flowered, Morning Glory, (Convolvulus Major, Giant
Japanese), Myosotis Palastris Forget-Me-Not, Nasturtium
(Dwarf Mixed, Tall Mixed), Pansy Very Large Flowering
Mixed, Petunia Mixed Hybrid, Phlox Drummond Grandiflori
Mixed, Poppy Carnation Double Mixed, Portulaca Single
Mixed, Ricinus Sanguineus (Castor Oil Bean), Salpiglossis
Large Mixed, Scabiosa Majus Dwarf Mixed, Smilax Boston,
Stock German Dwarf Mixed, Sunflower Double Globosus
Fislutosus, Swan River Daisy, Sweet William (double), Thunbergia
Mixed, Verbenas Hybrid Mixed, Wild Cucumber,
Quinnia Double Dwarf Mixed, Sunflower White Seeded,
Phoenis (Reclinata, Canariensis), Dracaena (Indivisa, Australis),
Snails, Wonus, Dolishos, Lablab White, Lagums
Ovatus, Avena Steralis, Coix Lachrymo, Zea Japinica, Ameranthus
Candatus
Sweet Peas.—America, Broeatton, Emily Eckford, Fire Fly,
Katherine Tracy, Navy Blue, Queen of England, Crossman's
Special Mixed
James J. Culbertson, Groveland. Silver medal
Wheat.—Gold Bullion, Dawson's Golden Chaff
Beans.—Marrow

Frank H. Cupp, Painted Post. Bronze medal
    Rye.—White
Albert J. Davis, Spencerport. Bronze medal
    Corn
Hiram Davis, Gansevoort. Bronze medal
    Corn
C. A. Davidson, Caton. Bronze medal
    Oats
W. H. Dettoes, Johnsonville. Bronze medal
    Corn
Henry Drudge, Clarence. Bronze medal
    Buckwheat
J. H. Durkee, Florida. Silver medal
    Wheat
F. E. Ebbing, Syracuse. Silver medal
    Seeds
Wm. Edminster, Painted Post. Silver medal
    Wheat and Oats
Frank H. Emery, Hornellsville. Silver medal
    Wheat
G. W. Engdalil, Ellington. Silver medal
    Barley and Oats
Frank A. Erwire, Painted Post. Silver medal
    Oats
P. E. Eysaman, Hammond. Bronze medal
    Corn
James Faucett, Bath. Silver medal
    Oats
Henry M. Fisher, Warsaw. Gold medal
    Wheat
Frank E. Ford, Painted Post. Bronze medal
    Grain
M. C. Frisbee, Ellington. Bronze medal
    Barley
M. E. Ferguson, Florida. Silver medal
    Wheat and Oats
M. L. Gamble, Groveland. Bronze medal
    Beans
John Gerow, Washingtonville. Bronze medal
    Corn
M. O. Gilbert, Ellington. Gold medal
    Buckwheat
Samuel Green, Florida. Bronze medal

Buckwheat
John E. Griffith, Ellington. Silver medal
  Oats
L. P. Gunson & Co., Rochester. Gold medal
  Oats
W. H. Haight, Fishkill. Bronze medal
  Wheat
W. H. Hall, Bath. Bronze medal
  Wheat
G. L. Halstead, Arlington. Bronze medal
  Wheat
J. M. Ham, Washington Hollow. Bronze medal
  Rye
George Harder, Bath. Bronze medal
  Wheat
A. G. Happul, Johnsonville. Bronze medal
  Corn
E. P. Harris, Elmira. Gold medal
  Beans
Charles Hathaway, Hartford. Bronze medal
  Oats
I. C. Hawkins, Middletown. Bronze medal
  Corn
Joe Hetzel, Florida. Silver medal
  Rye and Corn
J. M. Hewlett, Bath. Bronze medal
  Wheat
G. K. Higbie, Rochester. Gold medal
  Oats
C. B. Hill, Wellsville. Bronze medal
  Oats
Frank N. Holbrook, Charlton. Silver medal
  Buckwheat
John Houston, Florida. Bronze medal
  Grain
James K. Houston, Goshen. Silver medal
  Rye and Oats
J. C. Howard, Irondequoit. Silver medal
  Corn and Beans
John S. Howell, Elmira. Bronze medal
  Wheat
George W. Humphrey, Warsaw. Bronze medal
  Oats

C. L. Jesup, Florida
    Corn.—Peachblow, ears
    Wheat.—No. 2, Red
Fred Johannes, Filmore. Silver medal
    Barley.—Black
    Buckwheat.—Gray, Silver Hull
    Oats.—Clydesdale
Peter Johnson, Florida
    Buckwheat.—Silver Hull, Silver Gray
    Corn.—Extra Early Evergreen Sweet
A. N. Jones, LeRoy. Grand Prize
    Wheat
John Jones, Meriden. Bronze medal.
    Oats.—Pride of England
    Wheat.—Farmer's Friend
N. B. Keeney & Son, LeRoy. Gold medal
    Beans.—Saddle Back Wax, White Kidney, Dwarf Horticulture,
    Bush, Bismarck, Snow Flake Pea, Burpee's New Stringless
    Green Pod, Crimson Flageolet, Boston Small Pod, China Red
    Eye, Grant's Stringless Green Pod, Red Valentine, Celestial
    Wax, Improved Golden Wax, Currie's Rust Proof Wax, Improved
    Horticulture, Improved Black Wax, Burlingame's
    Medium, Early Mohawk, Davis Wax, Pencil Pod Black Wax,
    Golden-Eyed Wax, Golden Refugee, Maule's Butter Wax,
    Keeney's Rustless Golden Wax, White Wax, Longfellow Bush,
    Round Pod Kidney Wax, Round Pod Refugee, Brittle Wax,
    Yosemite Mammoth Wax, Extra Early Refugee, Challenger
    Black Wax, Flageolet Wax, Keeney's Stringless Refugee Wax
    Peas.—Abundance, Admiral, Advancer, Alaska, Ameer,
    American Champion, American Wonder, British Wonder,
    Champion of England, Claudit, Duke of Albany, Duke of York,
    Ever Bearing, Nott's Excelsior, Extra Early Pedigree, Extra
    Early Trial Ground, First and Best, Forcing Suttons, Forty-Fold,
    Glory, Gradus or Prosperity, Heroine, Hurst William,
    Juno, Prolific Laxtons, Laxton, Thos., Long Island Mammoth,
    Market Garden, Horsfords, Marrowfat (Black-Eyed, Early
    Marblehead, White), Premium Gem, Pride of the Market,
    Profusion, Prolific Early Market, Reliance Hursts, Seedling
    Suttons, Senator Improved, Shropshire Hero, Station, Stratagem,
    Sugar Mammoth Podded, Surprise Gregorys, Telegraph,
    Telephone, Tom Thumb, Yorkshire Hero
C. E. Knapp, Little Britain. Bronze medal
    Corn.—White Flint, ears

Frank Lawrence, Ellington. Bronze medal
   Barley.—Beardless
   Oats.—Siberian
E. D. Lee, Whitesville
   Corn.—White Flint, ears
James Livingston, Cobleskill. Silver medal
   Flax
   Timothy
Charles Lovell, Painted Post. Silver medal
   Oats.—English Wonder
   Wheat.—Gold Bullion
D. Macbeth, Kanona. Bronze medal
   Wheat.—Clawson
Mrs. S. E. Manning, Elmira Heights. Gold medal
   Wheat.—Red Russian
Frank Marley, Hornellsville
   Corn.—Red Blaze
Charles Martin, Hartford. Silver medal
   Beans.—Apple
Fred Martin, Fort Ann
   Corn.—King Phillip
Will Martin, Hartford
   Oats.—Lincoln
Jacob Marzolf, Clarence Center. Bronze medal
   Wheat.—Hundred Mark
E. P. Mattice, Middlebury
   Wheat.—Genesee Giant
Harry J. McCann, Elmira. Bronze medal
   Corn.—Queen's Golden Pop, Queen's Golden, ears
   Pumpkin.—Red Field
James McCann, Elmira. Silver medal
   Corn.—Klondike
   Buckwheat.—Gray
   Rye.—White
John McCann, Elmira. Silver medal
   Wheat.—Rochester Red, Clawson, Golden Coin
   Corn.—White Cap Yellow Dent, Queen's Golden Pop, ears,
    White Pearl Pop, ears
   Buckwheat.—Japanese
   Clover.—Crimson
   Beans.—Red Marrow, Gold Eye
   Rye.—Dark
   Oats.—Banner

S. J. McChesney, Kanona. Silver medal
  Wheat.—White Winter
John McConkie, Galway. Silver medal
  Oats.—White Swede, Welcome
E. J. McLean, Troupsburg. Silver medal
  Beans.—White Kidney
  Barley.—Black
  Buckwheat.—Silver Gray, Silver Hull
  Corn.—Pop Corn, ears
Stephen Merchant, Burnt Hills. Silver medal
  Rye.—White
D. W. Miller, Boonville. Bronze medal
  Oats.—Arctic
Romantie Miller, Scottsville. Bronze medal
  Wheat.—Longberry Red
George E. Minard, Filmore. Silver medal
  Barley.—Black, Beardless, Giant White
  Corn.—-Yellow Flint, ears
Howard Moore, Cobleskill. Bronze medal
  Corn.—Early Sunset Yellow
J. W. Moore, Fishkill Village. Bronze medal
  Wheat.—Gold Coin, White Winter
  Rye.—White Winter
  Corn.—White Dent, ears
Daniel Morris, Groveland. Bronze medal
  Wheat.—No. 8 Red Winter
Munger Bros., Warsaw. Silver medal
  Barley.—Beardless
  Oats.—Golden Prolific
J. Myers, Warnersville. Silver medal
  Beans.—Red Kidney
New York State Grange. Butler grand prize banner
  Collection of Grains
E. E. Nichols, South Onondaga. Bronze medal
  Rye.—Dark
  Wheat.—Gold Chaff, Red Winter
  Oats.—Swede, Lincoln, White Russian
  Peas.—Small Field
  Buckwheat.—Japanese
  Corn.—Eight-Rowed White Ears, Early Red Cory Sweet, 1900
  Sweet, Monarch Sweet
Will Norton, Hartford. Bronze medal
  Barley.—Beardless

Oats.—Lincoln
Oatka Farm, Scottsville. Silver medal
   Rye.—Dark
   Wheat.—Dawson's Golden Chaff
Hugh Osborne, East Hartford. Bronze medal
   Corn.—Atwood, ears
F. R. Payne, White Plains. Silver medal
   Beans.—White Marrowfat
Charles Perry, Wyoming. Silver medal
   Wheat.—Dawson's Golden Chaff
N. S. Pierson, Painted Post. Silver medal
   Rye.—Dark
I. B. Pipe, Prattsburg. Silver medal
   Buckwheat.—Silver Hull
   Oats.—Twentieth Century
F. C. Platt, Painted Post. Bronze medal
   Oats.—Golden
J. P. Platt, Bath. Gold medal
   Wheat.—Gold Coin
G. Pollock, East Hartford. Bronze medal
   Oats.—Probister
Peter Prechtel, Elmira. Bronze medal
   Wheat.—Clawson
Frank Qua, East Hartford
   Oats.—Swede, White Star
George R. Qua, Hartford. Gold medal
   Rye.—Siberian
G. L. Quick, Rochester Junction. Gold medal
   Wheat.—Dawson's Golden Chaff
   Oats.—Clydesdale
Anson Reed, Kanona. Silver medal
   Beans.—White Kidney, Golden Eyed
James H. Russell, Hopewell Junction. Bronze medal
   Corn.—Early Mastodon, ears
H. Brown Richardson, Lowville. Silver medal
   Maple Sugar
   Maple Syrup
John K. Roe, Florida. Bronze medal
   Corn.—Queen's Golden Pop
E. N. Rollins, Andover. Silver medal
   Wheat.—Gold Coin
W. H. Roper, Wyoming. Silver medal
   Oats.—Siberian

Wheat.—Genesee Giant

M. J. Sahler, Pattan Kunk. Silver medal

Oats.—Twentieth Century, American Improved

Buckwheat.—Japanese

Chas. F. Saul, Syracuse

Seeds

Peas.—Yorkshire Heroes, Everbearing, Telephone, McLean's
Advancers, Extra Early Premium Gem, Duke of York, Juno,
First and Best, McLean's Little Gem, Alaska, Prosperity, Champion
of England, Black-Eyed Marrowfat, American Wonder,
Horsford's Market Garden, Philadelphia Extra Early, Nott's
Excelsior

Beans.—Red Kidney, Large Lima, Long Yellow Six Weeks,
Horticultural, Henderson's Bush Lima, Sofa

Spelt

Rye.—Spring

Clover.—Medium, Mammoth, Crimson, White

Grass.—Orchard

Corn.—Eight-Rowed Yellow, Black Mexican

Barley.—Imperial Two-Rowed, Fancy Red Top

Wheat.—Spring

Kentucky Blue Grass

Hemp

Lettuce.—Boston

Onion.—Red Wethersfield

Squash.—Summer Crookneck, Hubbard

Canary Seed

Rape.—Dwarf Essex

Melon.—Rockford

Watermelon.—Ice Cream, Cobb's Gem

Celery

Beet

Carrot

Salsify

Parsnip.—Hollow Crown

Spinach

Radish

Turnip

Cow Peas

Field Pumpkin

Millet.—Japan

Cucumber.—Early Cluster

Kaffir Corn

Timothy

Will Saville, Hartford. Bronze medal
   Corn.—White Cap Dent

Sidney Schell, Theresa
   Oats.-Mortgage Lifter

I. L. Schofield, Wappingers Falls. Bronze medal
   Buckwheat.—Japanese

C. E. Schultz, Florida. Bronze medal
   Corn.—Eight-Rowed Yellow

R. F. Seeley, Waterloo. Silver medal
   Timothy
   Rye.—Mammoth White
   Corn.—Eight-Rowed Yellow
   Wheat.—Jones' Winter Fife, American Bronze
   Beans.—Red Kidney
   Buckwheat.—Japanese

Chas. J. Settle, Cobleskill
   Rye.—White

S. C. Shaver, Albany. Gold medal
   Hops.—Albany

A. M. Sleight, Arlington. Bronze medal
   Corn.—Eight-Rowed Yellow, ears

Fred W. Smith, Scottsville
   Oats.—Genesee Valley White

Ward L. Snyder, Carlisle Center. Bronze medal
   Oats.—Twentieth Century, Italian

Ed. Stevens, Warsaw. Bronze medal
   Buckwheat.—Gray

F. C. Stevens, Attica. Silver medal
   Wheat.—Silver Chaff, No. 6
   Rye.—Winter, Dark

Henry Stewart, Kanona. Gold medal
   Wheat.—Red Winter
   Barley

T. L. Stone, Craig Colony, Sonyea. Silver medal
   Corn.-Shakers' Pride, Pride of the North, White Shaker
   Wheat.—Red Winter Fife, Red Winter No. 8
   Oats.—Mixed

Stumpp & Walter Co., New York city. Gold medal
  Seeds
   Corn.—Evergreen Brown, Red Kaffir, White Kaffir, Snow
     White Dent, Stowell's Evergreen, Iowa Gold Mine, Yellow
     Dent, Improved Longfellow, Southern Horse Tooth, Cory

White Cob, Metropolitan, Yellow Mills Maize
Clover.—White Dutch, Red, Crimson
Millet.—German or Golden, Japanese
Grass.—Italian Rye, Rough Stalked Meadow, Orchard,
  Creeping Bent, Shady Place, Permanent Pasture, Rhode Island
  Bent, English Rye, Kentucky Blue, Canada Blue, English Cow,
  Hungarian
Hard Fescue
Timothy.—Fancy
Recleaned Red Top
Alfalfa
Alsike
Red Fescue
Meadow Fescue
Peas.—Daniel O'Rourke, American Wonder, Black-Eyed
  Cow, Canada Field, Telephone, Black-Eyed Marrowfat, Dwarf
  Sugar, Blue Beauty, Bliss Everbearing, Juno, Alaska, Nott's
  Excelsior, Horseford's Golden, Little Gem, Heroine, First
  of All
Beans.—Davis Kidney Wax, Best of All, Improved Golden
  Wax, Early Long Yellow Six Weeks, Red Valentine, Dwarf
  Horticultural, King of the Garden, Early Refugee, Improved
  Black Wax, Early Green Sofa, Velvet, Stringless Green Pod,
  Early Mohawk, Refugee or 1000 to 1, Burpee's Bush Lima,
  Lazy Wife, Bountiful
Oats.—Clydesdale, Russian, Lincoln
Sun Flower.—Mammoth Russian
Sea Island Cotton
Hemp
Wheat.—Silver Sheaf Winter, Red Winter, Jones' Red
  Chief, Saskatchewan
Barley.—Champion Beardless
Rice.—Unhulled
Pumpkin.—Large Cheese, Connecticut Field
Radish.—Early Scarlet Turnip, White-Tipped
Teosinte
Peas.—Sweet
Sorghum.—Early Amber, Early Orange
Spinach.—Roundleaf, Norfolk Savoy, Long Standing,
  Verofly
Australian Salt Bush
Rye.—Winter, Dark
Turnip.—Improved Purple Top Rutabaga, Yellowstone

Beet.—Mammoth Long Red Mangel, Champion Yellow
  Globe
Parsley.—Double-Curled
Lettuce.—California Cream Butter, Early Curled Simpson
Buckwheat.—Japanese
Field Lupins
Onions.—Wethersfield
Sainfoin
Amber Cane
Salsify.—Sandwich Island
C. O. Taylor, Petrolia. Bronze medal
  Oats.—Siberian
Morrison Taylor, Florida. Bronze medal
  Corn.—Eight Rowed Yellow
J. M. Thorburn & Co., New York city. Grand prize
  Field, Garden and Flower Seeds
  Bermuda.—Cedar
  Radish.—Early Turnip, Early Deep Blood Turnip, Half Long
    Delicacy, White Tipped, Non Plus Ultra, Round Scarlet China,
    Scarlet Turnip, Scarlet Globe, Olive Shaped Golden Yellow,
    Olive Shaped Red Rocket, White Tipped Scarlet, French
    Breakfast, Golden Summer, Scarlet Forcing, Winter, White
    Winter, White Olive Shaped, Black Spanish, Long White Icicle,
    White Tipped Summer White, Tipped Turnip, Long White
    Russian, Scarlet Chinese Winter, Woods Early Frame
  Lapania Borbonica
  Salsify.—Long White French
  Yellow Locust
  Cabbage.—Cow
  Beet.—Mammoth Long Red Mangel Wurzel, Queen of Denmark
    Sugar, Columbia, Golden Fleshed Globe Mangel Wurzel,
    Golden Tankard Mangel Wurzel, Red Globe Mangel Wurzel,
    Turin
  Tomato.—Blush Lemon, Aristocrat, Fagmore, Scarlet, Yellow
    Plum, Democrat, Thorburn's Novelty, Thorburn's 1903,
    Thorburn's Rosalind, Waldorf
  Parsley.—Moss Curled
  Asparagus
  Marigold.—Eldorado
  Coffee Tree.—Kentucky
  Millet.—Barn Yard, Red Siberian
  Watermelon.—Imperial, Iron Clad, Dark Iceing, Triumph,
    Hungarian, Van Cluse

Cucumber.—Small Gerkin, White Pearl
Oats.—Silver Mine, Black Tartarian
Squash.—Marblehead, White Chestnut, Canada Crookneck,
  Pineapple, Orange Marrow, Red China, Perfect Gem, Butmans,
  Pikes Peak, Der Wing, The Faxon, Japan Turban, French
  Olive
Silver Maple
Juglans Cardifornus
Celery.—Cooper's Cutting, Thorburn's Fin de Siecle
Sorrel.—Garden
Mignonette
Sun Flower.—Large Russian
Musk Melon.—Pineapple, Golden Gate
Teosinte
Grass.—Ribbed, Red Fescue, Meadow Fescue, Pepper, Hungarian
Curled Chervil
Borage
Pepper.—Sweet Spanish
Caraway
Savory.—Summer
Aera Caespitosa
French Thyme
Wheat.—Premium Red New York, Ruperts Giant, Red
  Rover
Poppy.—Double Peony Flowered
Calendula.—Prince of Orange
Koelreuteria Paniculata
Rough Rice
Chicory.—Large Rooted
Lettuce.—Thorburn's Mammoth Black Seeded, Black Seeded
  Tennis Ball, Thorburn's Maxumum, Hammersmith's Hardy,
  Green
Carrot.—Bellot, Carentan
Anthoxanthum Oderatum
Cherry.—Mahaleb
Coliander
Beech.—American
Crab Apple.—French
Cherry.—Black Mazzard
Leek.—Large Flag Winter
Dill
Juglans.—Sieboldii
Kentia.—Belmoreana

Musk Melon.—Ward's Nectar
Lupins.—Blue, White, Yellow
Turnip.—White Norfolk, Thorburn's Improved Purple Top
  Rutabaga
Onion.—Thorburn's Excelsior Pickling
Lavender
Dandelion
Apricot Pits
Endive.—White Curled
Sage
Fagus.—Sylvatica
Lolumi.—Italicum
Kale.—Sea
Canary.—Sicily
Connes Florida
Morning Glory
Holcus Lanatus
Lolucui Perenis.—Thorburn's Selected Dwarf
Prunes.—Serotina
Rhus.—Copallina
Clover.—Sand Crimson, Japan, White, Pea-vine
Spinach.—Winter, Long Standing, Lettuce Leaf, New
  Zealand, Summer
Beet.—Swiss, Chard
Ampelopsis Hederacea
Bene
Gourd.—Sugar Trough, Dish Cloth, Mock Orange
Catalpa
Lentils.—Spanish
Buckwheat.—Japanese, American Silver Hull
Butternut
Cypress.—Bald
Rye.—Excelsior Winter
Rice—Wild
Elm.—Common
Spelts
Burnet.—Common Field
Pumpkin.—Tennessee Sweet Potato
Sainfoin
Sera Della
Spring Tares
Fenn Greek
Linden.—American

Tree of Heaven
Kentia.—Fosteriana
Acer Coriaceum
Australian Salt Bush
White Birch
Timothy.—Fancy
Mushroom.—French Spawn
Spurry-Spergula Arvensis
Scotch Broom
Pinus.—Maritima
Candytuft
Festuca Ovina
Alsike.—Clover
Abies.—Nordmanniana
Cynosurus Ciristatus
Alfalfa
Kohl Rabi.—Large White
Acer.—Campestre
Calendula
Mustard.—-Broad Leaved
Corylus.—American
Aster
Alopecurus Pralensis
Pinus.—Cembra
Poppy
Nasturtium.—Tall Mixed
Sweet Marjoram
French Pear
Virginian Stock
Pinus.—Pinea
Parsnip.—Hollow Crown
Scorzouena
Acer.—Pseudo-platanus
Bromus Mollis
Cauliflower.—Gilt Edged
Laburnum
Anemone Coronaria
Poa Trivialis
Jute
Almes.—Oregonia
Thea Viridis
Brussells Sprouts
Faximus Excelsior

Calleopsis
Anise
Convolvulus.—Tricolor
Poa Annua
Sweet Fennel
Tulip Tree
Peas.—Stratagem, William Hurst, Prince of Wales, Horseford's
  Market Garden, Thorburn's Early Market, Sweet, Blue
  Beauty, Dr. McLean's, Alaska, Yorkshire Hero, Telephone,
  Premium Gem, Juno, McLean's Advancers, Clay Cow, Queen,
  Champion of England, American Wonder, Alpha, Telegraph,
  Pride of the Market, Heroine, Duke of Albany, Abundance,
  Nott's Excelsior, Gregory's Surprise, Gradus, Everbearing,
  Magnum Bonum
Corn.—Leaming, Virginia Horse Tooth, Snow Flake, Early
  Yellow Canada, Farmer's Favorite, Compton's Early Flint,
  Sanford's White Flint, Angel of Midnight, Hickory King,
  White Surprise, Longfellow, Thorburn's White Flint, Mastodon
  Dent, Golden Beauty, Stowell's Evergreen Sugar, Potter's
  Excelsior Sugar, Country Gentleman Sugar, Early Adams
  Sugar, Black Mexican Sugar, Egyptian Sugar, Triumph Sugar,
  Minnesota Sugar, Corn Salad, Perry's Hybrid Sweet ears,
  Black Mexican Sweet ears, Hickox Sweet ears, Early Minnesota
  Sweet ears, Early Crosby Sweet ears, Hickory King ears,
  King Phillip ears, Legal Tender ears, White Cap Yellow Dent
  ears, Compton's Early ears, Northern White Dent ears, Pride
  of the North ears, White Sanford ears
Beans.—Tall July Runners, Vienna Forcer, Sword (Long
  Pod) Challenger Lime, Improved Golden Cluster, English
  House, Velvet Wardwell Kidney Wax, Scarlet Runner, Kentucky
  Wonder, Golden Refugee, White Snowflake, Lightning,
  Yellow Sofa, Castor, Early Valentine, Pole, Ne Plus Ultra,
  Broad Windsor, Galega, Medium Eyed Sofa, Horticultural,
  Dun Colored, Byer's Dwarf, Marvel of Paris, Dwarf Chocolate,
  Canadian Wonder, Thornburn's Dwarf Lima, Longfellow Bush,
  Longfellow Six Weeks Bush, Early Mohawk Bush, Early China
  Bush, Everbearing Bush, Improved Golden Cluster Bush,
  Medium Early Green Bush, Round Pod Kidney Wax Bush,
  Lazy Wife Pole, Golden-Eyed Wax Bush, Scarlet Runner
  (Pole), Emperor of Russia (Pole), Round Six Weeks Bush,
  Southern Creeseback Bush, 1,000 to 1 Bush, Black Velentine
  Bush, Improved Golden Wax Bush, White Kidney Bush,
  White Marrow Bush

Peter S. Tower, Youngstown. Silver medal
    Wheat.—Early Arcadian
    Corn.—Eight-Rowed Yellow, ears
Miles Townsend, Bath. Silver medal
    Wheat.—Longberry Red
Morgan Vail, Stormville. Silver medal
    Oats.—White Tartar
    Rye.—White Winter
    Corn.—White Dent, ears
Vancott Bros., LaGrangeville. Bronze medal
    Corn.—Pride of New Jersey, ears
W. H. Dueson, Le Roy. Gold medal
    Wheat.—Red Clawson
Walter Van Loon, Bath. Gold medal
    Beans.—Marrowfat
Joseph Van Wyck, Arlington. Bronze medal
    Corn.—Eight-Rowed Yellow, ears
James Vick's Sons, Rochester. Silver medal
    Clover.—Crimson
    Cane.—Amber
    Flax
    Corn.—Champion White Pearl Pop, Early Mastodon, Pride of
    the North, Kaffir
    Pea.—Large White Marrowfat, Small Field
    Beans.—Black Butter, White Kidney, Black Wax, Large Marrowfat,
    Red Kidney
    Barley.—Bulless, Manshung
    Oats.—New Banner.
    Sun Flower.—White—Beauty, Mammoth Russian
F. L. Wailt, Ellington. Bronze medal
    Wheat.—White Winter
Walter Ward, Rochester Junction. Bronze medal
    Corn.—Longfellow Yellow, ears
John B. Y. Warner, Scottsville. Silver medal
    Barley.—Beardless
Charles Watrous, Warsaw. Bronze medal
    Wheat.—Red Clawson
    Oats.—Clydesdale, Probester
Mrs. Emogene Watrous, Warsaw. Silver medal
    Wheat.
Joseph L. Weed, Ballston Spa. Bronze medal
    Corn.—Eight-Rowed Yellow, ears, Twelve-Rowed Yellow,
    ears, Eight-Rowed Yellow Dent, ears

C. Weiting, Cobleskill. Silver medal
  Wheat.—Spring Red
W. H. Wheeler, Florida. Silver medal
  Wheat.—Red Winter, Fulcastor
C. W. & C. M. Wilcox, Delhi. Silver medal
  Maple Sugar and Syrup
James Wilder, Warsaw. Silver medal
  Rye.—White
Charles Willour, Painted Post. Bronze medal
  Wheat.—Long Medt
James M. Wisner, Edenville
  Corn.—Pedrick Perfect, ears
O. M. Wixon, Elinira. Bronze medal
  Wheat.—-Clawson
  Oats.—Early Scotch
C. S. Wright, Hammond
  Corn.—New England Fline, ears
Wyoming County Alms House, Varysburg. Silver medal
  Wheat and Oats
A. Young, Bath. Bronze medal
  Corn.—White Rice Pop, ears

Vegetables

Albany County. Silver medal
  Potatoes
Allegany County. Silver medal
  Potatoes
C. L. Allen, Sandy Hill. Silver medal
  Potatoes
C. W. Becker, Carlisle. Bronze medal
  Potatoes.—Salzer's Great Sunlight, Salzer's Million Dollar
John Bockeno, Baldwinsville. Bronze medal
  Onions.—Yellow Danvers, Prize Taker, Silver King, Southport
    Red, Southport White
F. E. Brown, Binghamton. Bronze medal
  Onions.—Red Wethersfield, Australian Brown, Yellow
    Danvers, Prize Takers, Southport White
Arthur L. Billings, Prattsburg. Silver medal
  Potatoes.—Hobson's Choice, Uncle Sam, White Gilial, New
    York Wonder, White Banner, Billings' Favorite, Billings'
    White Beauty, American Beauty, Billings' Surprise, Early

Gem, Sir Walter Raleigh, Sampson's Best, Vick's Early Perfection,
Beauty Hebron, Excelsior, Golden Nugget, White
Steuben

Fred Coe, Fulton. Silver medal
  Potatoes.—Blue Victor, World's Fair Prize, Early Northern,
    Early Michigan, Carmen No. 3, Bovee, Quick Crop, Late
    Hebron, Potentate, Burpee's Superior, Green Mountain, New
    Queen, Gold Coin, Delaware
  Beets.—Turnip Blood

James E. Cole, Fulton. Bronze medal
  Tomatoes.—Golden Queen, Burpee's Matchless
  Squash.—Hubbard

Miss Mabel Churchill, Fulton. Bronze medal
  Onions.—White Globe, Yellow Globe, Red Globe, Red
    Wethersfield
  Beets.—Red Turnip
  Potatoes.—White Mammoth

Jessie T. Carrier, Fulton. Bronze medal
  Potatoes.—Quick Crop, Early Market

Chemung County. Silver medal
  Potatoes

Cortland County. Silver medal
  Potatoes

Columbia County. Silver medal
  Potatoes

Cornell University, Ithaca. Grand prize
  Beets.—Lane's Sugar, Crimson Globe, Yellow Table, Sugar,
    Detroit Red, Long Red Mangel, Golden Tankard
  Radishes.—Summer, Winter
  Squash.—Dent Marrow, Yellow Bush Scallop, White Bush
    Scallop, Summer Crookneck, Turban, Boston Marrow, Warty
    Hubbard, Hubbard, Vegetable Marrow, Ford Hook
  Citron.
  Corn.—Eight-Rowed Yellow, 90 Day Monarch, Stowell's
    Evergreen
  Beans.—Lima
  Turnips.—Rutabaga, Purple Top Strap Leaf, White Sweet
    German, Sweet Russian, White Egg

Pumpkin.—Mammoth Chilian, Negro, Field, Mammoth
Cheese
Carrots.—Long Orange, Short Orange, Ox Heart
Salsify.
Onions.—Burpee's Australian Brown, Mammoth White,
Yellow Danvers, Red, Mills' White Portugal, Red Victoria,
Southport Red Globe, Red Wethersfield, Mills' New White
Queen, Mammoth Red Pompett, Mills' Brown Wonder, Ferr's
Early Red, Southport Yellow Globe, Mills' White Victoria,
Burpee's Early Golden Globe, Yellow Globe Danvers, Yellow
Dutch or Strasburg, Burpee's Cherry Pickle, Extra Early Red,
Michigan Danvers
Kohl Rabi.—Red, White
Parsnips.
Martynia.—Gourds
Celery.—White Plume
Turnips.—Sweet Rutabaga
Squash.—Delicate
Beets.—Early Egyptian, New Queen, Globe Mangel, Red
Mangel, Red Turnip
Squash.—Hubbard
Turnips.—Purple Top Rutabaga, Purple Top, White Rutabaga,
Flat Dutch, Purple Top Strap Leaf
Pumpkin.—Field
Potatoes.—Churchill Seedling, Rose of Erin, Uncle Sam,
Sir Walter Raleigh, Maule's Early, Chase's Early, Pan-American,
Early Fortune, Bliss Triumph, Nevada White, Chautauqua,
Ohio Victor, Burpee's Perfection, Celtic Beauty, Centennial
Blue, Livingston's Banner, Monarch of the West, Early
Janet, Late Rose, Hammond's Early, Blue Christy, Early
North, 20th Century, Maggie Murphy, Early Canada, Pure
Gold, Early Vermont, Early Six Weeks, Eam's Early
Cauliflower.
Swiss Chard.
Salsify.
Okra.
Celery.—Turnip Rooted, White Plume, Parsley
Cabbage.—White Flat, Round White

Leeks.

Beets.—Sugar, Detroit Red, Long Red Mangels

Kohl Rabi.—White

Parsnips.

Carrots.—White Belgian

Onions.—Yellow, White

Radish.—Red Chinese

Squash.—Summer Crookneck, Marrow

Pumpkin.—Red Gold

Corn.—Stowell's Evergreen

Potatoes.—Carmen No. 1, Burbanks

Celery.—Root's

Cabbage.—Danish Bullhead, Surehead, Autumn King

Turnips.—Garton's Pioneer Hybrid, Magnum Bonum Swedes, Purple Top Cow Horn, White Cow Horn, Golden Ball, Hartley's Top Rutabaga, Maule's Improved Purple Top, Aberdeen Yellow, Garton's Monarch Rutabaga, Green Top Scotch Yellow

Beets.—Golden Tankard, Sugar Beets, Garton's Long Red Mangel, Norbition Giant Mangels, Half Sugar Mangels, Yellow Globe Mangels, Chinks Castle Long Red Mangels, Sutton's Long Red Mangels

Carrots.—James Intermediate, Witshire Giant White, Yellow Belgium, Scarlet Intermediate, Lobberich's Agricultural

Parsnips.—Hollow Crown

Crossman Bros., Rochester. Grand prize

Beets.—Bassano, Dewings, Egyptian Dark Red, Long Dark Red Blood, White French Sugar, Yellow Chilian, Swiss Chard or Silver

Carrots.—Dutch Horn, Oxheart Guerands, Chautenay, Danvers Half Long, Long Orange, White Belgium, Chicory Large Rooted

Celeriac.—Smooth Prayer

Celery.—Paris Golden, S. B.

Cabbage.—Red Dutch, Danish Baldhead

Cucumbers.—Peerless White Spine, Hybrid Forcing

Cauliflower.—Snow Ball

Endive.—Broad Leaf Batavian, White Curled

Kohl Rabi.—Early Purple Vienna, Large Late Green

Leeks.—Monstrous Carenton

Mangels.—Mammoth Long Red

Kale.—Simi Dwarf Moss Curled

Onions.—Danvers Globe

Peppers.—Sweet Mountain

Parsnips.—Hollow Crown

Pumpkin.—King of the Mammoth, Mammoth Tours, Small
  Sugar

Parsley.—Hamburg Turnip Rooted, Champion Moss Curled

Salsify.—French

Squash.—Summer Crookneck, White Bush, Yellow Bush,
  Improved Hubbard American Turban, Louisiana, Mammoth
  Golden Crookneck, Ice Cream Pattipan

Turnips.—Purple Top Strap Leaf, Purple Top White Globe,
  Golden Ball, Snowball, Cow Horn, White Top Strap Leaf

Water Melons.—Red Seeded Citron

Earl Daniels, Bath. Silver medal

Potatoes.—Great Divide, White Giant, White Flower, Blue
  Bell, Victor, Early Minister, Golden Bell, Excelsior

C. W. Dearlove, Prattsburg. Silver medal

Potatoes.—Evert's Early, Rupert's Perfection, Free Silver,
  Rupert's Early, Stray Beauty, Rural New Yorker No. 2,
  Farmer's Beauty, Maine Rose, Adirondack, Sarvia Red, New
  Queen, Pride of the West, Cayuga Chief, Mammoth Pearl,
  Early Thoroughbred, Prize Taker, White Beauty, Mills' New
  Astonisher, Early Minister, Michigan Russet, Rose Early, Early
  Ohio, Earth Northern, English Russet, White Peachblow, Late
  Rose, Isle of Jersey, Pride of Jersey, Money Maker, Snow
  Drop, Late Prindaes

John DeGraw, Middletown. Bronze medal

Potatoes.—Early Northern, Blue Victor

G. M. Durland, Florida. Bronze medal

Potatoes.—Early Sunrise

Dutchess County. Silver medal

Potatoes.

A. Empie, Carlisle. Bronze medal

Potatoes.—Early White Michigan, Freeman

Leonard Fenton, Standards. Bronze medal
   Potatoes.—Early Giant
Charles W. Ford & Co., Fishers. Silver medal
   Potatoes.—Empire State, Queen
E. C. Foster, Standards. Bronze medal
   Potatoes.—Blue Victor
Geneva Experiment Station, Geneva. Silver medal
   Tomatoes.—Ponderosa, Earliana, Success, Trophy, Royal
   Red, Atlantic Prize, Golden Queen, Lester's Prolific, Beauty,
   Buckeye, Freedom, New Imperial
G. Gessell, South Lirna. Silver medal
   Celery
Burt Giddings, Fulton. Bronze medal
   Onions
Glendale Stock Farm, Glens Falls. Grand prize
   Squash.—Golden Bronze, Hubbard, Marblehead, Turban,
   Boston Marrow, Brazilian Sugar, Pineapple, Mammoth Whale,
   Canada Crookneck, Early Golden Bush, Silver Bush, Yellow
   Bush Scallop, Fordhook, Early White Scallop Bush, Red
   Hubbard, Summer Crookneck, Giant Summer Crookneck, Warty
   Hubbard, Red Hubbard, Mammoth, Chilian, Essex Hybrid,
   Ford Hook, Cocoanut, White Bush Scallop, New Mammoth
   White Bush, English Vegetable Marrow, Mammoth Yellow
   Bush, Golden Custard, White Summer Crookneck, White Pineapple,
   Early White Bush, Long White Marrow, Des Wing,
   Pike's Peak, White Chestnut, Delicate, Bronze, Golden Marrow,
   Giant Crookneck, Giant Straightneck, Striped Bush
   Beets.—Long Red, Red Globe, Yellow Globe, Table Beet
   Flat, Rose Half Sugar, Red Intermediate, Sugar, Long Yellow,
   Giant Yellow Intermediate, Half Long Turnip
   Mangels.—Wurzel Golden Tankard, Wurzel Mammoth Long
   Red, Wurzel Yellow Globe
   Cucumbers.—Short Green, Yellow Short, White Long, Improved
   Long Green
   Leek.—Musselburgh, Large Row
   Kohl Rabi.—Early Purple Vienna
   Parsnips.—Long White
   Carrots.—Long White, Half Short Ox Heart, Long Orange,

Short White

Turnips.—Yellow Rutabaga, Red Top, Globe Shaped, White
Strap-Leafed Flat

Pumpkins.—Cheese, Connecticut Field, Red Etampe, Cushaw,
Green Mountain, Early Sugar, Livingston Pie, Quaker
Pie, Brazilian Sugar, Negro, Tennessee Sweet Potato, Golden
Oblong, Genuine Mammoth, Winter Luxury, King of Mammoth,
Sandwich Island, Salzer's Mammoth, Jonathan, Calhoun,
Tours, Mammoth Globe, Sweet Pie, Golden Oblong, Japan
Crookneck

Tomatoes.—Acme, Canada, Cardinal, Dwarf Champion,
Early Conquerer, Essex Hybrid, General Grant, Jumbo, Livingston's
Beauty, Livingston's Favorite, Livingston's Perfection,
Mikado, New Queen, Optmus, Paragon, Pear-Shaped
Red, Pear-Shaped Yellow, Crimson Cushion, Yellow Cherry,
Red Cherry, Stone Cherry, Combination, Henderson's Ponderosa,
Mammoth Prize, Honor Bright, Burpee's Noble, Long
Keeper, Sutton's Best of All, Ford Hook First, Imperial,
Climax, Queen Table, Autocrat, Beauty, Golden Queen, White
Excelsior, Lemon Bush, Terra Cotta Lorillard, Yellow Peach,
Red Peach, Red Currant, Matchless, Yellow Plum, Red Pear,
Yellow Pear, Trophy, Volunteer

Water Melons.—Black Spanish, Boss, Cuban Queen, Green
and Gold, Kolb's Gem, Mammoth Iron Clad, Mountain Sweet,
Orange, Peerless Ice Cream, Cole, The Jones, Sweetheart, Black
Diamond, Florida's Favorite, Dixie, Seminole, Pride of Georgia,
Black Bolder, Duke Jones, Scarly Bark, Wonderful Sugar,
Phinney's Early

Peppers.—Celestial Cherry, County Fair, Chinese, Long Cayenne,
Long Red, Long Yellow, Ruby King, Sweet Mountain,
Black Unbian, Red Chili, Red Etruce, Elephant, Gold Upright,
Kaliscope, Red Cluster, Orange Rinkle, Bull Nose, Spanish
Montrous, Ox Heart, Red Cherry, Sweet Spanish, Yellow Chili

Cauliflower.

Cabbage.—Early York, Winnestadt, Summer, Jersey Wakefield,
Early Flat Dutch, Fowler's Short Stem, All Seasons, Henderson's
Succession, Stone Mason, Autumn King, Tildegrant,
Late Flat Dutch, Drumhead, Marblehead Mammoth, Nettie

Savoy, Drumhead Savoy, Early Red Erfust, Dwarf Flat Dutch,
Henderson's Early Spring, Selected All Seasons, Charlton
Wakefield, Thorburn's Collosal, Short Stem, Large Red Drumhead,
Red Polish Short Stem

Cucumbers.—Early Russian, Early Cluster, Early Green Prolific,
Early Frame, Early White Spine, Livingston's Evergreen,
Nichols' Medium, Long Green, Japanese Climbing, Cool and
Crisp, White Wonder, Snake, White Pearl, Paris Pickling,
Short Green Gherkins, West India Gherkins, Long Green Turkey,
White Spine Arlington

Brussells Sprouts.—Improved Half Dwarf, Improved Dwarf
German, Improved Long Island, Improved Perfection

Egg Plant.—Improved New York, Early Dwarf Purple,
Long Purple, Round French, Black Pekin, Mammoth Pearl,
Scarlet Chinese, Round White, Long White, Striped White,
Black Snake

Leeks.—Large Flag Winter, Large Rouen Winter, Large
Musselberg, London Summer

Parsnips.—Guerney, Long Smooth, Hollow Crown, Delmonico,
Abbot, Maltese, Student

Salsify.—Long White French, Sandwich Islands, Thick
Rooted

Brussells Sprouts.—Seven Dwarf, Tall, Green, Dwarf Prolific,
Lady Finger, White Velvet, Perkins Mammoth, Sugar
Trough, Dipper, Nest Egg, Spocen

Sage

Thyme

Summer Savory

Dill

Winter Savory

Martynia

Chicory

Carrots.—Ox Heart, St. Valery, Early Scarlet Horn, Half
Long Scarlet, Danvers Half Long; Long Yellow Stump Root,
Long Orange, Short White Vosges, White Belgian, Yellow
Belgian, Danvers, Henderson's New York, Early Forcing

Onions.—Yellow Globe Danvers, Yellow Strasburg, Early
Red, Red Wethersfield, Southport White Globe, Southport Red

Globe, Southport Yellow Globe, Early Cracker, Silver Skin,
Prize Taker, White Victoria Red, Early Barletta, Australian
Brown, White Portugal, Silver Ball, Large Red Globe, Improved
Michigan, Large White Globe, Giant Roco, Burpee's,
Gibralter, Queen, Ohio Yellow Globe

Beets.—Columbia, Dark Stinson, Early Blood Turnip, Egyptian,
Improved Arlington, Dewing's Improved Blood, Half
Long Blood, Lentz, Crimson Globe, Eclipse, Crosby's Egyptian,
Edmunds' Early Blood, Long Smith Blood Red, Bastian Half
Long Blood, Early Yellow Long, Early Bassano, Arlington's
Favorite, Electric, Detroit Dark Red, Jumbo, White Sugar
Rose Top, Lane's Improved, Vilmooric Improved, White Sugar
Green Top, Long Red Mangel Wurzel, Long Yellow Mangel
Wurzel, Giant Yellow Mangel Wurzel, Golden Tankard Wurzel,
Red Globe Wurzel, Yellow Globe Wurzel, Yellow Ovoid Wurzel,
Half Long Red Wurzel, Golden Flesh Globe Wurzel

Turnips.—Rutabaga, Golden Ball, Cow Horn, White Egg,
Yellow Stone, Yellow Globe, Red Top Strap Leaf

Celeric

Earth Almonds

String Beans

Potatoes.—Dewey, Early Sunrise, Grate, Freeman, Carmen
No. 1, Telephone, Early Rose, Delaware, White Mountain,
Stray Beauty, Snow Flake, Irish Queen, White Star, Burbank,
American Giant, White Elephant, Peerless, Blue Victor, Maine
Rose, Monroe Seedling, Sir Walter Raleigh, White Hebron,
Great Dixie, American Wonder, Lightning Express, Bovee,
Dexter, Clark No. 1, Pat's First Choice, Carmen No. 3, Early
Ohio, State of Maine, Early Vermont, Uncle Sam, Money
Maker, Late Rose, Empire State, Rose of Erin, Victor Rose,
Everett, Early Six Weeks, Howell, Free Silver, Sunrise, Red
Wonder, Early Market, Early Strawberry, Eureka, New Ideal,
Thorburn's Late Puritan, Hampton Beauty, Maule's Early
Thoroughbred, Glendale Seedling, White Lily, Early Chicago
Market, Gem of Bristol, Pan American, Early Ball, Early Harvest,
Hebron Beauty, Early Ohio, Jr., Early Northern, Kospangue,
Green Mountain, Great Divide, New Queen, St. Joseph,
Signal, Chinese Yams, Rural New Yorker, White Rose, Jersey

Red Sweet, Yellow Jersey, Lady Finger, Early Russett, Blue
Mercury, Early York, Bliss Triumph, Early Puritan

Lettuce.—Tennis Ball, Self Folding, Golden Queen, Big
Boston, Black-Seed Simpson, New York, Boston, Curled, Iceberg,
Silver Ball, Hanson, White Heart, Paris White Coe

Endive.—Green Curled, Moss Curled, White Curled, Broad
Leafed

Bert Groummore, Minetto. Bronze medal

Potatoes.—Carmen No. 2

Herkimer County. Silver medal

Potatoes

George K. Higbie & Co., Rochester. Gold medal

Potatoes

C.N. Holley, Glens Falls. Silver medal

Potatoes.—Early Thorburn, Early Hebron, Bovee, Rural
New Yorker No. 2, Early Norther, Carmen No. 1, Cream
Howell, Uncle Sam, Krine's Lightning, The Queen, Early
Fortune, Sweet Home, Pearl of Savory, Yellow Elephant,
White Elephant, Chicago Market, Green Mountain, Early
Whiton, Early Roberts, Dakota Red, Great American, Dewey's
Early, Potentate, Depew, Downing, Early Market, Rural New
Yorker No. 2, Pat's Choice, Early Norther, Clark's No. I, Blue
Centennial, Early Seedling, Burpee's Extra Early, Mammoth
Pearl, Early Sunrise, Irish Cobler, Early Six Weeks, Early
Ohio, Early Rochester, Henderson's Bovee

J. C. Howard, Irondequoit

Squash.—Summer Crookneck

Citron

W.W. Hull, Middletown. Bronze medal

Potatoes.—Seedless, Queen of the Highway

Jefferson County. Silver medal

Potatoes

Daniel Johnson, Lisle. Silver medal

Potatoes.—Carmen No. I, Bliss Triumph, Rural New Yorker No. 2,
Early Puritan, State of Maine, Bovee, Queen, Quick Crop

S. L. Johnson, Lisle. Silver medal

Potatoes.—Sir Walter Raleigh, Rural New Yorker No. 2, Early
Fortune, Early Puritan, Early Maine, Admiral Dewey, Lee's

Favorite, Quick Crop, Uncle Sam, Early York, Banner, Green
Mountain, White Giant, King of Michigan

M. L. Klock, Bath. Gold medal

Potatoes.—Celtic Beauty, Red Star, Ontario, Great Dundee,
Mills' New Astonisher, Carmen No. 3, New Ideal, Rupert's
Perfection, German Queen, Snow Flake, White Gilial, White
Mountain, New Queen, Mohawk Valley, Twilight, White Peachblow,
Cayuga Chief, Bliss Triumph, Early Hebron, Early Six Weeks,
Burpee's Early, Hammond's Up-to-Date, Golden Bell, Early
Chicago Market, Early Ohio, White Hebron, Rose White,
White Wax, Maine Rose, Farmer's Daughter, Isle of Jersey,
Housewife Favorite, Queen of the Valley, Early Crusader, Great
Steuben

W. S. Kisker, Summit

Potatoes.—Vick's Champion, Sir Walter Raleigh No. 1

Mrs. C. A. Knapp, Goshen

Potatoes.—Rural New Yorker

Lewis County. Silver medal

Potatoes

O. M. Lincoln, Newark. Gold medal

Potatoes.—Bliss Triumph, Irish Cobler, Rural New Yorker, Bill Nye,
Early Potentate, Strange Beauty, Blue Victor, Early Norther, White
Giant, Early Ohio, Early Fortune, Early Sunrise, World's Fair
Premium, Negro, June Eating, Quick Crop, White Russet, White
Beauty, Sir Walter Raleigh, Bovee, Star, Early Puritan, Early
Harvest, Early Albino, Maggie Murphy, Everetts, Dandy, Albino,
Carmen No. 1 & 2, World's Fair, Great Divide, Early Market, Early
Maine, Freeman, American Wonder, Pingree, Empire State,
Rochester Rose, State of Maine, Beauty of Hebron, Monroe Seedling,
Thorburn, New Queen

P. R. Loder, Bluff Point. Silver medal

Potatoes.—Abundance, Burpee's Extra Early, Early White
Sunrise, Polaris Early, Gold Coin, Rural New Yorker, Early
Rose, Late Rose, Late White, Cyclone, White Napoleon, Potentate,
Early Puritan

Prescott E. Maine, Canastota. Silver medal

Mangel.—Long Red, Golden Tankard

Beets.—Sugar

Squash.—Red Hubbard, Yellow Bush Scallop, Winter Crookneck, Mammoth Chilian
Pumpkin.—Early Sugar, Negro
Cucumber.—Long White
W. H. Manning, Elm Valley. Bronze medal
Potatoes.—Tuscarora, Mortgage Lifter
G. W. Manning, Elm Valley
Potatoes.—Mortgage Lifter
Asa Mapes, Howells. Bronze medal
Potatoes.—Green Mountain
E. N. Marsh, Fredonia. Gold medal
Potatoes.—Uncle Sam, Lincoln, White Rose, Mortgage Lifter, Ohio Junior, Early Sunrise, Sir Walter Raleigh, Early Burpee, Eureka, May Queen, Isle of Wight, Early Bovee, Great Divide, Acme, Early King, Astonisher, Early Minnesota, Polaris, Rochester Rose, Six Weeks, Ohio, Million Dollar Mark Hanna, Rural New Yorker, Mills' Prize, Express, Honeoye Rose, Salzer's Earliest, Early Rochester
Onions
Squash
Gourd
Kohl Rabi
C. H. Mason, Cortland. Bronze medal
Potatoes.—Clark's Seedling, Pride of Castle Dorn
A. A. Mitchell, Palmyra. Silver medal
Potatoes.—White Peachblow, Empire State, American Wonder, New Queen, World's Fair, Stray Beauty, Bliss Triumph, White Star, Sir Walter Raleigh, Early Ohio, Rupert's Perfection, White Russet, Rural New Yorker, Early Northern, Early Bovee, Early Hebron, Negro, Carmen Nos. 1, 2, 3, Irish Cobler, Wilson's First Choice, Honeove Rose, White Giant, Bill Nye, Rural New Yorker No. 2, State of Maine, Monroe Seedling, Burpee's Extra Early, Blue Victor, Dunkirk Seedling, Early Sunrise, Beauty of Hebron, Rochester Rose, Early Potentate, Pink Eye, Queen of the Valley, Early Rose
Monroe County. Silver medal
Potatoes
Montgomery County. Silver medal

Potatoes

A. J. Moore, Beaver Dam. Silver medal

    Potatoes.—American Wonder, Epitomes, Pride of Jersey,
Mohawk Valley, Pan American, Rural New Yorker No. a, Mr.
Dooley, Adirondack, Bovee, White Hebron, Early Puritan,
Clark's Nonesuch, Prize Taker, Michigan Russet, Early Sunrise

James D. McCann, Elmira. Bronze medal

    Potatoes.—American Giants

W. A. McCoduck, Sandy Hill. Silver medal

    Onions

New York State Exhibit of Vegetables. Grand prize

Onondaga County. Silver medal

    Potatoes

Ontario County. Silver medal

    Potatoes

Orange County. Silver medal

    Onions

Otsego County. Silver medal

    Potatoes

Fred B. Paine, South Granby. Bronze medal

    Potatoes.—Vermont Gold Coin, Carmen No. 3, Sir Walter
Raleigh, Stray Beauty, Green Mountain, Rural New Yorker
No. 2

A. J. Reed, Bath

    Beets

R. F. Russell, Westtown.

    Potatoes.—Queen of the Valley

M. J. Sahler, Pattaukunk

    Potatoes.—Ouick Crop, Early Dew Drop

Saratoga County. Bronze medal

    Potatoes

W. H. Saunders, South Lima. Silver medal

    Celery

Schenectady County. Silver medal

    Potatoes

Schoharie County. Silver medal

    Potatoes

Schuyler County. Silver medal

Potatoes

George Scott, Bath. Bronze medal

    Potatoes.—Rose White, Early Doe, Early Hero, Early Wheeler

Chas. J. Settle, Cobleskill. Bronze medal

    Potatoes.—Burbank, Sir Walter Raleigh, Money Makers,
      Carmen No. 1

Frank Shear, Standards

    Potatoes.—Endurance

W. C. Skiff, Davenport Center. Silver medal

    Potatoes.—Early Ohio, White Star, Early Puritan, Stray
      Beauty, Blue Victor, June Eating, Rock Rose, Early Sunrise,
      Everett, Calvert, White Peachblow, Carmen No. 1, White
      Beauty, Dandy, Early Harvest, Empire State, Early Market,
      New Queen, Bovee, Pingree, Bliss Triumph, Quick Crop, Sir
      Walter Raleigh, Beauty of Hebron, American Wonder, White
      Giant, Great Divide, Maggie Murphy

Chas. Slocum, Freetown Corners. Bronze medal

    Potatoes.—Polarus

C. C. Smith, Bath

    Carrots

    Mangels

Jay W. Smith, Fulton. Bronze medal

    Potatoes.—Vermont Gold Coin, Eureka, Potentate, Burpee's
      Extra Early, Early Northern, Irish Cobler

Steuben County. Silver medal

    Potatoes

Steuben Nature Study Workers, Bath

    Potatoes.—Cambridge Russet, Clark's No. 1, Allen's No. 1,
      Beauty of Hebron, King of the Roses, Clark's Nonesuch,
      Celtic Beauty, Salzer's Peachblow, Maggie Murphy, Blue Victor,
      Clark's Early, Abundance, Early Sunrise, Cream of the
      Field, American Beauty, Blue Bell, Rose No. 9, Cuban Giant,
      White Peachblow, Giant White, Pan American, World's Fair,
      Peachblow, Carmen No. 3, Hammond's Up-to-Date, Commercial,
      Wilson's First Choice, American Beauty Early, Cavuga
      Chief, White Flower, Vick's Favorite, Charles Downing, Rose
      Invincible, American Wonder White Star, Vick's Extra
      Early, Free Silver, Burpee's Empire State, John Bull, Samson's

Best, Early Hebron, The Epitomist, Blue Bell, Vick's
Harvest, Pride of the West, Uncle Sam, Twilight, Great Divide,
Troy Seedling, Vick's Early Perfection, Twentieth Century,
Snow Drop, Snow Flake, Rural New Yorker No. 2,
St. Patrick, Salzer's Earliest, Rupert's Perfection, Adirondack,
Rural New Yorker No. 1, Prize Taker, Early Wheeler, Washington,
Klondike, Sir Walter Raleigh, Rose Clay, Bliss Triumph,
The Tramp, Ted Roosevelt, Great Steuben, Trumbull,
Hammond's New Wonder, Rusty Coat, Oom Paul, Pride of
America, Purple Pole, Rupert's Early, Blue Mercer, Early
Six Weeks, Early Rose Improved, German Queen, Jersey Red,
American Beauty Late, Jersey Peachblow, Early Michigan,
Early Cuban Giant, Cobler, Beauty of Rochester, Rose Yo. 9;
Bovee Earlv, Mammoth Pearl, White Mountain, Monroe Seedling,
Rose Beauty, Early Harvest, Early Maine, Mills New
Astonisher, Early Minister, Maine Hebron, White Banner,
Golden Bell, Green Mountain, Mortgage Lifter, Mohawk Valley,
German Otteen, Early Pingree, State of Maine, White
Mammoth, Clark's Early, Columbia, Carmen No. 1, Early
Gem, Dakota Red, Irish Daisy, Irish Russet, Lee's Favorite,
Late Puritan, Early Norther, Stray Beauty, Rose Honeoye,
Radical Seedling, Early Hero, Earlv Snow Ball, White Wax,
Enormous, Rural Blush, Dewey, Housewife's Favorite, No
Equal, Real Star, Mills' Prize, Money Maker, Early Pride,
Rupert's Early, Early Crusader, Early Ohio, Early Chicago
Market, Early Puritan, English Russet, Early Thoroughbred,
Golden Nugget, Early Doe, Hammond's Pride of Briton, Early
Vermont, Michigan Russet, New Jersey, Long Keeper, Livingston's
Banner, Queen of the Valley, Early Gem, Summerset,
Himalaya, New Queen, Isle of Jersev, Pride of Jersey, Early
Freeman, Early Beauty, White Gilial, Early Fortune
Onions.—White Flat, Yellow Flat, Red Flat, White Round,
  Round Red
Turnips.—Purple Top Strap Leaf, Purple Top Rutabaga,
  White Strap Leaf
Squash.—Hubbard, White Bush Scallop, Summer Crookneck
Pumpkin.—Red Field, Negro
Cabbage.—Flat Dutch, Drumhead

Cucumbers.—Short Green
Radish.—White Winter
Parsnips.—Long
Beets.—Table Round, Table Long, Yellow Mangels
Carrots.—Half Long Orange, Long Orange

St. Lawrence County. Silver medal
Potatoes

Sunnyside Farm, Starkey. Gold medal
Onions.—Philadelphia Silver Skin, Giant Rocco, Large Yellow Globe, Large White Globe, Large Red Globe, Prize Taker, Austrian Brown, Red Weathersfield, White Pearl
Beets.—Lang's Improved Imperial Sugar, Golden Tankard, Detroit Dark Red, Burpee's Improved Blood, Brundage Red Sugar, Brundage Yellow Sugar, Orange Globe, Improved Wanglebee, Crimson Globe
Carrots.—Danver's Half Long, White Belgium, Ox Heart
Radish.—Round Black Spanish Winter
Gourds.—Common, Ornamental Pomegranate
Turnips.—White Neckless, Purple Top Strap Leaf, Burpee's Breadstone
Squash.—Large Crookneck, Mammoth White Bush Scallop
Parsnips.—Hollow Crown
Salsify.—Mammoth Sandwich Island
Musk Melons.—Banana
Cucumbers.—White Wonder, Ford Hook Pickling, Ivory Monarch, Cool and Crisp, Early Russian, Lemon, Wild, West Indies
Tomatoes.—Enornous Vine Peaches, Golden Queen, Matchless, Peach, Yellow Pear, Yellow and Red Cherry
Potatoes.—Early Ohio, Twilight, Irish Queen, Tuscarora, Crown Jewel, State of Maine, Livingston, Belle, White Giant, Early Fortune, Vermont Gold Coin, Jersey Peachblow, Mr. Dooley, Monroe Prize, Maine Pearl, Centennial, New Queen, White Chili, Garlick, Late Star, Hundred Fold, King's Excelsior, Carmen No. 3, St. Patrick, Pride of the East, Salzer's Beauty, White Peachblow, Seneca Beauty, Baltimore, Old Hemlock, Pan American, Allen's No. 1, Lake Erie, Republican, Golden Bell, Trumbull, White Michigan, Mullolly, Burpee's

Extra Early, Rutland Rose, Lady Finger, Early Triumph, Irish
Cups, Free Silver, Woodhull Seedling, Lincoln, Wall's Maggie
Murphy, Harvest Queen, Dermore, Table King, Eureka,
Commercial, Durand Seedling, Northern Spy, Jumbo Charley,
Queen Victoria, Irish Daisy, Pure Gold, Webster Rose, Charles
Oak, Summerset, June Eating, Ford's Late White, Empire
State, Signal, Washington, Green Mountain, Vick's Armstrong,
Early Freeman, Valley Queen, Red Star, Twentieth
Century, New Wonder, Snow Flake, Garfield, Isle of Jersey,
California, Million Dollar, Crandall, Limbo, White Elephant,
Bermuda, Overton No. g, Rural New Yorker No. 2, Derlove
No. 7, Farmer's Beauty, Allis' Seedling, Vick's Late White,
Peachblow Seedling, Belle of Nelson, New Jersey, Irish Cobler,
Vick's Baker, White Star, Stray Beauty, White Hebron, Cuban
Orange, Pullman Seedling, Dakota Red, American Beauty,
Red Chili, Drake's Bermuda, Home Comfort, World's Fair,
Strong Pride, Early Wonder, Rhode Island Peachblow, June
Holton, Roscow, Narragansett Red, Beaulah's North Star,
Fultz. Seedling, Irish Russet, Oepheart, Cow Horn, Monever
Pride, Irish Gray, Burpee's Early, Enormous, Red Astrican,
Prolific, Jr., White Whipper, Salina Red, Old Peachblow

Alfred Sweet, Glens Falls. Silver medal
    Potatoes.—North Star, Sir Walter Raleigh, Green Mountain,
      Early Ruby, Potentate, Early Rose, Aristoke Rose, Early Puritan,
      Weiss Rose, Sir Walter Raleigh, Early Ohio, Livingston
      Banner, Poodle, Rose of Erin, Early Vermont, Irish Cobler,
      Mortgage Lifter, Early York, Cuba Orange, American Giant,
      Burbank, Snow Flake, White Mountain, Early Rose, Carmen
      No. 1, Early Sunrise, Delaware, Yellow Jersey, Jersey Red,
      Irish Queen, Stray Beauty, White Elephant, Telephone, Freeman,
      Dewey, Money Maker, White Star

Morrison Taylor, Florida. Bronze medal
    Potatoes.—Green Mountain

J. M. Thorburn & Co., New York City. Grand prize
    Potatoes—Hewe's Early, Early Whiton, Green Mountain,
      Great American, White Elephant, Yellow, Dakota Red, Early
      Robert, Pearl of Savoy, Sweet Home, Chicago Market, Early
      Fortune, Carmen No. 1, Early Norther, Early Queen, The

Queen, Rural New Yorker No. 2, Bovee, Krine's Lightning,
Uncle Sam, Early Hebron, Crown Jewel, Early Thorburn,
Early Rose, Carmen No. 3, Bliss Triumph, Gold Coin
Sweet Corn.—Country Gentleman, Black Mexican, Striped
Evergreen, White Evergreen, Stowell's Evergreen
Sweet Potatoes.—Harrison's Seedling, Jersey Red, Pierson's
Yellow Jersey, Vineland Bush
Carrots.—Early Scarlet Horn, Guerandes, Half Long
Pointed, Half Long Stump Rooted, Nautes, Chautenay, Bellot,
Early Forcing, Early Round Parisian, White Vosges, St. Valery,
Short White, Long White, Luc, Half Long Danvers, Long
Orange
Beets.—Giant Yellow Intermediate Mangel, Red Globe
Tankard Mangel, Golden Tankard Mangel, Yellow Tankard
Mangel, Queen of Denmark Mangel, Long Yellow Mangel,
Mammoth Long Red Mangel, Green Top Mangel; Rose Top
Mangel, Yellow Ovoid Mangel, Yellow Globe Mangel, Electric,
Crimson Globe, Dewing Early, Detroit, Early Blood Turnip,
Crosby's Egyptian, Half Long Blood, Bassano, Bastian, Long
Smooth Blood
Squash.—Early Golden Scallop Bush, Mammoth Chilian,
Eauphine, Hubbard, Golden Warted, Warren, Boston Marrow,
Bay State, Marrow, Turban, Mammoth Whale, Brazilian,
Vegetable, Cocozell Bush, Canada Crookneck, Winter, White
Custard, Yellow Custard, Cocoanut, Green Streaked Bush,
Long Island White Bush, Early White Scallop, Giant Summer
Crookneck, Giant Summer Straightneck, Delicate, Golden
Hubbard, Ford Hook, Vegetable Marrow, Yellow Oblong,
Pineapple
Onions.—Prize Taker, Golden Globe, Small Yellow Globe,
Red Gargeniis, Roquette
Parsley.—Extra Curled, Moss, Fern Leaf, Beauty of the Pasture,
Hamburg
Pumpkin.—Cheese, Connecticut Field, Red Estanples,
Negro, Cushaw, Jonathan, Calhoun, Small Sugar
Peppers.—Long Red Cayenne, Squash, Sweet Golden, Red
Harold, Golden Queen, Ruby King, Sweet Mountain, Chinese
Giant, Sweet Italian, Sweet Spanish, Neapolitan, Red Pointed

Celebrese, Long Bell, Procople Giant, Ox Heart, Elephant's
Trunk, Yellow Cherry, Celestial, Red Chili, Red Cherry, Red
Chester, Long Black Mexican, Matchless, Honor Bright
Kohl Rabi.—Purple Vienna, White Vienna
Cauliflower
Egg Plant.-New York Improved, Black Snake, Long
Purple, Long White, Round White, Mammoth Pearl, Scarlet
Chinese
Gourd.—Striped Pear, Orange, Egg, Sugar Trough, Dipper,
Hercules Club
Radishes.—Round Black Spanish, Half Long Black Spanish,
Long Black Spanish, White Winter Spanish, Celestial,
White Mammoth, Scarlet Chinese
Chicory
Salsify
Burnet
Okra.—Long Green, White Velvet Pod, Dwarf Green Improved,
Green Prolific
Martynia
Tioga County. Silver medal,
Potatoes
Tompkins County. Grand prize
Vegetables
Walter Van Loon, Bath
Beets
W. P. Vanscoter, Bath
Onions
Parsnips
Salsify
H. S. Vermilyea, Chelsea. Silver medal
Potatoes.—Thorburn, Money Maker, Sir Walter Raleigh,
New Queen, Carmen No. I, Acme, Bovee, Irish Cobler, Carmen
No. 3, White Star
Warren County. Grand prize
Vegetables
Washington County. Silver medal
Potatoes
Wayne County. Silver medal

Potatoes

Westchester County. Silver medal

Potatoes

Charles Wheelhouse, Fulton. Bronze medal

Beets.—Detroit Red Blood

Onions.—Red Wethersfield, Yellow Danvers

D. M. White, Bath

Carrots

Mangels

——— Wrenwick, Wellsville

Potatoes.—Elephant

A. Young, Bath

Onions

GROUPS EIGHTY-FIVE, NINETY-ONE AND NINETY-TWO

Animal Food Products, Waters, Wines, etc.

John Abd-et-nour, New York city. Silver medal
  Silk worms and cocoons
J. A. Anderson, Mooers Forks. Silver medal
  Butter
Barson & Co., A. S., 40 West street, New York city. Gold medal
  Cigarettes
J. W. Beardsley's Sons, New York city. Gold medal
  Bacon, dried and smoked beef, shredded codfish and star boneless
    herring put up in glass and tin
Sarah Drowne Belcher, M. D., New York city. Bronze medal
  Book on clean milk
Borden's Condensed Milk, New York city. Gold medal
  Condensed milk
John Brand & Co., Packers, Elmira. Gold medal
  Leaf tobacco
Breesport Water Co., Elmira. Silver medal
  Carbonated table water
Brotherhood Wine Co., New York city. Grand prize
  Wines and champagnes
A. C. Brown, Cincinnatus. Silver medal
  Butter
Natural Mineral Water Co., Saratoga Springs. Gold medal
  Carbonated table water
Congress Spring Co., Saratoga Springs. Gold medal
  Carbonated table water
Curtice Brothers. Rochester. Gold medal
  Canned fruits, vegetables, meats and catsups in glass and tin
Dedrick & Son, P. K., Albany. Grand prize
  Hay presses
F. De Garmo, Rochester. Gold medal
  Tobacco
Jonas Dillenback, Cobleskill. Silver medal
  Pressed hops
Duffy's Malt Whiskey Co., Rochester. Gold medal
  Whiskies
J. H. Durkee, Collaborator, New York State Exhibit. Gold medal
  Collectively and installation specialty

Henry Eibert, Thorn Hill. Silver medal
    Butter
Erie Preserving Co., Buffalo. Gold medal
    Canned fruit and vegetables in tin and glass
Excelsior Springs Co., Saratoga. Gold medal
    Carbonated table water
France Milling Co., Cobleskill. Gold medal
    Buckwheat flour
Germania Wine Cellars, Hammondsport. Gold medal
    Champagnes
Gleason Grape Juice Co., Fredonia. Silver medal
    Grape juice
Gordon & Dilworth, New York city. Gold medal
    Canned fruits, meats and catsups in glass and tin
Emit Greiner, 78 John street, New York city. Silver medal
    Dairy glass ware
Hammondsport Wine Co., Hammondsport. Bronze medal
    Wines and champagnes
High Rock Spring Co., Saratoga Springs. Gold medal
    Carbonated table water
Irondequoit Wine Co., Rochester. Bronze medal
    Wines and champagnes
Lincoln Spring Co., Saratoga Springs. Gold medal
    Carbonated table water
New York State. Grand prize
    Exhibit of canned goods, meats, preserves
New York State Exhibit. Gold medal
    Cheese
New York State Exhibit. Gold medal
    Butter
Paterson's Mineral Springs, Saratoga Springs. Gold medal
    Carbonated table water
Quevic Spring Co., Saratoga Springs. Gold medal
    Carbonated table water
———— Randall. Silver medal
    Grape juice
H. Brown Richardson, Lowville. Gold medal
    Maple sugar and syrup
Ripin Wine Co., New York city. Silver medal
    Champagne
T. F. Rutherford, Madrid. Silver medal
    Butter
Saratoga Seltzer Spring Co., Saratoga Springs. Gold medal

Carbonated table water
Saratoga Vichy Water Co., Saratoga Springs. Gold medal
   Carbonated table water
Stachalberg & Co., A. M., New York city. Gold medal
   Cigars
Star Spring Co., Saratoga Springs. Gold medal
   Carbonated table water
The Genesee Pure Food Co., Le Roy. Gold medal
   Jello
The Natural Mineral Water Co., Saratoga Springs. Gold medal
   Carbonated table water
United Cigar Manufacturing Co., New York city. Grand prize
   Cigars
Urbana Wine Co., Urbana. Gold medal
   Wines and champagnes
S. E. Van Horn, Durham. Silver medal
   Butter
C. A. Weatherly & Co., Milford. Bronze medal
   Cheese
J. O. Weeks, New York city. Silver medal
   Ice cream powder
Welch Grape Juice Co., Westfield. Silver medal
   Grape juice
White Top Champagne Co., Hammondsport. Gold medal
   Champagne
Worcester Salt Co., New York city. Gold medal
   Table and dairy salt

The following is a catalogue of exhibitors in the Department of Live Stock with the awards, if any, received by each

GROUP NINETY-EIGHT

Cattle

AYRSHIRES—SEVEN HERDS COMPETING

W. P. Schenck, Avon
Bull, 3 years old or over. Fifth premium, $30.
Bull, 1 year and under 2 years. First premium, $50.
Cow, 3 years old or over. Fifth premium, $30.
Heifer, 2 years and under 4. Third and fourth premiums,
   $90.
Heifer, 1 year and under 2. Third premium, $30.
Get of one sire. Second premium, $65.
Produce of one cow. Second and fifth premiums, $105.

Aged herd. Fourth premium, $65.
Young herd. Third premium, $55.
Aged herd, bred by exhibitor. Second premium, $100.
Young herd, bred by exhibitor. Third premium, $55.

BROWN SWISS—SEVEN HERDS COMPETING

F. R. Hazzard, Syracuse
Bull, 3 years old or over. First and fifth premiums, $70.
Bull, 2 years and under 3. First premium, $50.
Bull, 18 months and under 2 years. Second and fifth
  premiums, $60.
Bull, 12 months and under 18. First and third premiums, $60.
Bull under 6 months. Second and fourth premiums, $50.
Cow, 3 years old or over. First and third premiums, $80.
Heifer, 2 years old and under 3. Second premium, $40.
Heifer, 18 months and under 24. First and third premiums, $80.
Heifer, 12 months and under 18. Third premium, $25.
Heifer, 6 months and under 12. Second and fifth premiums, $45.
Heifer, under 6 months. Third and fifth premiums, $40.
Get of one sire. First premium, $50.
Produce of one cow. Second and third premiums, $75.
Aged herd. First premium, $75.
Young herd. Third premium, $35.
Herd bred by exhibitor. Third premium.
Champion bull, 2 years old or over. $80.
Champion cow, 2 years old or over. $80.
Grand champion bull. $125.
Grand champion cow. $125.
McLaury Bros. & Freemeyer, Portlandville
  Bull, 3 years old or over. Fourth premium, $25.
  Bull, 2 years and under 3. Fifth premium, $40.
  Bull, 18 months and under 2 years. First premium, $50.
  Bull, 6 months and under 12. First premium, $35.
  Bull under 6 months. First premium, $35.
  Cow, 3 years old or over. Second and fifth premiums,
    $60.
  Heifer, 2 years old and under 3. First premium, $50.
  Heifer, 12 months and under IS. Fourth premium, $20.
  Heifer, 6 months and under 12. First premium, $35.
  Get of one sire. Second premium, $40.
  Produce of one cow. First and fourth premiums, $75.
  Aged herd. Third premium, $60.
  Young herd. First premium, $50.

Herd bred by exhibitor. $200.
Champion bull under 2 years old. $60.
Champion cow under 2 years old. $60.

JERSEYS—TEN HERDS COMPETING

McLaury Bros. & Freemeyer, Portlandville
Bull, 2 years old and under 3. Third premium, $50.
Cow, 3 years old and over. Fifth premium, $30.
Heifer, 2 years old and under 3. Fourth premium, $40.

KERRYS—ONE HERD COMPETING

G. M. Carnochan, New York city
One prize for herd

SCOTCH HIGHLANDS—ONE HERD COMPETING

Warner M. Van Worden, Rye
One prize for herd

GUERNSEYS—SEVEN HERDS COMPETING

C. C. Taylor, Lawton Station
Bull, 3 years old and over. First premium, $75.
Bull, 2 years old and under 3. Fifth premium, $30.
Bull, 1 year and under 2. Second premium, $40.
Bull under 1 year. Second premium, $40.
Heifer, 2 and under 3 years. Fourth premium, $40.
Heifer, 1 and under 2 years. Third premium, $30.
Heifer under 1 year. Third and fifth premiums, $50.
Get of one sire. Second premium, $65.
Produce of one cow. Fifth premium, $40.
Aged herd. Second premium, $100.
Young herd. First premium, $75.
Aged herd, bred by exhibitor. Second premium, $100.
Young herd, bred by exhibitor. First premium, $100.
F. B. Buckley, Schaghticoke
Cow, 3 years old or over. Fifth premium, $30.
Heifer, 1 and under 2 years. Fourth and fifth premiums, $45.
Get of one sire. Third premium, $55.
Produce of one cow. Fourth premium, $45.
Aged herd. Fourth premium, $65.
Young herd. Fifth premium, $40.
Young herd, bred by exhibitor. Fifth premium, $40.

GROUP NINETY-NINE

Sheep

SHROPSHIRES

SEVEN FLOCKS COMPETING—TWO FROM NEW YORK

L. D. Rumsey, Lewiston
Ram, 2 years old or over. Fifth prize, $20.
Ram, 12 months and under 16. Fourth prize, $30.
Ram, 6 months and under 12. Fifth prize, $15.
Ewe, 2 years old and over. First and fourth prizes, $80.
Ewe, 12 months and under 18. Second prize, $45.
Champion ewe, 1 year old or over. First prize, $80.
Grand champion ewe. First prize, $100.
Four animals, get of one sire. First prize, $60.
Two animals, produce of one ewe. First prize, $40.
Aged flock. Fourth prize, $25.
Young flock. Second prize, $40.

H. L. Wardwell, New York city
Ram, 12 months and under 18. Fifth prize, $20.
Ram, 6 months and under 12. First prize, $35.
Ram under 6 months. Second prize, $30.
Ewe, 2 years old and over. Second prize, $45.
Ewe, 12 months and under 18. Fourth prize, $30.
Ewe, 6 months and under 12. Fifth prize, $15.
Ewe under 6 months. Second and fourth prizes, $50.
Champion ram under 1 year old. First prize, $50.
Four animals, get of one sire. Second prize, $50.
Two animals, produce of one ewe. Fourth prize, $20.
Aged flock. Third prize, $30.
Young flock. Third prize, $25.

CHEVIOTS

EIGHT FLOCKS COMPETING—ONE FROM NEW YORK

William Curry & Son, Hartwick
Ram, 2 years old or over. Second prize, $30.
Ram, 18 months and under 24. First prize, $35.
Ram, 12 months and under 18. Second prize, $30.
Ewe, 2 years old or over. First prize, $35.
Ewe, 18 months and under 24. Third prize, $25.
Ewe, 12 months and under 18. Fourth prize, $20.
Ewe, 6 months and under 12. Third prize, $15.
Champion ewe, 1 year old or over. First prize, $60.
Grand champion ewe. First prize, $75.

Four animals, get of one sire. Second prize, $30.
Two animals, produce of one ewe. First prize, $25.
Aged flock. First prize, $50.
Young flock. Second prize, $30.
Breeder's flock. First prize, $150.

MERINOS

THIRTEEN FLOCKS COMPETING—ONE FROM NEW YORK

D.K. Bell, Brighton

Ram, 2 years old or over. First and second prizes, $65.
Ram, 12 months and under 18 months. First and second prizes, $65.
Ram under 6 months. Second and third prizes, $35.
Ewe, 2 years old or over. First and second prizes, $65.
Ewe, 18 months and under 24. First prize, $35.
Ewe, 12 months and under 18. First and second prizes, $60.
Ewe under 6 months. First and fourth prizes, $35.
Champion ram, 1 year old or over. First prize, $60.
Champion ewe over 1 year old. First and second prizes, $40.
Champion ewe under 1 year old. First prize, $40.
Grand champion ram. First prize, $75.
Grand champion ewe. First prize. $75.
Four animals, get of one sire. First and second prizes, $70.
Two animals, produce of one ewe. First and second prizes,
    $45
Aged flock. First and second prizes, $90.
Young flock. First and second prizes, $70.
Breeder's flock. First prize, $150.
Exhibitor's flock. First prize, diploma.

HAMPSHIRES

FOUR FLOCKS COMPETING—ONE FROM NEW YORK

Chilmark Farm, Ossining
Ram, 2 years old or over. Second prize, $30.
Ram, 18 months and under 24. Fourth and fifth prizes, $35.
Ram, 12 months and under 18. First and third prizes, $60.
Ram, 6 months and under 12. Fourth prize, $10.
Ewe, 2 years old or over. First and fifth prizes, $50.
Ewe, 18 months and under 24. First and third prizes, $60.
Ewe, 6 months and under 12. Fifth prize, $8.
Ewe under 6 months. Second and fourth prizes, $30.
Champion ewe, 1 year or over. First and second prizes, $60.
Grand champion ewe. Second prize, diploma.
Four animals, get of one sire. First and fourth prizes, $60.
Two animals, produce of one ewe. Third prize, $15.

Aged flock. First and fourth prizes, $70.
Young flock. Third prize, $25.

GROUP ONE HUNDRED ONE

SWINE

TWO HERDS OF SWINE WERE EXHIBITED FROM NEW YORK

YORKSHIRE

A. Vroman, Carthage
Boar, 2 years old or over. Fifth prize, $15.
Sow, 2 years old or over. Third prize, $25.

CHESHIRES

S. G. Otis, Sherwood
Herd bred by exhibitor. First prize, $150.

GROUP ONE HUNDRED THREE

BELGIAN HARES

Jennie M. Lockwood, Reading Center
Doe, 4 and under 6 months, Daisy 91. Second prize
Charles Hilts, Cobleskill
Doe under 4 months, Anona 94. Second prize
Black Belgian buck, over 6 months, Black Jack, Jr., 102. First prize
White Belgian Doe, over 6 months, Lady Day 96. First prize
White Belgian doe, under 6 months, Opal 95. First prize

GROUP ONE HUNDRED FOUR

Poultry

Edgewood Farm, Ballston Lake
Buff Plymouth Rock, cock. First prize
Buff Plymouth Rock, cockerel. Sixth prize
Buff Plymouth Rock, pullet. Second prize
Buff Plymouth Rock, breeding pen. Seventh prize
Greystone Poultry Farm, Yonkers
White Plymouth Rock, cock. Third prize
Single Comb Black Minorcas, pullet. Fourth prize
Single Comb Black Minorcas, pullet. Sixth prize
Single Comb Black Minorcas, breeding pen. First prize
George W. Hillson, Amenia
White Plymouth Rock, pullet. First prize
Dark Brahma Bantam, breeding pen. First prize

Dark Brahma Bantam, breeding pen. Second prize
Dark Brahma Bantam, breeding pen. Fifth prize
Light Brahma Bantam, cock. Fifth prize
Light Brahma Bantam, cock. Sixth prize
Light Brahma Bantam, hen. First prize
Light Brahma Bantam, hen. Second prize
Light Brahma Bantam, hen. Third prize
Light Brahma Bantam, pullet. Fifth prize
Light Brahma Bantam, pullet. Sixth prize
Light Brahma Bantam, pullet. Seventh prize
Light Brahma Bantam, breeding pen. Second prize
Light Brahma Bantam, breeding pen. Fourth prize
W.T. Lord, Troy
Buff Wyandotte, cock. Third prize
Buff Wyandotte, cock. Fifth prize
Buff Wyandotte, cockerel. First prize
Buff Wyandotte, cockerel. Fourth prize
Buff Wyandotte, cockerel. Fifth prize
Buff Wyandotte, hen. Sixth prize
Buff Wyandotte, hen. Seventh prize
Buff Wyandotte, pullet. First prize
Buff Wyandotte, pullet. Second prize
Buff Wyandotte, pullet. Third prize
Buff Wyandotte, pullet. Fourth prize
Buff Wyandotte, breeding pen. Second prize
Buff Wyandotte, breeding pen. Third prize
Buff Wyandotte, breeding pen. Fifth prize
E.G. Wyckoff, Ithaca
Partridge Wyandotte, hen. Seventh prize
Partridge Wyandotte, pullet. Sixth prize
Partridge Wyandotte, breeding pen. Second prize
Silver Penciled Wyandotte, cock. First prize
Silver Penciled Wyandotte, cock. Second prize
Silver Penciled Wyandotte, cockerel. First prize
Silver Penciled Wyandotte, hen. First prize
Silver Penciled Wyandotte, hen. Second prize
Silver Penciled Wyandotte, pullet. First prize
Silver Penciled Wyandotte, pullet. Second prize
Silver Penciled Wyandotte, breeding pen. First prize
Silver Penciled Wyandotte, breeding pen. Second prize
Black Leghorn, cock. First prize
Black Leghorn, cock. Fourth prize
Black Leghorn, cockerel. Second prize

Black Leghorn, hen. Second prize
Black Leghorn, hen. Third prize
Black Leghorn, pullet. Second prize
Black Leghorn, pullet. Fourth prize
Black Leghorn, breeding pen. First prize
Black Leghorn, breeding pen. Third prize
Single Comb Buff Leghorn, cock. First prize
Single Comb Buff Leghorn, cock. Fifth prize
Single Comb Buff Leghorn, cockerel. Second prize
Single Comb Buff Leghorn, breeding pen. First prize
Single Comb White Leghorn, cock. Second prize
Single Comb White Leghorn, cockerel. Third prize
Single Comb White Leghorn, hen. Third prize
Single Comb White Leghorn, hen. Fourth prize
Single Comb White Leghorn, pullet. Third prize
E.A. Parks, Syracuse
Partridge Wyandotte, breeding pen. Fifth prize
R.F. Alden, Deposit
Silver Wyandotte, pullet. Sixth prize
W.R. Curtiss & Co., Ransomville
White Wyandotte, hen. Sixth prize
White Wyandotte, breeding pen. Third prize
Pekin Ducks, cock. Seventh prize
Pekin Ducks, hen. Fifth prize
D. Lincoln Orr, Orr's Mills
White Wyandotte, pullet. Sixth prize
Dark Brahma Bantams, breeding pen. Third prize
Dark Brahma Bantams, breeding pen. Fourth prize
Dark Brahma Bantams, breeding pen. Sixth prize
Dark Brahma Bantams, breeding pen. Seventh prize
Light Brahma Bantams, cock. First prize
Light Brahma Bantams, cock. Second prize
Light Brahma Bantams, cock. Third prize
Light Brahma Bantams, cock. Fourth prize
Light Brahma Bantams, hen. Fourth prize
Light Brahma Bantams, hen. Fifth prize
Light Brahma Bantams, hen. Sixth prize
Light Brahma Bantams, hen. Seventh prize
Light Brahma Bantams, pullet. First prize
Light Brahma Bantams, pullet. Second prize
Light Brahma Bantams, pullet. Third prize
Light Brahma Bantams, pullet. Fourth prize
Light Brahma Bantams, breeding pen. First prize

Light Brahma Bantams, breeding pen. Third prize
J.M. Linnett, Baldwinsville
Light Brahma, breeding pen. Seventh prize
J.F. Knox, Buffalo
White Langshans, hen. First prize
White Langshans, hen. Fourth prize
White Langshans, pullet. Fifth prize
White Langshans, breeding pen. First prize
Black Cochin Bantams, cock. Third prize
Black Cochin Bantams, cock. Sixth prize
Black Cochin Bantams, cock. Seventh prize
Black Cochin Bantams, cockerel. Sixth prize
Black Cochin Bantams, cockerel. Seventh prize
Black Cochin Bantams, hen. Third prize
Black Cochin Bantams, pullet. Second prize
Black Cochin Bantams, pullet. Fifth prize
Black Cochin Bantams, breeding pen. First prize
Edwin H. Morris, Sparkill
Houdans, cock. Fourth prize
Houdans, hen. Fourth prize
Houdans, pullet. Sixth prize
Houdans, breeding pen. Fourth prize
Black East Indian Ducks, cock. Second prize
Black East Indian Ducks, cock. Third prize
Black East Indian Ducks, hen. First prize
Black East Indian Ducks, hen. Third prize
Black East Indian Ducks, pullet. Second prize
Rouen Ducks, cock. Fourth prize
Rouen Ducks, cock. Seventh prize
Rouen Ducks, cockerel. Fifth prize
Rouen Ducks, cockerel. Sixth prize
Rouen Ducks, hen. Third prize
Rouen Ducks, hen. Seventh prize
Rouen Ducks, pullet. Fourth prize
Rouen Ducks, pullet. Fifth prize
E.F. McAvoy, Schenectady
Houdans, cockerel. Third prize
Houdans, hen. First prize
Houdans, pullet. Fourth prize
Houdans, breeding pen. Third prize
Henry Scheyer, Lake View
Anconas Mottled, hen. Fourth prize
Anconas Mottled, hen. Fifth prize

Anconas Mottled, pullet. First prize
R.H. Quackenbush, Baldwinsville
    Blue Andalusians, cock. Fourth prize
    Blue Andalusians, pullet. Sixth prize
Storm King Poultry Yards, Cornwall-on-Hudson
    Blue Andalusians, pullet. Fourth prize
E.B. Cridler, Dansville
    S.C.B. Leghorns, cockerel. Fourth prize
    S.C.B. Leghorns, pullet. Third prize
    S.C.B. Leghorns, pullet. Fourth prize
    S.C.B. Leghorns, breeding pen. Fourth prize
William T. Liddell, Greenwich
    S.C.B. Leghorns, pullet. Fifth prize
    Rose Comb Brown Leghorns, cock. First prize
    Rose Comb Brown Leghorns, cockerel. Fifth prize
H.S. Lamson, Cameron
    Rose Comb Brown Leghorns, hen. Third prize
S.E. Smith, Norwich
    Single Comb White Leghorns, cockerel. Sixth prize
Irving F. Rice, Cortland
    Single Comb White Leghorns, hen. First prize
J.H. Santee, Yonkers
    Single Comb Black Minorcas, cock. Second prize
    Single Comb Black Minorcas, cock. Sixth prize
    Single Comb Black Minorcas, hen. Third prize
Mrs. George E. Monroe, Dryden
    Single Comb Black Minorcas, cock. Third prize
    Single Comb Black Minorcas, pullet. Second prize
    Single Comb Black Minorcas, breeding pen. Second prize
Gedney Farm, White Plains
    Single Comb Black Minorcas, hen. Fourth prize
Charles L. Seely, Afton
    White Crested Black Polish, cock. Second prize
    White Crested Black Polish, cock. Fifth prize
    White Crested Black Polish, cock. Sixth prize
    White Crested Black Polish, cockerel. Fourth prize
    White Crested Black Polish, hen. Second prize
    White Crested Black Polish, hen. Fifth prize
    White Crested Black Polish, hen. Seventh prize
    White Crested Black Polish, pullet. First prize
    White Crested Black Polish, pullet. Third prize
    White Crested Black Polish, breeding pen. First prize
Dr. A.H. Phelps, Glens Falls

Black Cochin Bantams, hen. Seventh prize
Black Japanese Bantams, hen. First prize
Black Japanese Bantams, hen. Sixth prize
Black Japanese Bantams, breeding pen. First prize
Black Tailed Japanese Bantams, cock. Fifth prize
Black Tailed Japanese Bantams, hen. Fifth prize
Black Tailed Japanese Bantams, breeding pen. Second prize
Booted White Bantams, cock. Second prize
Booted White Bantams, hen. Second prize
Dark Brahma Bantams, cock. First prize
Dark Brahma Bantams, hen. Third prize
Dark Brahma Bantams, pullet. First prize
Cochin Partridge Bantams, cock. Fifth prize
White Cochin Bantams, cock. Sixth prize
Polish Buff Laced Bantams, cock. First prize
Polish Buff Laced Bantams, cock. Second prize
Polish Buff Laced Bantams, hen. First prize
Polish Buff Laced Bantams, hen. Second prize
White Crested White Polish Bantams, cock. Second prize
White Crested White Polish Bantams, hen. Fourth prize
White Crested White Polish Bantams, hen. Fifth prize
White Crested White Bearded Polish Bantams, cock. Third prize
White Crested White Bearded Polish Bantams, cockerel. Fourth prize
White Crested White Bearded Polish Bantams, hen. Second prize
White Crested White Bearded Polish Bantams, pullet. Fifth prize
Black African Bantams, cock. Seventh prize
White African Bantams, cock. Third prize
White African Bantams, cockerel. Fourth prize
White African Bantams, hen. Fourth prize
White African Bantams, pullet. Fifth prize
Golden Seabright Bantams, hen. Second prize
Silver Seabright Bantams, cock. Sixth prize
Birchen, cock. First prize
Birchen, hen. First prize
Black Breasted Red Bantams, cock. Second Prize
Black Breasted Red Bantams, hen. Fourth prize
Golden Duckling, cock. First prize
Golden Duckling, cockerel. Second prize
Golden Duckling, pullet. Second prize
Silver Duckling, cock. Second prize
Silver Duckling, cockerel. First prize
Silver Duckling, hen
Silver Duckling, pullet. Second prize

Red Pyle Game Bantams, cock. Second prize
Miscellaneous Frissles, cock. Second prize
Miscellaneous Frissles, cock. Third prize
Miscellaneous Frissles, hen. Second prize
Miscellaneous Frissles, hen. Sixth prize
Miscellaneous Silkies, cock. Third prize
Miscellaneous Silkies, hen. First prize
Miscellaneous Sultans, pullet. Second prize
Indian Game Bantams, cock. Second prize
Indian Game Bantams, cockerel. First prize
Indian Game Bantams, hen. Second prize
Indian Game Bantams, pullet. Second prize
N.Y. Salmon Faverolles, cock. First prize
N.Y. Ermine Faverolles, cock. First prize
N.Y. Salmon Faverolles, cock. Second prize
N.Y. Black Faverolle, cockerel. First prize
N.Y. Salmon Faverolle, cockerel. First prize
N.Y. Salmon Faverolle, cockerel. Second prize
N.Y. Ermine Faverolle, hen. First prize
N.Y. Salmon Faverolle, hen. First prize
N.Y. Salmon Faverolle, hen. Second prize
N.Y. Ermine Faverolle, pullet. First prize
N.Y. Blue Faverolle, pullet. First prize
N.Y. Black Faverolle, pullet. First prize
N.Y. Salmon Faverolle, pullet. First prize
N.Y. Salmon Faverolle, pullet. Second prize
N.Y. Salmon Faverolle, breeding pen. First prize
N.Y. Salmon Faverolle, breeding pen. Second prize
Barred White Plymouth Rock, bantams, cock. First prize
Barred White Plymouth Rock, cockerel. First prize
Barred White Plymouth Rock, pullet. First prize
Barred White Plymouth Rock, breeding pen. First prize
Rumpless, cock. Second prize
Rumpless, hen. Second prize
Sicilian, cock. First prize
Sicilian, hen. First prize
Campinos, hen. First prize
Gray Japanese Bantam, cock. Second prize
Gray Japanese Bantam, hen. Second prize
Lakenfelders, cock. First prize
Lakenfelders, cock. Second prize
Lakenfelders, cock. Fourth prize
Lakenfelders, cockerel. First prize

Lakenfelders, cockerel. Second prize
Lakenfelders, cockerel. Third prize
Lakenfelders, cockerel. Fourth prize
Lakenfelders, hen. First prize
Lakenfelders, hen. Second prize
Lakenfelders, hen. Third prize
Lakenfelders, hen. Fifth prize
Lakenfelders, pullet. First prize
Lakenfelders, pullet. Second prize
Lakenfelders, pullet. Third prize
Lakenfelders, pullet. Fifth prize
Lakenfelders, breeding pen. First prize
Lakenfelders, breeding pen. Second prize
Lakenfelders, breeding pen. Third prize
Lakenfelders, breeding pen. Fourth prize
Campines, pullet. First prize
Campines, breeding pen. First prize
Cuckoo Cochins, cock. First prize
Cuckoo Cochins, cockerel. First prize
Cuckoo Cochins, hen. First prize
Cuckoo Cochins, pullet. First prize
Rose Comb Blues, cock. First prize
Rose Comb Blues, cockerel. First prize
Rose Comb Blues, hen. First prize
Rose Comb Blues, pullet. First prize
W.A. Smith, Whitney's Point
    Black African Bantams, hen. Third prize
    Black Cochin Bantams, hen. Second prize
    Brown Red Game Bantams, cockerel. Second prize
    Brown Red Game Bantams, pullet. Second prize
    Buff Cochin Bantams, hen. Seventh prize
    Gray Call Ducks, cock. First prize
    White Call Ducks, hen. First prize
J.A. Sprakers, Sprakers
    White Game, cockerel. Second prize
    White Game, pullet. Second prize
    White Game, pullet. Third prize
    White Game, breeding pen: Second prize
G.B. Babcock, Jamestown
    Toulouse Geese, cock. Seventh prize
    Toulouse Geese, cockerel. Second prize
    Toulouse Geese, cockerel. Fourth prize
    Toulouse Geese, hen. Fourth prize

Toulouse Geese, pullet. Second prize
Toulouse Geese, pullet. Fourth prize
Jonas Hayner, Livingston
S.C. White Orpingtons, cockerel. Seventh prize

Pigeons

J.F. Knox, Buffalo
Red or Yellow Fantail, cock. Second prize
Red Fantail, hen, Second prize
Red or Yellow Fantail, 1904. Sixth prize
Any Color Saddle Fantail, cock. Third prize
Any Color Saddle Fantail, cock. Fourth prize
Any Color Saddle Fantail, hen. First prize
Any Color Saddle Fantail, 1904. Third prize
Any Color Saddle Fantail, 1904. Fourth prize
Black Pigmy Pouter, hen. Second prize
Black Pigmy Pouter, hen. Third prize
Black Pigmy Pouter, 1904. Fifth prize
Black Pigmy Pouter, 1904. Sixth prize
Blue Pigmy Pouter, cock., Second prize
Blue Pigmy Pouter, cock. Third prize
Blue Pigmy Pouter, hen. Fourth prize
Red or Yellow Pigmy Pouter, cock. Second prize
Red or Yellow Pigmy Pouter, 1904. Third prize
Red or Yellow Pigmy Pouter, 1904. Fourth prize
Red or Yellow Pigmy Pouter, 1904. Seventh prize
White Pigmy Pouter, hen. First prize
White Pigmy Pouter, hen. Fifth prize
White Pigmy Pouter, 1904. Second prize
J.H. Duer, Buffalo
White Working Homer, cock. Third prize
White Working Homer, hen. Sixth prize
White Working Homer, 1904. First prize
White Working Homer, 1904. Second prize
White Working Homer, 1904. Fourth prize
White Working Homer, 1904. Fifth prize
Dr. L.H. Jones, Rome
Black Pigmy Pouter, cock. Fourth prize
Black Pigmy Pouter, 1904. Second prize
Black Pigmy Pouter, 1904. Fourth prize
Blue Pigmy Pouter, cock Sixth prize
Blue Pigmy Pouter, hen. Second prize
Blue Pigmy Pouter, hen. Sixth prize

Blue Pigmy Pouter, 1904. Second prize
Blue Pigmy Pouter, 1904. Fourth prize
Blue Pigmy Pouter, 1904. Sixth prize
Red or Yellow Pigmy Pouter, cock. Fourth prize
Red or Yellow Pigmy Pouter, hen. First prize
Red or Yellow Pigmy Pouter, 1904. Second prize
Red or Yellow Pigmy Pouter, 1904. Fifth prize
Silver Pigmy Pouter, hen. Second prize
Silver Pigmy Pouter, 1904. Second prize
White Pigmy Pouter, cock. Third prize
White Pigmy Pouter, hen. Third prize
White Pigmy Pouter, hen. Fourth prize
White Pigmy Pouter, 1904. First prize
White Pigmy Pouter, 1904. Fourth prize
Any Other Color Pigmy Pouter, hen. Second prize
Any Other Color Pigmy Pouter, 1904. First prize
Any Other Color Pigmy Pouter, 1904. Fourth prize
Any Other Color Pigmy Pouter, 1904. Fifth prize
J.A. Sprakers, Sprakers
Blue Runts, hen. Third prize
Damascene, cock. First prize
Damascene, hen. First prize
A. Samuels, Buffalo
Black Snip Swallow, cock. Second prize
Black Snip Swallow, hen. Second prize
Black Snip Swallow, hen. Fourth prize
Black Snip Swallow, 1904. Second prize
Black Snip Swallow, 1904. Third prize
Blue Snip Swallow, cock. Second prize
Blue Snip Swallow, cock. Third prize
Blue Snip Swallow, hen. Third prize
Blue Snip Swallow, hen. Fourth prize
Blue Snip Swallow, 1904. First prize
Blue Snip Swallow, 1904. Second prize
Red Snip Swallow, cock. Second prize
Red Snip Swallow, cock. Third prize
Red Snip Swallow, hen. First prize
Red Snip Swallow, hen. Second prize
Red Snip Swallow, 1904. First prize
Red Snip Swallow, 1904. Second prize
Any Other Color Snip Swallow, cock. Third prize
Any Other Color Snip Swallow, hen. Third prize
Full Head White Barred Swallow cock. Second prize

Full Head White Barred Swallow, cock. Third prize
Full Head White Barred Swallow, hen. First prize
Full Head White Barred Swallow, hen. Third prize
Full Head White Barred Swallow, 1904. Second prize
Full Head White Barred Swallow, 1904. Third prize
Yellow Full Head White Barred Swallow, cock. Second prize
Yellow Full Head White Barred Swallow, cock. Third prize
Yellow Full Head White Barred Swallow, hen. First prize
Yellow Full Head White Barred Swallow, hen. Second prize
Yellow Full Head White Barred Swallow, 1904. First prize
Yellow Full Head White Barred Swallow, 1904. Second prize
Roller Parlor Tumblers, cock. First prize
Roller Parlor Tumblers, hen. Second prize

[Illustration: TRANSPORTATION BUILDING]

CHAPTER XII
Horticulture Exhibit and Schedule of Awards

HORTICULTURE EXHIBIT

By CHARLES H. VICK

Superintendent of Horticulture

[Illustration]

At a meeting of the Louisiana Purchase Exposition Commission of the State of New York, held June 10, 1903, Charles H. Vick, of Rochester, N.Y., was appointed as Superintendent of Horticulture, and an appropriation of $15,000 was made for the exhibit in that department. This amount was subsequently increased to $20,000. The work was inaugurated July first, and offices were opened at 46 Elwood building, Rochester, N.Y.

METHODS OF SOLICITING FRUIT

Many hundred letters were mailed to the fruit growers of the State soliciting the donation of fruit for an exhibit at St. Louis. The number of replies received was so small that it was necessary again to circularize the growers offering to pay a reasonable price for exhibition fruit. Even this offer did not bring forth anything like a sufficient quantity of fruit to make a suitable exhibit. The State was then divided into six sections and competent men appointed to canvass thoroughly each section and buy fruit. A large collection of fine specimens of fruit were procured by this method, and as a result of this canvass exhibits were procured from every fruit growing county in the State. This fruit was all collected at the Gleason cold storage warehouse at Brighton, near Rochester, N.Y., and on December 1, 1903, a shipment of two cars, containing four hundred barrels of apples, fifty-five bushel boxes of pears and forty baskets of grapes were forwarded to the Mound City cold storage warehouse at St. Louis.

LOCATION OF EXHIBIT

The exhibit was housed in the Palace of Horticulture, which, although located in a somewhat remote part of the grounds, received its full share of Exposition visitors, all of whom were deeply interested in the magnificent displays of fruit found there.

The State of New York was assigned 4,000 square feet of space advantageously located near the northeast corner of the building. To the west were the exhibits of Illinois and Missouri, and to the east those of Minnesota and Washington, while Colorado bounded New York on the south and Pennsylvania on the north. In August, New York was assigned the space surrendered by Pennsylvania, approximately 1,200 square feet, to accommodate the large exhibit of grapes from the Central New York growers and from the Chautauqua Grape and Wine Association.

THE INSTALLATION

The space included three distinct sections, Nos. 40, 41 and 43, completely surrounded by aisles, thus affording an excellent opportunity of viewing the exhibit from all sides. On account of this an open installation was erected. Around section 43 was thrown an open facade, consisting of columns supporting a handsome cornice, which bore the coat of arms of the State and the words "The State of New York" on each side. On the cornice rested fifteen fine specimens of Boston ferns.

The fruit was displayed upon tables of varying lengths and from three to four feet in width. In the center of this space was the office of the Superintendent. Sections 40 and 41 were within the zone in which low installation was required by the Exposition authorities, so that no facade was erected in these sections, the name of the State being shown upon handsome ornamental gilt signs, placed upon the tables and suspended over the exhibit. The entire installation was of white enamel, kept spotlessly clean. The plates used were of special design. The center was white, with the monogram in green letters, "L. P. E., 1904," and a wide green border, with a gold band. The white and green furnished a most appropriate background for the varicolored fruit and the effect was most pleasing as the eye swept over the whole exhibit.

A WORD OF COMMENDATION

On the opening day of the Fair, April thirtieth, New York's exhibit of fruit was complete in every detail. In fact of the thirty-five States, Canada and Mexico represented, New York was the only State to have its exhibit installed and ready for exhibition when the doors of the Palace of Horticulture were thrown open to the public, which called forth a special word of commendation from the Chief of the Department of Horticulture, Honorable F. W. Taylor. Owing to the fact that at that time the other States were not prepared to make a display, it was deemed inadvisable to exhibit a large number of varieties, so that while the entire space was covered with fruit, the exhibit consisted of but thirty-one varieties of apples, ten of pears and three of grapes, as follows:

Apples: Fallawater, Swarr, Golden Russet, Snow, Belleflower, Sweet Russet, Cline's Red, Red Rock, Holland Pippin, Hubbardston Nonesuch, Deacon Jones, Judson, Sklanka Bog, Peach, Sutton Beauty, Flower of Genesee, Baldwin, Lady, Kirkland Pippin, Greening, Spitzenburg, Northern Spy, Walbridge, Seek-no-Further, McIntosh, Grimes' Golden, Wagener, Mann, Roxbury, Russet, King, Canada Red

Pears: Kieffer, Duchess, Vergalieu, Josephine, Diel, Beurre d'Anjou, Beurre Bosc, Lawrence, Mt. Vernon, Beurre Clairgeau

Grapes: Virgennes, Diana, Catawba

A HIGH STANDARD OF EXCELLENCE

From the opening to the close of the Fair, December first, New York's exhibit of fruit was maintained at a uniformly high standard of excellence. The total number of varieties of fruit exhibited was as follows:

Apples .... 424 varieties
Cherries .... 31 "
Currants .... 4 "
Gooseberries ... 1 "
Grapes .... 150 "
Pears .... 152 "
Plums .... 129 "
Quinces .... 8 "
Peaches .... 14 "
Strawberries ... 1 "

The Empire State far outstripped her sister States as to number of varieties of fruit, displaying twice as many varieties of apples, pears and plums, and more than three times as many varieties of grapes as her nearest competitor, and this be it said, in a display of fruits never before equaled either in size, variety or quality.

RECORD OF ENTRIES

Over 2,000 individual entries of fruit were made during the season, and as all of the fruit was entered twice, once for the general collection of the State and again for the grower, the total number of entries was nearly five thousand. An accurate record was kept of all entries, the following information being carefully tabulated: The name and address of the exhibitor. Date of removal from cold storage. Date placed upon the table. Date of removal from the table. Remarks concerning its condition.

FRUIT of 1904

The new fruit of the fall of 1904, while free from rust and of good color, was somewhat smaller in size than the fruit of 1903; nevertheless it made a grand display, and from the opening to the close of the Fair from 2,000 to 2,500 plates of fruit, including never less than 150 varieties of apples, were admired by the thousands of visitors.

APPLES

The apples placed in cold storage at St. Louis in December of 1903 were found to be in almost perfect condition when opened in April, and, with a few exceptions, continued so throughout the season. Most of the apples were wrapped first in tissue and then in oiled paper and firmly packed in barrels well lined with corrugated paper, with excelsior cushions in each end.

Owing to the fact that so much depends upon the condition of fruit when picked, and the necessity of placing it in cold storage as soon as picked, it was a difficult matter to make a comparative test of the keeping qualities of the different varieties. For instance, of two different collections of Baldwins (one of the best keepers), placed on the tables at the same time, one lot held up in perfect condition for several weeks while the other went down in as many days.

The varieties showing the best keeping qualities were Baldwin, Spitzenberg, Russet, Northern Spy and Canada Red. These varieties were kept in cold storage and placed on the tables as late in the season as November fifteenth, when they were found to have retained their color, firmness and flavor.

Some of the fall varieties, which are ordinarily supposed to be poor keepers, came out of cold storage in perfect condition and kept remarkably well after being placed on the tables. Among these the Alexander, Fallawater, Holland Pippin, McIntosh and Rome Beauty were the best.

A collection of Fallawaters from W.R. Fitch, of Rushville, N.Y., were placed on the tables April twenty-ninth, when they attracted considerable attention on account of their unusual size and fine color, and remained in splendid condition for weeks. While somewhat shriveled and dried up, they showed no signs of decay when removed from the tables July twentieth. The same is true of a collection of Holland Pippins and McIntoshes placed on exhibition at the same time.

A collection of Alexanders from J.B. Collamer, of Hilton, will serve as an illustration of the advantages of picking at the proper time, handling with care and placing in cold storage immediately. These apples were exhibited for a week at the State Fair held at Syracuse in September of 1903. They were then wrapped, packed and sent to St. Louis, where they were kept in cold storage until June twenty-sixth, when they were placed on exhibition until after the visit of Governor Odell, June twenty-ninth. On June thirtieth they were rewrapped and repacked and sent back to cold storage until a few days before the State Fair at Syracuse in September of 1904, when they were shipped to Syracuse and again exhibited for a week. At the close of the State Fair they were again returned to St. Louis and exhibited for two weeks.

The Newtown Pippin is another variety which showed excellent keeping qualities. On August twelfth a collection of forty-six plates from Henry D. Lewis, of Annandale, was taken out of cold storage and placed on exhibition. They held up in good condition until the thirtieth of August, during the hottest weather of the season.

The Greenings, while large in size, of fine color, and apparently in perfect condition when packed, invariably came out of cold storage badly scalded and discolored. In fact, there were only three or four lots which were entirely free from scald.

In September, large additions of new fruit were made to the exhibit from individual growers, and also from the New York Agricultural Experiment Station at Geneva.

George W. Anderson, Charles N. Baker, Samuel J. Wells and T.H. King are among the exhibitors who deserve special mention for the quality and extent of their exhibits.

A complete list of the 424 varieties of apples exhibited appears following the list of exhibitors.

GRAPES

The grape industry of New York had adequate and successful representation at the St. Louis Exposition, as a department of the general Horticultural Exhibit. This industry in New York is one of large and steadily increasing importance. The State ranks second only to California in the production of grapes, and the showing made in the Horticulture building was a revelation to thousands of visitors who there obtained their first knowledge of the extent of the viticulture industry in New York.

This sign was conspicuously displayed over the exhibit of grapes:

"NEW YORK LEADS IN TABLE GRAPES

"600,000 acres; 30,000,000 vines; crop worth $2,763,711 annually."

These figures are from census reports, and represent an advance of 198 per cent in the industry over its condition as represented at the Columbian Exposition in 1893. There is scarcely another such record of increase in the whole range of industries of the United States.

No attempt was made to show viticulture in any other way than by its product, but an almost continuous display of grapes was kept on the tables from the opening of the Exposition to its close. This in itself was a noteworthy achievement, for it included a display of cold storage grapes from the crop of 1903 up to the second week of July, 1904, something never before attempted. A display of forced fruit and early varieties began shortly after that date.

A collection of hot-house grapes grown by Mr. David M. Dunning, of Auburn, was an interesting feature of the grape exhibit and amazed crowds of visitors on account of their size and handsome appearance. The varieties were Barbarossa and Muscat Hamburg. One cluster of the latter variety weighed nine pounds and measured seventeen inches in length, exclusive of stem. This collection of grapes far surpassed anything of the kind shown in the Horticulture building, not even excepting California specimens.

The varieties in cold storage were as follows: Catawba, Diana, Iona, Isabella, Niagara, Salem and Virgennes. Of these varieties, the Catawba and Virgennes kept the longest. They were taken from cold storage July third and placed upon exhibition for a week, at the end of which time they were found to have retained their color and flavor perfectly. This was fully one month later than grapes were preserved at the Pan-American Exposition, notwithstanding the difference in distance between Buffalo and St. Louis from the vineyards. The Diana and Iona were close seconds in keeping qualities, while the Isabella rattled badly and the Niagara showed discoloration, though both retained fairly good flavor.

The display proper of the 1904 crop began early in September. This display was entirely made up of fruit contributed by the growers of the Chautauqua and Keuka Lake districts. These two districts were represented about in proportion to their acreages and products.

The grapes were well wrapped in paper and packed in a new style paper grape basket, furnished by Mullen Bros. Paper Company, of St. Joseph, Michigan. These baskets were packed in spring crates, and the grapes, with a very few exceptions, carried in perfect condition.

The grape exhibit was made adjacent to the rest of the New York exhibit. The tables afforded room for about 2,000 plates. The display was made up largely of Concord, Catawba, Niagara, Virgennes, Campbell Early and other commercial varieties.

The rarer varieties, however, were not neglected, as will be seen from the list of one hundred and fifty varieties appearing elsewhere.

PEARS

In October of 1903, fifty-five bushel boxes of pears were placed in cold storage to be used for the Exposition. Of this number, twenty-five boxes were purchased from David K. Bell, of Brighton, and the balance came in single bushels from some of the best growers of the State. The pears, like the apples, were wrapped first in heavy tissue paper and then in oiled paper.

The following is a list of the varieties kept in cold storage: Beurre d'Anjou, Beurre Bosc, Beurre Clairgeau, Beurre Diel, Angouleme, Columbia, Duchess, Howell, Josephine of Malines, Kieffer, Lawrence, Mt. Vernon, Rutter and Vergalieu.

On April twenty-fifth, when the boxes were examined and a selection made for the opening day, the Duchess was found in poorer condition than any of the other varieties. Notwithstanding this fact, a continuous exhibit of Duchess pears was made until May thirtieth. All the other varieties were in prime condition, and were displayed in lots of fifty plates until May twenty-sixth, when one grand exhibit was made, consisting of four hundred plates of fifteen varieties. This display continued in good condition until the sixteenth of June, in spite of the extreme hot weather at that time, the Anjou, Angouleme, Bosc, Clairgeau, Columbia, Howell and Kieffer keeping extremely well until that date.

The display in the fall of 1904 attracted a great deal of attention, not alone from visitors, but also from the superintendents of horticulture from the other States and from fruit growers in general. On September nineteenth, one hundred and forty-two varieties were exhibited from Ellwanger & Barry, of Rochester; on September twenty-first, twenty varieties were exhibited from David K. Bell, of Brighton, in addition to the general display from almost every section of the State, making an exhibit of pears never before equaled.

A complete list of the one hundred and fifty-two varieties of pears exhibited will be found following the list of exhibitors.

PLUMS

As the result of a bountiful plum crop, the display of this luscious and popular fruit was unusually large and fine. The first shipment, consisting of Early Red June, was received from F. E. Dawley, of Fayetteville, on August fifth, and from that time until September twenty-sixth, additions were made almost daily. One hundred and twenty-eight varieties, arrayed on hundreds of plates, and occupying nearly a third of the New York space, compelled the attention and admiration of every passer-by. And indeed, it was an attractive sight, from the stand-point of color alone, comprising, as it did, nearly every shade of green, yellow, purple, blue, orange and red.

The varieties attracting the most attention were Abundance, Arch Duke, Burbank, Coe's Golden Drop, Grand Duke, Quackenboss and St. Lawrence.
The display of Burbank was the largest and finest ever shown, the best two lots coming from Fred H. Teats, of Williamson, and T. H. King, of Trumansburg.

Splendid collections were also received from F. E. Dawley, of Fayetteville, consisting of eleven varieties; S. D. Willard, of Geneva, twenty-three varieties; New York Agricultural Experiment Station, at Geneva, one hundred and five varieties.

A total of one hundred and twenty-eight varieties were exhibited; all of the varieties are listed following the list of exhibitors.

CHERRIES

Thirty-one varieties of cherries were exhibited, the largest exhibit coming from the New York Agricultural Experiment Station. No other State excelled in number of varieties.

See the list following the list of exhibitors.

PEACHES

New York's peach crop was not up to the usual standard, being more or less infected with rust and lacking in color. It was also found to be a difficult matter to get shipments to St. Louis in good condition.

There were liberal quantities of such varieties as were shown, a list of which appears following the list of exhibitors.

QUINCES

The crop of 1904 was unusually small and inferior in quality. Nevertheless a fairly good exhibit was made.

The varieties shown appear following the list of exhibitors.

CURRANTS

It was impossible to make a general display of small fruits, owing to the distance from New York to St. Louis. Four varieties of currants were shown, however, the Perfection Currant, from C. G. Hooker, of Rochester, excelling in size, quality and flavor any currant exhibited.

A list of varieties appears following the list of exhibitors.

GOOSEBERRIES

The gooseberry crop was a total failure in New York, and only one small exhibit was made of the Downing.

STRAWBERRIES

It was the intention to make a large exhibit of strawberries, and arrangements were partially made with Mr. L. J. Farmer, of Pulaski, to collect this exhibit, but owing to the very poor condition of shipments received from Illinois, Missouri and other nearby States, the plan was abandoned, as it was feared that the berries would be spoiled in transit. One exhibit, however, was made. This was the Ryckman strawberry and came from G. E. Ryckman, of Brocton. Owing to extreme care in packing, this small exhibit came in fairly good condition, and excited much comment on account of its size, color, fine flavor and prolific production.

PLANTS AND FLOWERS

The exhibit of plants and flowers was, for the most part, made out of doors in beds, which were attractively laid out in the grounds surrounding the Horticulture and Agriculture buildings. The extent of the grounds afforded opportunity for the massing of the different varieties of hardy plants, such as roses, peonies, hydrangeas, and also of the newer varieties of cannas and geraniums. In the conservatory adjoining the Horticulture building proper were exhibited fine collections of ferns and a large display of gladiolas, and also one of peonies.

SOME GRATIFYING COMPARISONS

The following statistics from the United States census of 1903 may be of interest:

New York leads in the production of fruit, exclusive of subtropical fruits. Twelve and one-tenth per cent of the fruit production of the United States is in New York.

Orchard fruit of 1903 was valued at $10,542,272
Grapes of 1903 were valued at 2,763,711
Small fruits of 1903 were valued at 2,538,363

The following table will give an idea of the extensive cultivation of small fruits:

	Acres	Product-quarts
Raspberries	12,376	17,575,530
Strawberries	7,311	13,846,860
Currants	2,594	4,584,080
Blackberries	2,060	3,167,090
Other berries	710	862,107

	Number of vines	Product-pounds
Grapes	29,636,316	247,689,056

From the following a comparison may be drawn between the number of trees and apple product of the two leading apple states:

	Number of trees	Product-bushels
New York	15,054,832	24,111,257
Missouri	20,040,399	6,496,436

The average number of apple trees per farm in the United States was 74.5; the same for New York was 86.2. The average production in bushels per farm in the United States was 64.8; the same for New York was 138.1.

A considerable proportion of the trees in Missouri, quoted above, are young trees, and the relative products will soon show far different results unless New York fruit growers awake to the situation. In all of the western fruit growing states the annual planting of young trees is rapidly increasing, a precaution which our fruit growers are not taking to any great extent. Moreover, the lack of interest on the part of New York growers in expositions and the opportunity there afforded for advertising the superiority of New York products is a subject for comment. It is in marked contrast to the interest and progressive spirit of the growers in the western states who never lose such an opportunity, and are gradually working into the front ranks of fruit production. In many of the western states no public funds nor machinery were provided for a horticultural exhibit at St. Louis, but very creditable exhibits were prepared, the entire expense of the same being borne by fruit growers' associations. In marked contrast is a rather unfortunate precedent heretofore adopted in the State of New York, and of necessity followed at St. Louis, viz.: That the State, in order to obtain a creditable exhibit, must pay a fancy price for fruit for exhibition purposes and allow the seller to receive the award upon fruit which is no longer his own property.

THE STAFF

In addition to the superintendent the staff connected with the department consisted of James G. Patterson, of Sheridan, assistant superintendent; John W. Coughtry, of New Scotland, and Sherman T. Lewis, of Johnsonburg, assistants in charge of fruit exhibit; A. M. Loomis, of Fredonia, assistant in charge of viticulture, and Miss Bessie J. Hutchinson, of Rochester, stenographer. One and all they served the Commission and the State faithfully and efficiently.

AWARDS

The State received a total of 295 awards, divided as follows: A grand prize for installation, a grand prize for the collective State exhibit of fruit, 19 gold medals, 142 silver medals and 132 bronze medals. Owing to the rules and regulations governing the system of awards, however, prizes were not so freely distributed as at the World's Fair at Chicago, or the Pan American Exposition at Buffalo. Heretofore it has always been the custom to allow the exhibitor a medal for a collection of apples, another for a collection of pears, another for plums, etc., while at St. Louis only one award was allowed an exhibitor for his entire collective exhibit. The jury in the Department of Horticulture was on duty throughout the Exposition period, and as soon as an exhibit was placed upon the tables it was promptly passed upon by the jury, due application having been made.

Catalogue of Exhibitors in the Department of Horticulture, with the Award, if Any, Received by Each

GROUP ONE HUNDRED SEVEN

Pomology

F. M. Adams, Fredonia. Bronze medal
Grapes
  Pocklington, Martha, Concord
Frank Abbott, Pulteney. Silver medal
Grapes
  Catawba, Concord, Eumelan, Diana, Delaware
George Aldrich, Sheridan. Bronze medal
Grapes
  Concord, Niagara, Pocklington
B. C. Allen, Holley. Silver medal
Apples
  Roxbury, Russet, Snow
James Allen, Nliddleport. Silver medal
Apples
  Baldwin, Greening, Twenty Ounce, King
M. L. Allen, Seneca Falls. Silver medal
Apples
  Gilliflower, Northern Spy
Clark Allis, Medina
Apples
  Stump
G. W. Anderson, South Onondaga. Silver medal
Apples
  Twenty Ounce, King, Tallman Sweet, Peck's Pleasant, Northern Spy,
  Red Canada
W. W. Anderson, Gasport. Silver medal
Apples
  Northern Spy, Greening, Snow
Marcus Ansley, Geneva. Bronze medal
Pears
  Kieffer, Duchesse, Beurre Bosc
Lewis Archer, Hilton. Bronze medal
Apples

Baldwin, Cooper's Market, Roxbury Russet
Charles E. Artman, Le Roy. Bronze medal
 Apples
 King
George Bacon, Scriba. Bronze medal
 Apples
 Baldwin
Charles N. Baker, Selkirk. Silver medal
 Apples
  Peck's Pleasant, Northern Spy, Langford Seedling, Black Twig,
  Bagdanoff, Baldwin, Salome, Red Russet, Wagener, Scott's Winter,
  Winter Sweet, Newtown Pippin, Sutton Beauty, Tallman Sweet, Phoenix,
  Gilliflower, Golden Russet, Roxbury Russet, Willow Twig, Vandervere,
  McIntosh, Pound Sweet, Mother, Wolf River, Milding, Yellow
  Belleflower, Esopus Spitzenberg
C. M. Bailey, Pulteney. Bronze medal
 Grapes
  Concord, Catawba
Fred Baright, Van Wagoner. Bronze medal
 Apples
  Red Belleflower, Stark
R. A. Barnes, Lockport. Silver medal
 Pears
  Bartlett
W. A. Bassett, Farmer. Bronze medal
 Apples
  King, Peck's Pleasant, Hendrick Sweet
R. Bassett, Hilton. Bronze medal
 Apples
  Baldwin
 Peaches
  Late Crawford
F. M. Beattie, Brighton. Bronze medal
 Apples
  Northern Spy
C. Bechstedt, Oswego. Silver medal
 Apples
  Stump, Garden Royal, Unknown

David K. Bell, West Brighton. Silver medal
  Apples
    Mother
  Quinces
    Rhea's Mammoth
  Pears
    Josephine, Diel, Columbia, Clairgeau, Anjou, Winter Nellis,
    Bartlett, Superfin, Bose, Kieffer, Duchesse, Kinsessing, Louise
    Bonne, Pitmaston, Doyenne Boussock, Lawrence, Bergamot, Easter,
    Seckel, White Doyenne, Fred Clapp, Sheldon
L. J. Bellis, Crosby. Bronze medal
  Grapes
    Diana, Iona
E. S. Bender, New Scotland. Silver medal
  Apples
    Pewaukee, Rambo, Spitzenberg, Greening, Northern Spy,
    Lady Sweet, Pomme Grise, Roxbury, Russet
W. T. Benjamin, Fredonia. Silver medal
  Grapes
    Martha, Worden, Delaware
David W. Bennett, New Salem. Silver medal
  Apples
    Snow, Northern Spy, Baldwin, Rome Beauty
James Berryman, Bluff Point. Silver medal
  Grapes
    Catawba, Salem, Concord, Isabella, Niagara, Moore's Diamond,
      Pocklington
William Bradley, Pavilion. Bronze medal
  Apples
    Babbett, Cooper's Market, Northern Spy
L. G. Brainard, Ellington. Bronze medal
  Apples
    Gilliflower
E. T. Brizzee, Canandaigua. Bronze medal
  Apples
    Bailey Sweet, Belleflower
W. H. Brower, Arlington. Bronze medal
  Apples

Crow Egg, Lawver, Gilliflower, Newtown Pippin, Baldwin
W. D. Brown, Pulteney. Bronze medal
Grapes
Delaware, Concord, Niagara, Catawba
E. J. Brwen, Albion. Silver medal
Apples
King, Canada Red, Baldwin, Roxbury Russet, Northern Spy
A. B. Boyd, Pulteney. Silver medal
Grapes
Delaware, Concord, Worden, Ives' Seedling, Niagara, Brighton
J. V. Boyd, Pulteney
Grapes
Catawba, Concord
John W. Bullock, Brocton. Bronze medal
Grapes
Concord
F. D. Burger, Pulteney
Grapes
Catawba, Iona, Isabella
Mrs. Hiram Burgess, Newark. Bronze medal
Apples
White Graft, Smokehouse
F. W. Campbell, Esopus. Silver medal
Apples
Greening
Thomas Cant, Clarksville. Silver medal
Apples
Spitzenberg, Fall Pippin, McIntosh
Pears
Lawrence, Sheldon, Anjou, Howell
O. J. Chamberlain, Brocton. Bronze medal
Grapes
Concord, Niagara
Austin L. Champion, Schenectady. Bronze medal
Apples
Spitzenberg, Baldwin, Northern Spy, Red Winter Pippin
E. W. Chapman, Gasport. Silver medal
Apples

Snow, Nonesuch, Northern Spy
William Chillson, Fairdale. Bronze medal
Apples
Pound Sweet
M. A. Christman, Pavilion. Silver medal
Apples
Seek-no-Further
Fred W. Clark, Pavilion. Bronze medal
Apples
Northern Spy, Spitzenberg
J. E. Cline, Massena. Silver medal
Apples
Golden Russet, Snow, Belleflower, Sweet Russet, Cline's Red,
Red Rock, Ben Davis, Blue Pearmain, Sweet
H. B. Clothier, Silver Creek. Silver medal
Grapes
Concord, Niagara
F. B. Clothier, Silver Creek. Silver medal
Grapes
Concord
I. D. Cook & Son. South Byron
Apples
Peck's Pleasant, Tallman Sweet, Corey Pippin, Seek-no-Further
F. H. Cookingham, Cherry Creek
Apples
McIntosh, Maiden Blush, Mann
J. B. Collamer & Sons, Hilton. Silver medal
Apples
Alexander, Sweet Bough, Wealthy, Baldwin
Plums
Burbank
E. J. Cole, Sheridan. Silver medal
Grapes
Delaware, Salem, Concord, Niagara, Jessica
James E. Cole, Fulton
Apples
Rhode Island Greening
Ed. Colvin, Fredonia. Silver medal

Grapes
  Niagara, Worden, Campbell's Early
E. R. Concklin, Pomona. Bronze medal
  Apples
  Sutton Beauty, Baldwin, Pomeroy, Wagener
J. J. Conroy, Hilton. Silver medal
  Apples
  Baldwin, Nonesuch
J. B. Corkhill, Seneca Falls. Bronze medal
  Apples
  Gilliflower, Canada Red, Lady
H. A. Cosman, Hilton. Bronze medal
  Apples
  Canada Red, Ben Davis, Snow
Charles Covell, Lockport. Silver medal
  Apples
  King
F. Cozzens, Appleton. Silver medal
  Apples.
  Rhode island Greening, Tallman Sweet
Craig Colony, Sonyea. Bronze medal
  Apples
  Surprise, Sweet Henry, Pearmain, Dakota Sweet, Rhode
  Island Greening, Tallman Sweet, Baldwin, Gilliflower,
  Northern Spy, Bell Bond, Sweet Russet, Pound Sweet
A. B. Cranston, Sheridan. Bronze medal
  Grapes
  Delaware, Worden
S. S. Crissey, Fredonia. Silver medal
  Grapes
  Worden, Hartford, Green Mountain, Empire State, Wyoming
  Red, Ives' Black, Iona, Martha, Telegraph, Moore's
  Diamond, Concord, Pocklington
Fred Crosby, Crosby. Silver medal
  Grapes
  Empire State, Moore's Diamond, Catawba, Martha, Duchesse,
  Jefferson, Diana, Concord
John W. Crosier, Hall's Corners. Silver medal

Apples
  Pearmain, Canada Red, Baldwin
A. S. Cross, Pulteney. Bronze medal
  Grapes
  Concord
Cross & Uhl, Arlington. Silver medal
  Apples
  King, Snow, Northern Spy
Crossgrove Bros., Ripley. Bronze medal
  Grapes
  Concord, Niagara
Robert B. Crowell, Walkill. Silver medal
  Apples
  Russet Greening, Rambo, Pewaukee, Fallawater, Newtown
  Pippin, Snow, Grimes' Golden, Red Canada, Lady Sweet
Culver Bros., Bluff Point. Silver medal
  Grapes
  Delaware, Catawba, Concord, Niagara, Moore's Diamond,
  Pocklington
O. P. Curtis, Hilton. Bronze medal
  Pears
  Clapp's Favorite
  Plums
  Burbank
James Curtis & Son, Hilton. Bronze medal
  Apples
  Greening, King, Snow, Holland Pippin, Baldwin
  Pears
  Duchesse
F. E. Dawley, Fayetteville. Silver medal
  Apples
  Sweet Bough, Early Harvest, Red Astrachan, Yellow Transparent,
  Primate, Strawberry, Summer Pippin, Hawley,
  Grimes' Golden, Wine, Bismarck, English Streak, Red
  Romanite
  Cherries
  Dawley
  Pears

Clapp's Favorite, Seckel, Japanese
Plums
Seedling Japanese, Abundance, Primate, Red June, Burbank,
Japanese Wineberry, Red Negate, Shropshire Damson,
Tragedy Prune, Cooper, Lombard
Day Bros., Dunkirk. Silver medal
Grapes
Ives, Diana, Concord, Martha, Marion
David Dean, Oswego
Apples
Northern Spy
H. Dean, Aurora. Bronze medal
Grapes
Concord
John DeWitt, Bluff Point. Silver medal
Grapes
Catawba
George Dorman, Fredonia. Bronze medal
Grapes
Niagara
A. C. Doty, Sheridan. Bronze medal
Grapes
Brighton, Pocklington, Niagara, Delaware
C. E. Drake, Stanley. Silver medal
Apples
Smokehouse, Swaar, Winter Pippin, King, Bell Bond,
Ontario
Charles W. Driggs, Elba. Silver medal
Apples
Roxbury Russet, Baldwin, Northern Spy
R. C. Dunkelberger, Gasport. Silver medal
Apples
Baldwin, Roxbury Russet, Mann, Ben Davis, Cranberry
Pippin
David M. Dunning, Auburn. Gold medal
Apples
Alexander, King
Grapes

Barbarosa, Muscat Hamburg
Pears
Clairgeau
N.J. Durfee, Pavilion. Bronze medal
Apples
Snow, Baldwin, Northern Spy, Wagener
Sylvester Edeck, Olcott. Bronze medal
Apples
Cranberry Pippin
Pears
Kieffer
L.L. Edmunds, Holley. Silver medal
Apples
Lady Sweet, Spitzenberg, Nonesuch, Pound Sweet, Gilliflower,
Martin
John Elliott, Morton. Silver medal
Apples
Nonesuch, Holland Pippin
Ellwanger & Barry, Rochester. Gold medal
Apples
Arabskoe, Alexander, Albion, Amasias, Aucuba-leaved Reinette,
Ballarat Seedling, Bismarck, Black Detroit, Black Gilliflower,
Belle de Boskopp, Baldwin, Bohanan, Blanche de Bournay,
Blanche d'Espagne, Beauty of Kent, Ben Davis, Belle
d'Angers, Brittle Sweet, Brownlee's Russet, Barry, Buckingham,
Christiana, Cox's Pomona, Court Penduplat, Coe's Scarlet
Perfume, Canada Reinette, Danford, Duke of Devonshire, Dr.
Oppel's French Pippin, Dumclow's Seedling, Downing's Paragon,
English Royal Russet, Evening Party, Equimetely, Excelsior,
Esopus Spitzenberg, Fall Pippin, Flower of Kent, Fall
Orange, Fameuse, Fameuse Sucre, Glidden No. 3, Golden
Sweet, Gelber Richard, Grosse Bohnapfel, Golden Russet,
Hurlbut, Hester, Hartford Sweet, Hubbardston Nonesuch,
Hennepin, Idaho, Julia, Jackson, Johnson, Jonathan, Josephine
Kreuter, Keswick Codlin, King of Pippins, Krouzex,
Kelsey, Kikitia, Klaproth, Knox Russet, Lord Suffield, Lindenwald,
London Pippin, Lowell, Lady Hennicker, Liberty,
Lehigh, Long Stem, Magneta, Menagere, Minister, Mother,

Monmouth Pippin, McLellan, Marston's Red Winter, Milding,
Neversink, Nickajack, Nicolayer, Norton's Melon, Northern Spy,
Oustin's Pippin, Peter No. 12, Plumb's Cider, Pryor's
Red, Pickman, Pomme Grise, Pigeon de Schibler, Reinette
Monstrouse, Rhode Island Greening, Reinette Jaune Hative,
Reinette Bretagne, Riviere, Reinette gris de Versailles, Ribston
Pippin, Red Warrior, Red Canada, Roxbury Russet, Red
Beitingheimer, Sheppard's Perfection, Signe Tilisu, Schackleford,
Smokehouse, Swaar, Sol Edwards, Stott's Seedling, Seneca
Sweet, Summer Hagloe, Sweet Pearmain, Stump, Stark, Sutton
Beauty, Spaeth's Sameling, Soulard, Transparent de Croucels,
Turn-off Lane, Shannon, Twenty Ounce, Virginia Greening,
Wealthy Wagener, White Pippin, White Robinson, Winter
Pearmain, Winesap, Washington Strawberry, Wormsley's Pippin,
York Imperial, Yellow Belleflower

Pears

Admiral Cecil, America, Angelique le Clerc, Angouleme,
Angouleme Bronzee, Anjou, Ansault, Antoine Lormier, Auguste
Royer, Bergamot Buffo, Bergamot Heitrich, Bergamot
Royal d'Hiver, Beurre Alex Lucas, Beurre d'Aremburg,
Beurre Benoist Noveaux, Beurre Capiaumont, Beurre Diel,
Beurre Dumont, Beurre gris d'Hiver, Beurre Mauxion, Beurre
Moire, Bezi de la Motte, Black Worcester, Bonchretian Vermont,
Boussock, Brockworth Park, B. S. Fox, Buffam, Cabot,
Canandaigua, Catherine Gardette, Catinka, Chapman, Church,
Clairgeau, Columbia, Col. Wilder, Comice, Comte de Lamy,
Comte de Paris, Conseiller de la Cour, Delices d'Huy, Delices
de Mons, DeLamartine, Desiree Cornelis, Dix, Dorset, Dow,
Doyenne d'Alencon, Doyenne Boussock, Doyenne Dillon,
Doyenne Gray, Doyenne Jamain, Doyenne Robin, Doyenne
Sieulle, Dr. Nellis, Duchesse de Bordeaux, Duchesse Precoce,
Duhamel du Monceau, Eastern Belle, Easter Beurre, Edmunds,
Emile d'Heyst, Figue d'Alencon, Figue de Naples,
Fred Clapp, Gansel's Bergamot, Gansel's Seckel, Hardy, Homewood,
Hoosic, Island, Jackson, Jalousie de Fontenay, Jones,
Kieffer, Kingsessing, Kirtland, Knight's Seedling, Lady Clapp,
La France, Langalier, Lawrence, Le Comte, Lodge, Louise
Bonne de Jersey, Loveaux, Mace, Magnate, Miller, Minister,*

Dr. Lucius, Mount Vernon, Mme. Blanche Sannier, Mme.
Treyve, Napoleon, Oswego Beurre, Pardee's Seedling, Passe
Crasanne, Pater Noster, Paul Ambre, P. Barry, Pierre Corneille,
Pitmaston Duchesse, Poire Louise, Pound, President
Gilbert, Prince Consort, Prince's St. Germain, Rapalje's Seedling,
Raymond de Montlaux, Reeder, Refreshing, Rousselet
Bivort, Sarah, Seckel, Secretaire Rodin, Serrurier, Sheldon,
Soulard Bergamot, Souv. d'Esper, Souv. de Lens, Souv. de la
Marcau Trou, Souv. de la Reine des Belges, Souv. Sannier
Pere St. Andre, Sterling, Superfin, Tyson, Urbaniste, Van
Buren, Vergalieu No. 4, Washington, White Doyenne, Winter
Nelis
B. C. Fairchild, Willsboro. Bronze medal
Apples
Northern Spy, Fallawater, Wagener
William H. Falls, Gasport. Silver medal
Apples
King, Nonesuch, Lawyer, Baldwin, Tallman Sweet, Golden
Russet, Roxbury Russet
E. H. Fay, Portland. Bronze medal
Grapes
Stark Star
A. A. Fay, Brocton. Silver medal
Grapes
Concord, Niagara, Delaware
Finch & Horrocks, Bluff Point. Bronze medal
Grapes
Catawba, Niagara, Moore's Diamond
W. R. Finch & Son, Rushville. Silver medal
Apples
Fallawater, Swaar, Spitzenberg
Foster & Griffith, Fredonia. Silver medal
Apples
Fall Pippin, Abundance, Bradshaw, Red Beitengheimer,
Alexander, Black Detroit, Northern Spy, King, Ox, Maiden
Blush, St. Lawrence, Plunker Sweet, Fallawater, Orange
Pippin, Twenty Ounce, Duchess of Oldenburg
Grapes

Iona Red Rare, Vergennes, Delaware, Agawam, Jessica
White, Lucile, Lindley Rogers No. 9, Moyer Red
B. W. Frazer, Fredonia. Bronze medal
  Grapes
    Concord, Catawba
Howard S. Fullager, Penn Yan. Bronze medal
  Apples
    Northern Spy, Greening, Wagener
J. H. Gamby, Bluff Point. Silver medal
  Grapes
    Concord
John B. Garbutt, Middleport. Silver medal
  Apples
    Duchess of Oldenburg, Wealthy
J. V. Gaskell, Gasport. Silver medal.
  Apples
    Northern Spy, Pound Sweet, King
Geneva Experiment Station, Geneva. Gold medal
  Apples
    Albion, Alexander, Amasias, Aporte Orientale, August,
    Benoni, Bismarck, Bohana, Breskorka, Canada Baldwin,
    Canada Reinette, Caroline Red June, Charlock Reinette,
    Christiana, Coon Red, Count Orloff, Crott's, Deacon
    Jones, Dickinson, Doctor, Dudley Winter, Duncan, Edwards,
    Elgin Pippin, Enormous, Etowah, Ewalt, Excelsior,
    Fall Pippin, Ferdinand, Fishkill, Gideon, Gideon Sweet, Golden
    Medal, Golden Russet, Grandmother, Grand Duke Constantine,
    Great Mogul, Groscoe Slenka Greenle, Grundy, Hartford
    Rose, Haskell Sweet, Haywood, Herefordshire Beefing, Holland,
    Iowa Beauty, Jacob Sweet, Jones' Seedling, Jonathan
    Buler, Judson, Juicy Krimtartar, July Cluster, Keswick, Kirkland,
    Landsbergere Reinette, Lawver, Manchester, Magog Red
    Streak, McIntosh, McMahon, Milding, Milon, Milligan, Millott,
    Monmouth, Monroe, Moon, Moore Sweet, Mother, Mountain
    Sweet, Moyer's Bride, Munson, Nelson, Newman's Seedling,
    Northwestern Greening, Ohio Pippin, Olive, Paragon, Paul's
    Imperial Crab, Peach, Pear, Persian Bogdanoff, Piper, Pride
    of Texas, Reinette Coux, Rhodes Orange, Rolfe, Roxbury

Russet, Salome, Scott's Winter, Skelton, Sklanka Bog, Small's
Admirable, Standard, Stark, Stayman's Winesap, Striped Winter,
Stuart Golden, Sutton Beauty, Swaar, Swinku, Thompson,
Titus Pippin, Tobias, Tobias Black, Tobias Pippin, Tom Putt,
Van Hoy, Wabash Red Winter, Wallace Howard, Washington
Royal, Washington Strawberry, Watwood, Western Beauty,
White Zurdell, Williams Favorite, Winter Bananna, Winter
Golden, York Imperial

Cherries

Hoke, Ida, May Duke, King's Amarelle, Esel Kirche, Elton,
Double Nattie, Dyehouse, Orel No. 23, Gov. Wood, Black
Tartarian, Mercer, Rockport Bigarreau, Knight's Early Red,
Early Purple Guigne, Large Montmorency, Abesse de Pigmes,
Transcendant, Downer's Late, Napoleon Yellow Spanish,
Windsor, Bay State, Mezel, Olivet, Rapp, Luelling, Reine
Hortense, Sparhawk's Honey, Montmorency

Grapes

Hicks, Moyer, Canandaigua, Telegraph, Champion, Early
Victor, Riehl No. 22, McPike, Elvibach, Marion, Niagara, Isabella
Seedling, Rupert, Arminia, Corby, Hartford, Livingston,
Riehl No. 10, Janesville, August Giant, Eumelan, Merrimack,
Prentiss, Dracut Amber, Manito, Mary Favorite, Greene,
Horner No. 1, Diamond, Lucile, Mary Washington, Adirondack,
Browne, Worden, Colerain, Presley, Concord, Moore's
Early, Riehl No. 21, Cayuga, St. Louis, Rockwood, Jewell,
Campbell, Emerald, Waupanuka, Butler No. 1, R. W. Munson,
Essex, Barry, Pulaski, Thompson No. 7, Paragon, Wyoming
Red, Nectar, Herbert, Gold Coin, Perfection, Creveling,
Rebecca, Campbell's Early, Caywood No. 50, Brighton,
Winchell, Dr. Hexamer, Delaware, Faith, Peabody, Requa,
Etta, Chautauqua, Jessica, Lutie, Poughkeepsie, Olita, Berckman,
America, Golden Grain, Osage, Thompson No. 5, Columbian
Imperial, Northern Muscatine, Rogers No. 13, Red Eagle,
Agawam, Wilder, Hercules, Little Blue, Maxatawney, Kensington,
Helen Keller, Massasoit, Gold Dust, Martha, Station
No. 797

Plums

Yosebe, Engre, Japanese Seedling, Shiro, Oullin Golden,

Prunus Simoni, Climax, Hale, King of Damson, Berger,
Duane's Purple, Coe's Golden Drop, Monarch, Newman, Chabot,
Grand Duke, White Nicholas, Saunders, Burbank, Washington,
Mariana, De Caradenec, St. Lawrence, Field, Shipper,
Hector, Early Orange, World Beater, Normand, Poole's Pride,
Robe de Sargent, Harriet, Abundance, Bartlett, Merunka,
Combination, Pacific, Bailey, Imperial Gage, Yellow, Baray's Green
Gage, White Kelsey, Paragon, Maru, Orient, Mogul, Arch
Duke, Royal Hative, Pottawatamie, Gold, Niagara, Hiederman
Sand Cherry, Victoria, Autumn Comport, Baker, Pond's Seedling,
Miles, Palatine, America, October Purple, French Prune,
Quackenboss, King of Damson, Transparent, Spalding, Late
Black Orleans, Shropshire, Damson, Ungarrish Prune, Wickson,
Sweet Botan, Coe's Purple Drop, Reine Claude, Grant
Prune, Dame Aubert, Pringle Blue, Freestone Damson,
Pringle Purple, Clingstein, Hudson River Purple Egg, Wild
Goose, G. No. 44, Jones, McLaughlin, Eagle, Yeddo, Goliath,
Jefferson, Gold Drop, Belgian Purple, Diamond, Tennant,
Tragedy Prune, Mikado, Kirk, Yellow Egg, Cabot, Uchi Beni,
Union Purple, Geuthrie Late, Saratoga, Monroe
George Geringer, Childs. Silver medal
  Apples
  Baldwin, Northern Spy
John Gibson, Catawba. Bronze medal
  Grapes
  Niagara
Edwin S. Gifford, Lockport. Bronze medal
  Apples
  Greening
John D. Gilligan, Crown Point. Bronze medal
  Apples
  Northern Spy, Bethel
George A. Gilson, Sheridan. Bronze medal
  Grapes
  Agawam, Concord, Martha, Worden
P. Gleavey, Bluff Point. Silver medal
  Grapes
  Concord, Moore's Diamond, Niagara

E. J. Gleason, Keuka. Bronze medal
  Grapes
    Catawba
E. P. Gould, Rochester. Bronze medal
  Pears
    Beurre Clairgeau
J. H. Giffin, Catawba. Bronze medal
  Grapes
    Catawba, Isabella
S. S. Grandin, Westfield. Bronze medal
  Grapes
    Concord, Niagara
C. B. Gray, Albion. Silver medal
  Apples
    Golden Russet, Hubbardston Nonesuch, King
E. A. Guest, Fredonia. Bronze medal
  Grapes
    Concord, Cottage, Niagara, Vergennes, White Chautauqua
J. A. Hall, Catawba. Silver medal
  Grapes
    Alvira, Catawba, Concord, Delaware, Diana, Dutchess, Isabella,
    Pocklington
M. H. Hamilton, Westfield. Silver medal
  Grapes
    Concord
E. E. Hamlet, Sheridan. Silver medal
  Grapes
    Delaware, Moore's Early, Niagara, Worden
James H. Hanlon, Linwood. Bronze medal
  Apples
    Baldwin, Duchess of Oldenburg, King, Red Astrachan,
    Northern Spy
  Plums
    White Japan, Burbank
W. C. Harden. Stanton Hill. Silver medal
  Apples
    Pomeroy, Sutton Beauty
F. P. Hardenburg, Brocton. Silver medal

Grapes
  Concord
E. T. Hart, Fredonia. Bronze medal
Grapes
  Catawba, Clinton, Isabella
F. P. Hazelton, Le Roy. Silver medal
Apples
  Alexander, Black Gilliflower, Cooper's Market, Lady, Swaar,
  St. Lawrence
Pears
  Beurre Bosc
J. A. Hepworth, Marlboro. Silver medal
Apples
  Domine, Lady Sweet, Snow
Currants
  Filler
Pears
  Beurre Bosc, Clairgeau, Duchesse
Grant G. Hitchings, South Onondaga. Silver medal
Apples
  Pewaukee, Rhode Island Greening, Wealthy, Jonathan,
  Seek-no-Further, Red Canada, Spitzenberg, Fallawater,
  Northern Spy, Romanite, Gilliflower, Cranberry Pippin,
  Ben Davis, Walbridge, Hubbardston Nonesuch, Pound
  Sweet
Elton B. Holden, Hilton. Silver medal
Apples
  Cooper's Market, Cranberry Pippin, York Pippin
C. G. Hooker, Rochester. Gold medal
Currants
  Perfection
E. R. Hopkins, Sheridan. Silver medal
Grapes
  Lindley, Concord
S. O. Hubbard, Pavilion. Bronze medal
Apples
  Northern Spy, Snow
J. A. Hulbert, South Onondaga. Bronze medal

Apples

Douse

T. S. Hubbard Nursery Co., Fredonia. Silver medal

Grapes

Eaton, Moore's Diamond, Wyoming Red, Empire State,
Cynthiana, Brilliant, Woodruff Red, Early Daisy, Rommel,
Berckman Red, Brighton, Dracut Amber, Gaertner, Moyer,
Niagara, Goethe, Campbell's Early, Telegraph, Lutie Red,
Janesville, Early Ohio, White Diamond, Etta, Concord,
Early Victor, Cottage, Jessica, Norton, Green Mountain,
Lucile, Moore's Reissling, Delaware

Elias B. Hutchinson, Pavilion. Silver medal

Apples

Golden Russet, Peck's Pleasant, Phoenix

J. S. Hutt, Cobleskill. Bronze medal

Apples

Hook

J. Corwin Jacks, Batavia. Bronze medal

Apples

Flower of Genesee

Ira S. Jarvis, Hartwick Seminary. Bronze medal

Apples

English Russet, Ross, Nonpareil

George S. Josselyn, Fredonia. Gold medal

Grapes

Campbell's Early, Eaton, Barry, Pocklington, Dracut Amber,
Lindley, Massasoit, Diana, Victoria, Herbert, Montefiore,
Amenia, Wyoming Red, Wilder, Moyer, Catawba, Telegraph,
Concord, Esther, Martha, Green Mountain, Lucile,
Worden, Brighton, Early Victor, Vergennes, Salem,
Woodruff Red, Alice, Cottage, Noah, Ulster Prolific, Agawam,
Etta, Clinton, Goethe, Niagara, Delaware, Moore's
Diamond, Janesville, Moore's Early, Jefferson

F. I. Judd, Batavia. Silver medal

Apples

Golden Russet, Greening, Roxbury Russet, Northern Spy

Alfred Jorgensen, Bluff Point. Bronze medal

Grapes

Concord, Niagara
M. H. Kelly, Wyoming. Silver medal
  Apples
    Roxbury Russet
Herman L. Kent, Westfield. Silver medal
  Grapes
    Catawba, Concord, Isabella, Kent's Favorite
John G. Kettle, Schodack Landing. Bronze medal
  Apples
    Baldwin, Blush Pippin, Bristol, Esopus Spitzenberg, Greening,
    Mann, Pomeroy Sweet, Stark
John C. Ketchum, Schenectady. Bronze medal
  Apples
    Baldwin, N ewtown Pippin, Northern Spy, Spitzenberg, Vandevere
George M. Kinner, Fredonia. Silver medal
  Grapes
    Concord, Salem, North Carolina, Worden, Niagara, Perkins,
    Rogers No. 15, Massasoit, Catawba, Delaware, Rogers No.
    9, Rogers No. 8 Black, Rogers No. 33 Black, Martha
P. W. King, Athens. Bronze medal
  Apples
    Baldwin, Northern Spy, Roxbury Russet, Spitzenberg
T. H. King, Trumansburg. Silver medal
  Apples
    Hendrick Sweet, Northern Spy, Seek-no-Further, Hubbardston
    Nonesuch, King, McIntosh, Ben Davis, Fall Pippin
  Peaches
    Carman, Elberta, Hill's Chili, Kalamazoo, Stevens' Rare Ripe
  Pears
    Kieffer
  Plums
    Burbank
E. H. Kinyoun, Bluff Point. Silver medal
  Grapes
    Concord, Moore's Diamond, Niagara
Frank P. Kinyoun & Co., Penn Yan. Silver medal
  Grapes
    Concord, Niagara

Judson N. Knapp, Syracuse. Bronze medal
  Apples
    Knapp's Prolific, Pound Sweet
E. Ben Knight, Bluff Point. Silver medal
  Grapes
    Concord
Lake View Nursery Co., Sheridan. Bronze medal
  Grapes
    Eaton, Agawam, Lindley, Clinton
E. W. Lamont, Cobleskill. Bronze medal
  Apples
    Baldwin, Ben Davis, Greening, Hannah Kazoot, Kirkland
    Pippin, Lady, Spitzenberg
A. R. Lathrop, Brocton. Silver medal
  Grapes
    Concord
Fred B. Leibring, Gasport. Bronze medal
  Apples
    Greening, King
C. N. Leonard, Penfield. Silver medal
  Apples
    Cooper's Market, Golden Russet, Greening, Northern Spy,
    Phoenix
Henry D. Lewis, Annandale. Silver medal
  Apples
    Newtown Pippin
H. J. Lewis, Ripley. Bronze medal
  Grapes
    Concord, Niagara
S. T. Lewis, Johnsonburg. Bronze medal
  Plums
    Burbank, Mary, Delaware, Bradshaw, Giant Prune, Imperial
    Gage, juicy, Jefferson, General Hand, Apple, Satsuma,
    Osto Smomo, Pearl, Gueii
P. R. Loder, Bluff Point. Silver medal
  Grapes
    Vergennes
C. W. Mackey, Coxsackie. Silver medal

Apples
Baldwin, Pomeroy, Snow, Spitzenberg
H. Manchester, Lockport. Bronze medal
Apples
Cranberry Pippin, Northern Spy, King
Willis T. Mann, Barker. Silver medal
Apples
Boiken, Cranberry Pippin, Mann, Sutton Beauty
Arlington Mapes, Stanley. Bronze medal
Apples
Crown.
U. P. Markham, Fredonia
Grapes
Delaware
I. H. Marvin, Albion. Bronze medal
Apples
Greening, Hubbardston Nonesuch, King
H. R. Mason, Ripley. Bronze medal
Grapes
Concord
O. C. Mather, Albion. Bronze medal
Apples
Lady
A. Ross Matheson, Pomona. Silver medal
Apples
Baldwin, Fallawater
A. G. Meiklejohn, Putnam Station. Silver medal
Apples
Ben Davis, Bethel, Blue Pearmain, Greening, McIntosh Red,
Northern Spy, Tallman Sweet, Snow
W. D. Merrick, Albion
Pears
Anjou, Clairgeau, Duchesse, Howell
W. W. Metcalf, Castile. Bronze medal
Apples
Baldwin, Canada Red, Greening, Northern Spy
H. R. McNair, Dansville. Bronze medal
Apples

Grimes' Golden, Mann, McIntosh, Peck's Pleasant,
Seekno-Further, Wagener, Walbridge
W. S. Millard, Joshua. Silver medal
  Apples
  Rhode Island Greening
Fred Miller, Penn Yan. Bronze medal
  Apples
  Gilliflower, Greening, King, Northern Spy, Smokehouse,
  Spitzenberg, Tallman Sweet
George Miller, Naples. Silver medal
  Grapes
  Catawba, Salem, Vergennes
Robert Miller, Sheridan. Silver medal
  Grapes
  Agawam, Brighton, Catawba, Concord, Delaware, Diana,
  Martha, Moore's Diamond, Pocklington
C. D. Mills, Wellsville. Bronze medal
  Apples
  Wolf River
C. D. Miner, Lima. Silver medal
  Apples
  Duchess of Oldenburg, King, Red Astrachan, Sweet Bough
A. A. Mitchell, Palmyra. Bronze medal
  Apples
  Canada Reinette, Domine, Vandevere
W. C. Moore, Bluff Point. Bronze medal
  Grapes
  Niagara
W. Seward Mudge, Gasport. Silver medal
  Apples
  Baldwin, Greening, Northern Spy
G. E. & E. H. Munt, Le Roy. Bronze medal
  Apples
  Rambo
Mrs. I. Neff, Bluff Point. Silver medal
  Grapes
  Delaware, Brighton, Agawam, Moore's Diamond
William Newton, Henrietta. Bronze medal

Pears
  Anjou, Lawrence
New York State. Collective exhibit. Grand prize
  Apples
    424 varieties
  Cherries
    31 varieties
  Currants
    4 varieties
  Gooseberries
    1 variety
  Grapes
    150 varieties
  Peaches
    14 varieties
  Pears
    152 varieties
  Plums
    129 varieties
  Quinces
    8 varieties
  Strawberries
    1 variety
New York Grape Growers' Association. Gold medal
  Grapes
O'Brien & Morse, Sheridan. Bronze medal
  Grapes
    Agawam, Moore's Early
H. H. Ostrander, Salt Point. Bronze medal
  Apples
    Canada Red, Snow.
Gottlieb Otto, Gasport. Bronze medal
  Apples
    Northern Spy
John J. Ovens, Crosby. Bronze medal
  Grapes
    Catawba
Levi A. Page, Seneca Castle. Silver medal

Apples

Baldwin, Canada Red, Gilliflower, Roxbury Russet

George D. Parker, Bluff Point. Silver medal

Apples

Northern Spy

James G. Patterson, Sheridan. Silver medal

Apples

Duchess of Oldenburg, Virginia Sweet, Western Beauty

Plums

Burbank

J. W. Patterson, Ripley. Bronze medal

Grapes

Concord

S. Patterson, Bluff Point. Silver medal

Grapes

Concord, Delaware, Empire State, Moore's Diamond, Niagara,
Pocklington

Fayette E. Pease, Lockport. Bronze medal

Apples

Baldwin, Jonathan

William B. Pepper, Branchport. Bronze medal

Grapes

Concord, Delaware, Diana, Empire State, Golden Pocklington.

D. Perry, Bluff Point. Bronze medal

Grapes

Niagara

J. E. Perry, Pulteney. Bronze medal

Grapes

Concord

W. R. Perry, Rushville. Bronze medal

Pears

Vergalieu

George Pettit, Lyndonville. Bronze medal

Apples

Roxbury Russet

Mrs. Laura Pettit, Brocton. Bronze medal

Grapes

Agawam, Moore's Early

Merton Phelps, Castile. Bronze medal
  Apples
  Belleflower, Blue Pearmain, Peck's Pleasant, Tallman Sweet
  Unknown
M. F. Pierson, Stanley. Silver medal
  Apples
  Boiken, Canada Red, Cooper's Market, Delaware Red, Winter,
  Ewalt, Gano, Kirkland, Lady, Lady Sweet, Rome Beauty,
  Scott's Winter, Sutton Beauty
  Pears
  Columbia, Kieffer
W. H. Pillow, Canandaigua. Silver medal
  Peaches
  Lemon Cling, Late Crawford, Elberta, Champion, Old
  Nixon, Willet
  Pears
  Vermont Beauty, Howell, Clairgeau, Louise Bonne, Pitmaston
  Duchesse
  Plums
  Grand Duke, Frost Damson, Blue Damson, Reine Claude,
  Arch Duke, Stanton, Italian Prune, French Prune
  Quinces
  Orange
E. C. Porter, Sauquoit. Silver medal
  Apples
  Gloria Mundi, Spitzenberg
George T. Powell, Ghent. Silver medal
  Apples
  Fall Pippin, Fall Strawberry, Gravenstein, Hubbardston
  Nonesuch, King, Jonathan, Red Winter Sweet, Roxbury
  Russet, Lady Sweet, Sutton Beauty, Twenty Ounce,
  Transcendant Crab
Jesse A. Putnam, Fredonia. Bronze medal
  Grapes
  Cottage, Eaton, Lucile, Pocklington, Telegraph, Worden
H. J. Rater, Ripley. Silver medal
  Grapes
  Concord

George H. Remer, Penn Yan. Bronze medal
Grapes
  Concord, Delaware, Moore's Diamond
George P. Reed, Honeoye. Silver medal
Grapes
  Vergennes
George S. Reeves, Marion. Bronze medal
Apples
  Rome Beauty
A. Reisinger, Naples. Bronze medal
Grapes
  Catawba, Diana, Isabella, Iona
J. F. Riker, Lakeside. Bronze medal
Apples
  Fall Pippin, King
John T. Roberts, Syracuse
Apples
  Fall Pippin
William Roberts, Lockport. Bronze medal
Apples
  King
Barney Roach, Penn Yan. Bronze medal
Grapes
  Concord, Delaware, Moore's Diamond, Niagara
William H. Roeper, Wyoming. Silver medal
Apples
  Northern Spy, Roxbury Russet, Red Astrachan, Sweet Bough,
  Black Detroit, Duchess of Oldenburg, Strawberry, Black
  Gilliflower, Steele's Red, Bottle Greening
Pears
  Bartlett, Tyson
Lewis Roesch, Fredonia. Silver medal
Grapes
  Early Daisy, Moore's Diamond
Plums
  Shipper's Pride, Satsuma
Charles R. Roff, Pulteney. Silver medal
Grapes

Niagara, Catawba

W. P. Rogers, Williamson. Silver medal

Apples

Baldwin, Gravenstein, Greening, King, Maiden Blush

William H. Rossiter, Despatch. Silver medal

Apples

King

L. A. Rowe, Barnard. Bronze medal

Apples

Canada Red, Henry Sweet, Hubbardston Nonesuch

G. E. Ryckman & Son, Brocton. Silver medal

Grapes

Lutie, White Delaware, Green Mountain, Agawam, Diana,
Isabella, Martha, Niagara, Delaware Seedling, Diamond

Strawberries

Ryckman

Lemons

American Wonder

L. R. Ryckman, Brocton. Silver medal

Grapes

Niagara

B. H. Sackett, Keuka. Bronze medal

Grapes

Empire State, Niagara

J. V. Salisbury, Phelps. Silver medal

Apples

Greening, Hendrick Sweet, Swaar, Seek-no-Further, Spitzenberg,
Tallman Sweet, Fall Pippin, Twenty Ounce, King

Joseph Sanderson, Bluff Point. Silver medal

Grapes

Concord, Catawba, Diana, Niagara, Salem

R. Sanderson, Pulteney. Bronze medal

Grapes

Delaware, Moore's Diamond, Niagara, Pocklington, Salem

E. L. Seely, Lafayette. Silver medal

Apples

English Stripe, Gilliflower, Prior's Red, Rock, Sweet Greening,
Spitzenberg

A. F. Selby, Williamson. Bronze medal
Apples
Baldwin, Geniton
Guy A. Selmser, Waterloo. Silver medal
Apples
Baldwin, Greening, Northern Spy, Pewaukee, Rambo, Vandevere
J. D. Sherman, Castile. Silver medal
Apples
Baldwin, Black Gilliflower, Fallawater, Swaar, Seek-no-Further,
Yellow Belleflower
Aaron Shofmyer, Schenectady. Silver medal
Apples
Northern Spy, Spice, Spitzenberg
John D. Silsby, Lockport. Bronze medal
Apples
King, Greening
I. M. Slingerland, Fayetteville. Bronze medal
Apples
Cranberry Pippin, Hendrick Sweet, Seek-no-Further, Slingerland
Henry Smith, Fredonia. Silver medal
Grapes
Brighton, Fredonia, Niagara, Woodruff Red
W. I. Smith, Hilton. Gold medal
Apples
Alexander, Fall Pippin, Northern Spy, Spitzenberg,
Seek-no-Further, Twenty Ounce
Peaches
Elberta
Smith & Boyce, Holley. Bronze medal
Apples
Snow
F. H. Snyder, Ghent. Bronze medal
Apples
Alexander, Gravenstein, Wealthy
M. A. Soverhill, Newark. Bronze medal
Apples
Lady, Rambo, Willow Twig
S. Stace, Barnard. Bronze medal

Apples
  Baldwin, Greening, King
C. L. Stearns, Clay. Bronze medal
  Apples
    Baldwin, Belleflower, Northern Spy, Peck's Pleasant, Rome
    Beauty, Sterns, Winter Pippin
Jason L. Stearns, Cardiff. Silver medal
  Apples
    Red Astrachan, Maiden Blush, Strawberry
  Pears
    Clapp's Favorite, Flemish Beauty, Sheldon
Willis C. Streeter, Fulton. Silver medal
  Apples
    Twenty Ounce, Ribston Pippin, Fall Strawberry,Red Astrachan,
    Ox, King, Rhode Island Greening, Northern Spy,
    Sops of Wine, English Russet, Lowell, Mother, Gilliflower,
    Roxbury Russet, Golden Russet, Rock Greening,
    Egg Top, Golden Sweet, Pound Sweet, Spice, Duchess,
    Cranberry Pippin, Belleflower, Sweet Russet, McIntosh,
    Alexander, Monmouth Pippin, Twenty Ounce Pippin, Red
    and Green Sweet, Detroit Red, Culbert, Bitter Sweet,
    Early Strawberry, Porter, Peck's Pleasant, Phoenix, Cabashea,
    Yellow Belleflower, Spitzenberg
John Striker, Pulteney. Silver medal
  Grapes
    Catawba
Tallman & Christy, Ripley. Bronze medal
  Grapes
    Concord
Fred H. Teats, Williamson. Silver medal
  Plums
    Burbank
Delos Tenny, Hilton. Silver medal
  Apples
    Greening, Roxbury Russet
W. S. Teator, Upper Red Hook. Bronze medal.
  Apples
    Baldwin, Fallawater, Greening, Northern Spy, Stark

Clarence Tenny, Hilton. Bronze medal
Apples
Baldwin
N. Tenny & Sons, Hamlin. Bronze medal
Currants
Pres. Wilder, Black Champion
Gooseberries
Downing
Mrs. H. J. Thayer, Fredonia. Silver medal
Apples
Red Astrachan
A. M. Thayer, Pulteney. Silver medal
Grapes
Catawba, Concord
James K. Thayer, Penn Yan. Bronze medal
Grapes
Catawba, Concord, Niagara
Fred Tillman, Catawba. Bronze medal
Grapes
Concord, Delaware, Diana, Niagara
E. B. Tolles, Sheridan. Bronze medal
Grapes
Agawam, Concord, Martha, Wyoming Red
Howard H. Tozer, Naples. Silver medal
Apples
Rambo, Seek-no-Further
Pears
Flemish Beauty
S. J. Turk, Fredonia. Bronze medal
Grapes
Niagara
John S. Van Allen, Selkirk. Bronze medal
Apples
Baldwin, Northern Spy
J. P. Van Buren, Stockport. Silver medal
Apples
Lady
Robert L. Van Dusen, Newark

Pears
Rutter
F. E. Van Eps, Stanley. Silver medal
Apples
Primate, Astrachan, Autumn Strawberrv, Yellow Transparent,
Spitzenberg, Vandevere, Smokehouse, Gravenstein,
Maiden Blush
W. H. Van Sickles, Union Springs. Bronze medal
Apples
Tallow Pippin
W. H. Van Vliet, South Schodack. Bronze medal
Apples
Newtown Pippin
Abram Van Vranken & Sons, Vischer's Ferry. Bronze medal
Apples
Northern Spy
H. S. Vermilyea, Chelsea. Bronze medal
Apples
Baldwin, Northern Spy
James Vick's Sons, Rochester. Silver medal
Apples
Rhode Island Greening
F. Vroom, Pulteney. Bronze medal
Grapes
Concord, Niagara, Salem
S. W. Wadhams, Clarkson. Bronze medal
Peaches
Crosby, Elberta
J. E. Wakeman, Lockport. Silver medal
Apples
Spitzenberg, Northern Spy
Ward Fruit Co., Ravena. Silver medal
Apples
Fall Pippin, Greening, Northern Spy, Spitzenberg
Henry D. Warner, Clifton Springs
Apples
Limber Twig
Ira Watson, Fredonia. Silver medal

Apples

   Alexander, Sweet Bough

H. E. Wellman, Kendall. Silver medal

   Apples

   Baldwin, Golden Russet, Rhode Island Greening

Samuel J. Wells, Fayetteville. Silver medal

   Apples

   King, Fall Pippin, Pound Sweet, Fall Greening, Swaar,
   Onondaga Sweet, Seek-no-Further, Rambo, Gilliflower,
   Alfred Sweet, Hubbardston Nonesuch, Rome Beauty, Lady
   Sweet, Steele's Red Winter, Spitzenberg, Red Astrachan,
   Yellow Transparent, Sweet Bough, Cornell, Golden Sweet

   Grapes

   Niagara, Isabella, Iona, Diana, Vergennes

   Pears

   Comet

Walter E. Wetmore, Wilson. Silver medal

   Apples

   Mann

T. D. Whitney, Flint. Silver medal

   Apples

   Dutchess, Primate, Sweet Bough

E. P. Willard, Cayuga. Bronze medal.

   Pears

   Beurre Bose, Clairgeau, Duchess

S. D. Willard, Geneva. Gold medal

   Apples.

   Stump, Martha Crab, Windsor Chief, Wealthy, North Star,
   Red Russet, Swaar, Black Gilliflower, Duchess, White
   Streak

   Peaches.

   Horton River, Wadell.

   Pears.

   White Doyenne, Beurre Clairgeau, Worden Seckel.

   Plums.

   America, Hale, Quackenboss, Arch Duke, Imperial Gage,
   Palmer's Favorite, Copper, Blue Damson, Coe's Golden
   Drop, Hudson River Purple Egg, Peters' Yellow Gage,

Smith's Late Blue, Reine Claude, Grand Duke, Monarch,
Geuii, Middleburgh, Lombard, Stanton's Seedling, Coe's
Late Red, Shropshire, Wickson
Quinces
Orange
A. H. Wilcox, Gasport. Silver medal
Apples
Baldwin, Greening
I. A. Wilcox, Portland. Bronze medal
Grapes
Campbell, Clinton, Delaware, Moore's Early, Vergennes
J. H. Windsor, Brockton. Silver medal
Grapes
Concord, Moore's Diamond, Niagara
M. Witherby, Brockton. Bronze medal
Grapes
Concord
Albert W. Wood & Son, Carlton Station. Silver medal
Apples
Cabashea, King, Hubbardston Nonesuch, Roxbury Russet
William W. Yost, Waterloo. Silver medal
Apples
Hendrick Sweet, King
Philip Zimmer, Keuka. Silver medal
Grapes
Catawba, Niagara
George Zorn, Hilton. Silver medal
Apples
Northern Spy, Roxbury Russet, Spitzenberg, Swaar

GROUP ONE HUNDRED EIGHT

Trees, Shrubs, Ornamental Plants and Flowers

Fred Beaulieu, Woodhaven, L. I., hose support. Silver Medal
Charlton Nursery Co., Rochester, peonies. Gold Medal
Cottage Garden Co., Queens, L. I., peonies. Silver Medal
Ellwanger & Barry, Rochester, trees and shrubs. Gold Medal
J. Roscoe Fuller, Floral Park, cannas. Silver Medal
Samuel Gilbert Harris, Tarrytown, roses. Gold Medal
William F. Kasting, Buffalo, cannas. Gold Medal
William F. Kasting, Buffalo, ferns. Gold Medal
F. R. Pierson & Co., Tarrytown, ferns. Gold Medal
John Scott, Brooklyn, ferns. Gold Medal
Siebrecht & Sons, New Rochelle, ferns. Gold Medal
Siebrecht & Sons, New Rochelle, trees and shrubs. Gold Medal
J. M. Thorburn & Co., New York, bulbs. Silver Medal
Arthur Cowee, Berlin, gladiolas

General Collaborator

Charles H. Vick, Rochester, Superintendent of Horticulture. Gold
Medal

The following is a list of the varieties of fruits exhibited:

Apples

Albion
Alexander
Alfred Sweet
Amasias
America
Ananarnoe
Arabskoe
Arkansas Beauty
Aporte Orientale
Aucuba-leaved Reinette
August
Autumn Strawberry
Austin Pippin
Babbitt
Bagdanoff

Bailey Sweet
Baldwin
Barry
Beauty of Kent
Bell Bond
Belle de Boskoop
Belle d' Angers
Belleflower
Ben Davis
Benoni
Bethel
Bietingheimer
Bismarck
Bitter Sweet
Boiken
Black
Black Detroit
Black Gilliflower
Black Twig
Blanche de Bournay
Blue Pearmain
Blanche d'Espagne
Blush Pippin
Bohana
Bottle Greening
Breskora
Bristol
Brittle Sweet
Brownlee's Russet
Buckingham
Cabashea
Canada Baldwin
Canada Reinette
Canada Red
Carlaugh
Caroline Red June
Cathead Russet
Centennial
Chenango Strawberry
Chillicothe Sweet
Christiana
Clark
Cline's Red

Coe's Scarlet Perfume
Coffey's Beauty
Colvert
Coon Red
Cooper's Market
Corey Pippin
Cornell
Count Orloff
Court Penduplat
Cox's Pomona
Cranberry Pippin
Crow Egg
Crown
Crott's
Culbert
Cullum's Keeper
Dakota Sweet
Danford
Deacon Jones
Delaware Red Winter
Denton Seedling
Detroit Red
Dickinson
Doctor
Domine
Douse
Downing's Paragon
Dr. Opple's French Pippin
Duchess of Oldenburg
Dudley Winter
Duke of Devonshire
Dumclow's Seedling
Duncan
Early Joe
Early Strawberry
Edwards
Egg Top
Elgin Pippin
English Russet
English Royal Russet
English Stripe
Enormous
Equimetely

Esopus Spitzenberg
Etowah
Evening Party
Ewalt
Excelsior
Excelsior Crab
Fallawater
Fall Pippin
Fall Greening
Fall Jenneting
Fall Orange
Fall Strawberry
Fameuse
Fameuse Sucre
Fanny
Ferguson Stat
Ferdinand
Fishkill
Flemish Spitzenberg
Flower of Genesee
Flower of Kent
French Pippin
Gano
Garden Royal
Gelber Richard
Gen. Grant Crab
Geniton
Gideon
Gideon Sweet
Gilliflower
Gladstone
Glidden No. 3
Gloria Mundae
Golden Medal
Golden Russet
Golden Sweet
Grandmother
Grand Duke Constantine
Gravenstein
Great Mogul
Greasy Pippin
Greening
Green Crimean

Grimes' Golden
Grosse Bohnapfel
Groscoe Slenka Greenle
Grundy
Haas
Hannah Kazoot
Hartford Sweet
Hartford Rose
Haskell Sweet
Hawley
Haywood
Hendricks Sweet
Hennepin
Henry Sweet
Herefordshire Beefing
Hermiker
Hester
Holland
Holland Pippin
Hook
Hubbardston Nonesuch
Hurlbut
Hyslop Crab
Idaho
Iowa Beauty
Jackson
Jacob
Jacob Sweet
Johnson
Jones' Seedling
Jonathan
Jonathan Buler
Josephine Kreuter
Judson
Juicy Krimtartar
Julian
July Cluster
Kelsey
Keswick
Keswick Codlin
Kikitia
King
King of Pippin

Kirkland
Kirkland Pippin
Klaproth
Knapp's Prolific
Knox Russet
Krouzex
Lady
Lady Crab
Lady Elgin Crab
Lady Henniker
Lady Sweet
Landsberger Reinette
Langford Seedling
Lawver
Lehigh
Liberty
Limber Twig
Lindenwald
Long Stem
Lord Nelson
Lord Suffield
Louden Pippin
Lowell
Maiden Blush
Magenta
Marston's Red Winter
Mann
Manchester
Magog Red Streak
Mannington Pearmain
Martha Crab
Menagerie
McIntosh
McIntosh Red
McLellan
McMahon
Milding
Milan
Milligan
Millot
Minister
Monmouth
Monmouth Pippin

Monroe
Moon
Moore Sweet
Mother
Mountain Sweet
Moyer's Pride
Munson
Nelson
Newtown Pippin
Newman's Seedling
Neversink
Nickajack
Nicolayer
Northern Spy
North Star
Northwestern Greening
Norton's Melon
Ohio Pippin
Olive
Onondaga Sweet
Ontario
Orange Crab
Orange Pippin
Ornament de Table
Oustin's Pippin
Ox
Paragon
Paul's Imperial Crab
Peach
Pear
Pearmain
Peck's Pleasant
Pennock
Persian Bagdanoff
Peter No. 12
Pewaukee
Phoenix
Pickman
Pigeon de Schiller
Piper
Parrish Bly
Plumb's Cider
Plunker Sweet

Pomeroy
Pomeroy Sweet
Pomme Grise
Porter
Pound Pippin
Pound Sweet
Pride of Texas
Priestly
Primate
Prior's Red
Queene Anne
Rambo
Rawle's Janet
Red Astrachan
Red Beitingheimer
Red Belleflower
Red Rock
Red Russet
Red Siberian Crab
Red Winter Pippin
Red Winter Sweet
Red Warrior
Reinette Bretagne
Reinette Coux
Reinette grin de Versailles
Reinette Jaune Hative
Reinette Monstrouse
Rhode Island Greening
Rhodes' Orange
Ribston Pippin
Richards
Riviere
Rock
Rock Greening
Rolfe
Romanite
Rome Beauty
Rose Sweet
Ross Nonpareil
Roxbury Russet
Russian No. 1
Russian Queen
Russian Seedling

Salome
Sandy Glass
Schackleford
Scott's Winter
Seedling No. 11
Seedling No. 12
Seedling No. 13
Seedling No. 19
Seedling No. 21
Seedling No. 22
Seek-no-Further
Seneca Favorite
Seneca Sweet
Shannon
Sheppard's Perfection
Siberian Crab
Signe Tilissu
Skelton
Sklanka Bog
Slingerland
Small's Admirable
Smokehouse
Snow
Sol Edwards
Soulard
Sour Russet
Spaeth's Sameling
Spice
Spitzenberg
Standard
Stark
Stayman's Winesap
Steele's Red Winter
Sterns
St. Lawrence
Stott's Seedling
Strawberry
Striped Astrachan
Striped Winter
Stuart Golden
Stump
Summer Hagloe
Summer Pippin

Summer Rambo
Surprise
Sutton Beauty
Swaar
Sweet Bough
Sweet Greening
Sweet Pearmain
Sweet Russet
Sweet Russian
Swinku
Tallman Sweet
Tallow Pippin
Tewksbury
Thompson
Titus Pippin
Tobias
Tobias Black
Tobias Pippin
Tom Putt
Transcendant Crab
Transparent de Croucels
Turn-off Lane
Twenty Ounce
Twenty Ounce Pippin
Un-named
Vandevere
Van Hoy
Virginia Greening
Virginia Sweet
Wabash Red Winter
Wagener
Walbridge
Wallace Howard
Washington Royal
Washington Strawberry
Watwood
Wealthy
Welker Beauty
Welker's Seedling
Western Beauty
White Graft
White Pippin
White Robinson

White Streak
White Zurdell
Whitney's Crab
Williams Favorite
Willow Twig
Windsor Chief
Wild Crab
Wine
Winesap
Winter Banana
Winter Golden
Winter Pearmain
Winter Pippin
Winter Sweet
Wolf River
Wormsley's Pippin
Yellow Belleflower
Yellow Transparent
York Imperial
York Pippin

Grapes

Adirondack
Agawam
Alice
Alvira
America
Armenia
August Giant
Barbarosa
Barry
Berckman
Berckman Red
Brighton
Brilliant
Brown
Butler No. 1
Campbell
Campbell's Early
Canandaigua
Catawba

Cayuga
Champion
Chautauqua
Clinton
Colerain
Columbia Imperial
Concord
Corby
Cottage
Creveling
Cynthiana
Delaware
Delaware Seedling
Diamond
Diana
Dracut Amber
Dutchess
Early Daisy
Early Ohio
Early Victor
Eaton
Elvibach
Emerald
Empire State
Essex
Esther
Etta
Eumelan
Faith
Fredonia
Gaertner
Goethe
Gold Coin
Gold Dust
Golden Grain
Golden Pocklington
Greene
Green Mountain
Hartford
Helen Kellar
Herbert
Hercules
Hicks

Horner No. 1
Iona
Iona Red Rare
Isabella
Isabella Seedling
Ives
Ives Black
Ives Seedling
Janesville
Jefferson
Jessica
Jessica White
Jewell
Kent's Favorite
Kensington
Lindley Rogers
Little Blue
Livingston
Lucile
Lutie
Lutie Red
Manito
Marion
Martha
Mary Favorite
Mary Washington
Massasoit
Maxatawny
McPike
Merrimack
Montefiore
Moore's Diamond
Moore's Early
Moore's Reissling
Moyer
Moyer Red
Muscat Hamburg
Nectar
Niagara
Noah
North Carolina
Norton
Northern Mascadine

Olita
Osage
Paragon
Peabody
Perkins
Perfection
Pocklington
Poughkeepsie
Presley
Prentiss
Pulaski
Rebecca
Red Eagle
Requa
Riehl No. 10
Riehl No. 21
Riehl No. 22
Rockwood
Rodgers No. 8 Black
Rodgers No. 9
Rodgers No. 13
Rodgers No. 15
Rodgers No. 32
Rodgers No. 33 Black
Rommel
Rupert
R. W. Munson
Salem
Station No. 797
Station No. 2612
Stark Star
St. Louis
Telegraph
Thompson No. 5
Thompson No. 7
Ulster Prolific
Vergennes
Victoria
Waupanuka
White Diamond
White Delaware
Wilder
Woodruff Red

Wordon
Wyoming Red

Pears

Admiral Cecil
America
Angelique le Clerc
Angouleme
Angouleme Bronzee
Anjou
Ansault
Antoine Lormier
Arbre Courbe
Auguste Royer
Bartlett
Baylor
Bergamot Buffo
Bergamot Easter
Bergamot Heitrich
Bergamot Royal d'Hiver
Beurre Alex Lucas
Beurre d'Aremburg
Beurre Bosc
Beurre Benoist Noveaux
Beurre Capiaumont
Beurre Diel
Beurre Dumont
Beurre gris d'Hiver
Beurre Mauxion
Beurre Noire
Bezi de la Motte
Black Worcester
Bonchretian Vermont
Boussock
Brockworth Park
B. S. Fox
Buffum
Cabot
Canandaigua
Catherine Gardette
Catinka

Chapman
Church
Clairgeau
Clapp's Favorite
Columbia
Col. Wilder
Comet
Cornice
Comte de Lamy
Comte de Paris
Conseiller de la Cour
Delices d'Huy
Delices de Mons
De Lamartine
Desiree Cornelis
Dix
Dorset
Dow
Doyenne d'Alencon
Doyenne Boussock
Doyenne Dillon
Doyenne Gray
Doyenne Jamain
Doyenne Robin
Doyenne Sieulle
Dr. Nelis
Duchesse
Duchesse de Bordeaux
Duchesse Precoce
Duhamel du Monceau
Eastern Belle
Easter Beurre
Edmunds
Emile d'Heyst
Figue d'Alencon
Figue de Naples
Flemish Beauty
Fred Clapp
Gansel's Bergamot
Gansel's Seckel
Garber
Hardy
Homewood

Hoosic
Howell
Island
Jackson
Jalousie de Fontenay
Japanese
Jones
Josephine
Kieffer
Kingsessing
Kirtland
Knight's Seedling
Lady Clapp
La France
Langalier
Lawrence
Le Comte
Lodge
Louise Bonne de Jersey
Loveaux
Lucy Duke
Mace
Magnate
Miller
Minister Dr. Lucius
Mount Vernon
Mme. Blanche Sannier
Mme. Treyve
Napoleon
Oswego Beurre
Pardee's Seedling
Passe Crassane
Pater Noster
Paul Ambre
P. Barry
Pierre Corneille
Pitmaston Duchesse
Poir Louise
Pound
President Gilbert
Prince Consort
Princes St. Germain
Rapalje's Seedling

Raymond de Montlaux
Reeder
Refreshing
Rousselet Bivort
Rutter
Sarah
Sekel
Secretaire Rodine
Serrurier
Sheldon
Soulard Bergamot
Souv. d'Esper
Souv. de Lens
Souv. de la Marcau Trou
Souv. de la Reine des Belges
Souv. Sannier Pere
St. Andre
Sterling
Superfin
Tyson
Urbaniste
Van Buren
Vermont Beauty
Vergalieu
Vergalieu No. 4
Washington
White Doyenne
Winter Nelis
Worden Seckel

Plums

Abundance
America
Apple
Arch Duke
Arkansas Lombard
Autumn Comport
Bailey
Baker
Baray's Green Gage
Bartlett

Belgian Purple
Berger
Blue Damson
Bradshaw
Burbank
Cabot
Chabot
Climax
Clingstein
Coe's Golden Drop
Coe's Late Red
Coe's Purple Drop
Combination
Copper
Dame Aubert
De Caradenec
Delaware
Diamond
Duane Purple
Eagle
Early Orange Prune
Engre
French Prune
Freestone Damson
Frost Damson
Field
General Hand
Geuii
Giant Prune
Gold
Gold Drop
Goliath
G. No. 44 Jones
Grand Duke
Grant Prune
Geuthrie Late
Hale
Harriet
Hector
Hiederman Sand Cherry
Hudson River Purple Egg
Imperial Gage
Italian Prune

Japanese Seedling
Jefferson
Juicy
King of Damson
Kirk
Late Black Orleans
Lombard
Mariana
Maru
Mary
McLaughlin
Merunka
Middleburgh
Mikado
Miles
Mogul
Monarch
Monroe
Newman
Niagara
Normand
Ocheeda
Octi Smomo
October Purple
Orient
Oullin Golden
Pacific
Palatine
Paragon
Palmer's Favorite
Pearl
Pond's Seedling
Poole's Pride
Pottowatamie
Pringle Blue
Pringle Purple
Prunus Simoni
Quackenboss
Red June
Red Negate
Reine Claude
Robe de Sargent
Royal Hative

Saratoga
Satsuma
Saunders
Shipper
Shipper's Pride
Shiro
Shropshire
Shropshire Damson
Smith's Late Blue
Spalding
Stanton
Stanton's Seedling
St. Lawrence
Sweet Botan
Tragedy Prune
Transparent
Tennant Prune
Uchi Beni
Ungarrish Prune
Union Purple
Victoria
Washington
Wickson
Wild Goose
White Japan
White Kelsey
White Nicholas
World Beater
Yeddo
Yellow Egg
Yellow Gage
Yosebe

Cherries

Abesse d'Oignies
Bay State
Black Tartarian
Centennial
Downer's Late
Double Nattie
Dyehouse

Early Purple Guigne
Elton
Esel Kirsche
Governor Wood
Hole
Ida
King's Amarelle
Knight's Early Red
Large Montmorency
Luelling
May Duke
Mercer
Mezel
Montmorency
Napoleon
Olivet
Orel No. 23
Rapp
Reine Hortense
Rockport Bigarreau
Sparhawk's Honey
Transcendant
Windsor
Yellow Spanish

Currants

Perfection
Black Champion
Filler
President Wilder

Peaches

Carman
Champion
Crosby
Elberta
Greensboro
Hill's Chili
Horton River

Kalamazoo
Late Crawford
Lemon Cling
Old Mixon
Stevens' Rare Ripe
Waddell
Willet

Quinces

Champion
Japanese
Orange
Pink Japan
Red Japan
Rea's Mammoth
Sweet Winter
White Japan

[Illustration: VIEWING THE GUNS]

CHAPTER XIII}
Forest, Fish and Game Exhibit and Schedule of Awards

FOREST, FISH AND GAME EXHIBIT

BY A. B. STROUGH

Special Agent of the Forest, Fish and Game Commission, State of New York

The State exhibit in the Forest Fish and Game Department was prepared and installed by the Forest, Fish and Game Commission, with funds furnished by the Louisiana Purchase Exposition Commission of the State of New York.

A SPORTSMAN'S CAMP

A modern sportsman's camp of rustic design, fourteen feet by seventeen feet in size, was constructed and furnished after the general style and appearance of the usual summer residence in the Adirondack mountains. The contractor for the erection of this camp was the firm of Messrs. D. B. & D. F. Sperry, of Old Forge, N. Y. Mr. D. F. Sperry, "Frank," as he is known to visitors to the Adirondacks, had personal charge of the construction and was something of an exhibit himself. Being a lifelong Adirondack guide, and having been employed by many prominent people, among others, ex-President Harrison, any rustic work from his hand was sure to attract attention.

It was unfortunate that it was impossible to have him, or some other Adirondack guide, in attendance at the "camp" all through the season, as many visitors wished to see and talk with some such person. Some of them, seeing the Sperry name-plate on the end of a log of the camp, inquired for "Frank," expecting to find him in attendance. He has had many inquiries from people residing at widely separated places in various parts of the country, for duplicates of the camp exhibit, or for some other design of rustic building.

CONSTRUCTION OF THE CAMP

The camp was constructed of Adirondack spruce logs and the chimney was of the same external construction. The roof was covered with spruce bark. All the material showing inside the camp was, as far as possible, left in natural condition, the logs with the bark on, and the underside of the roof boards unplaned, showing the coarse saw marks.

Innumerable inquiries were made by interested visitors, particularly those coming from the southern and western States, as to the species of timber used in constructing the camp. When informed that the logs were of spruce much interest was shown. Many had never seen spruce before.

THE FURNITURE

A part of the furniture was built by Mr. Sperry, and the remainder by another Adirondack guide, Mr. E. E. Sumner, of Saranac Lake, N. Y. Mr. Sperry made the bedstead, the window settee and the center table, after a style that is common in the Adirondack camps. The woodwork was of spruce, turned smooth and stained a light smoke color to give it a finished appearance. Mr. Sumner constructed the other furniture in the best rustic style, the framework being of white cedar with the bark on, and the bottoms of the chairs and settees of white birch bark. Both of these guides have had many inquiries for duplicates of their handiwork as exhibited. The "atmosphere" of the camp was that of everyday life in the forest. The bed was "made up" as though the owner was expected to occupy it at night. Garments and articles that had seen service, such as a leather hunting jacket, a gun case, "pack" baskets, fish reels and snow shoes were hung on the walls in proper places.

ATTRACTIVE FEATURES

The mantel and fireplace particularly attracted attention. The mantel was of spruce with the bark on, and the fireplace was constructed with a stone facing and lining, showing andirons and birch logs in place as in actual use. In one corner there was shelving for bric-a-brac, fishing tackle, ammunition, etc., constructed by utilizing a discarded fishing boat, cutting the same across the center into two parts and placing shelves at convenient intervals, fastening the same on the ribs of the boat.

In another corner was a swing table that could be hung up against the wall when not in use. On the mantel were placed articles of rustic work that harmonized with the surroundings—a rustic clock, wooden pipes and smoking set to match, a stein and mug of wood, together with other articles of ornament and utility. A piece of library shelving of unique design and special construction was provided and furnished with standard publications on fish, birds and animals, and stories of life in the forest and of the chase. Thirty books were shown, a number of which were kindly furnished by Messrs. Doubleday, Page & Co., of New York city. On the center table were kept the current numbers of the leading sporting magazines, both weekly and monthly.

WALL DECORATIONS

The walls were decorated with bright colored Indian blankets, flags and souvenir paddles, on which were painted various national flags and camping scenes. The paddles being of a very white spruce and the background being the spruce logs of the camp with dark colored bark, the effect was pleasing and attracted much attention.

An interesting and valuable feature of the furnishing and decoration of the camp, and, incidentally, souvenirs of the chase, were a large fine moose head over the mantel, an elk's head on the gable outside, bucks' heads at the sides of the porch in front of the camp, and the furs of red foxes, deer and black bear. Some of the furs were specially prepared for rugs and placed on the floor of the camp, giving the interior an air of comfort and cheerfulness.

HUNTING AND FISHING OUTFIT

The hunting and fishing outfit consisted of two repeating rifles, one a Savage and the other a Winchester, a double-barreled shotgun, three fishing rods, one each of steel, split lancewood and split bamboo, and a collection which included trout flies, landing nets, minnow pail, reels, lines, cartridge belt, loading set and other paraphernalia. A guide-boat of the latest style and of superior workmanship was a part of the sportsman's outfit. This boat was kindly loaned by the manufacturer, Mr. Fred W. Rice, formerly of Saranac Lake, N. Y., but now living at Seattle, Wash. His son continues the manufacture of guide-boats at Lake Placid, N. Y.

BALSAM PILLOWS

On the settee and bed in the camp were a number of balsam pillows. A large and particularly fine one came from the Higby camp on Big Moose lake in the Adirondacks. It was made by Miss Lila Daisy Higby, a little lady only seven years of age, whose needlework decorating the cover showed artistic ability of great merit for one so young. Many visitors admired it, and some of them have written her in complimentary terms.

The odor from these pillows filled the camp, and instantly attracted the attention of visitors. One of the questions usually asked first of the attendant was where the perfume came from and what it was. Some supposed it to be from the logs of which the camp was constructed. Many visitors wanted to know where they could obtain such pillows. Those purchased for the camp came from Mr. A. M. Church, Boonville, N. Y., who also furnished the gun rack so much admired, and also the fur rugs.

FIRE NOTICE

On the side of the camp in a conspicuous place was posted a fire notice such as may be found in thousands of places along the trail throughout the Adirondacks and Catskills. Visitors that had been through our mountains recognized this feature instantly, for these notices may be found at all the hotels and public places, and also on a great many of the private camps. This little placard printed on cloth attracted much attention. It contains our forest fire rules and much of the law relative to woodland fires. Many persons interested in forestry, many of them from foreign countries, copied the notice verbatim. It is probable that similar rules and regulations will be incorporated in the forestry laws of other states and countries.

An attendant was employed at the camp who answered the numerous questions as to where the various articles of furniture and decoration might be obtained. Much information was also sought by visitors in relation to the Adirondack forests and the summer resorts of New York in general.

This sportsman's camp was the only exhibit of the kind shown at the Fair. Sportsmen and lovers of life in the woods from all parts of the land visited it; many were ecstatic in its praises; some complimented it by saying it was the most artistic feature of the whole forestry, fish and game exhibit. It was photographed perhaps more than one hundred times during the season and in one instance by nine different persons on a single day.

ANIMALS AND BIRDS

The fur and game animals and birds of the State were represented by mounted specimens prepared by professional taxidermists. In many instances they were shown in pairs, male and female.

The space in front of the camp and also at one side was inclosed by a rustic fence built of round spruce. In the yard at the side was placed a tree about twelve feet high, and under it was prepared an artificial ground work in imitation of a woodland area after a recent snow storm. In and about this tree, and forming a part of the picture, were placed in position, as true to life and natural conditions as possible, specimens of practically all of the birds that remain with us during the winter season, as follows:

Bald Eagle
Golden Eagle
Osprey
Red-tailed Hawk
Cooper Hawk
Marsh Hawk
Ruffed Grouse
Spruce Grouse
Quail
Kingfisher
Three-toed Woodpecker
Pileated Woodpecker
Goshawk
Red-shouldered Hawk
Sharp-shinned Hawk
Broad-winged Hawk
Rough-legged Hawk
Duck Hawk,
Gray Gyrfalcon
Snow Owl
Barred Owl
Great-horned Owl
Long-eared Owl
Short-eared Owl
Acadian Owl
Screech Owl
Great Gray Owl
Hawk Owl
Barn Owl

Richardson Owl
Hairy Woodpecker
Downy Woodpecker
Flicker
Pine Grosbeak
Red-winged Crossbill
White-winged Crossbill
Redpoll
Blue Jay
Horned Lark
Lapland Longspur
English Sparrow
Winter Wren
Chickadee
Northern Shrike
Snowflake
Moose Bird
Raven
Crow

SONG AND PERCHING BIRDS

In and about another tree placed in front of the camp were shown practically all of the song and perching birds of the State other than the ones shown in the winter scene at the side of the camp. The birds in this collection were as follows:

Cardinal
Summer Tanager
Scarlet Tanager
Yellow-billed Cuckoo
Black-billed Cuckoo
Red-headed Woodpecker
Red-bellied Woodpecker
Yellow-bellied Sapsucker
King Bird
Cat Bird
Towhee
Robin
Meadow Lark
Prairie Horned Lark
Baltimore Oriole
Orchard Oriole
Whip-poor-will
Night Hawk
Pigeon Hawk
Sparrow Hawk
Mourning Dove
Rose-breasted Grosbeak
Evening Grosbeak
Purple Finch
Red-winged Blackbird
Rusty Blackbird
Bobolink
Mocking Bird
Starling
Purple Grackle
Humming Bird
Yellow-breasted Chat
Blue-gray Gnatcatcher
Tufted Titmouse
Brown Creeper

House Wren
Marsh Wren
Brown Thrasher
Wood Thrush
Hermit Thrush
Wilson Thrush
Water Thrush
Chimney Swift
Bank Swallow
Rough-winged Swallow
Cliff Swallow
Barn Swallow
Song Sparrow
Tree Sparrow
Blue Bird
Indigo Bunting
Ruby-crowned Kinglet
Golden-crowned Kinglet
Oven Bird
Yellow Throat
Goldfinch
Bohemian Waxwing
Cedar Waxwing
Phoebe
Wood Pewee
White-eyed Vireo
Blue-headed Vireo
Yellow-throated Vireo
Warbling Vireo
Black and White Warbler
Worm-eating Warbler
Myrtle Warbler
Prairie Warbler
Palm Warbler
Tennessee Warbler
Black-throated Blue Warbler
Cerulean Warbler
Prothonotary Warbler
Blackburnian Warbler
Black-throated Green Warbler
Hooded Warbler
Golden-winged Warbler
Connecticut Warbler

Mourning Warbler
Canadian Warbler
Blue-winged Warbler
Chipping Sparrow
Field Sparrow
Swamp Sparrow
Ipswich Sparrow
White-crowned Sparrow
Olive-sided Flycatcher
Yellow-bellied Flycatcher
Loggerhead Shrike
Purple Martin
Cow Bird
Pine Warbler
Kentucky Warbler
Nashville Warbler
Parula Warbler
Cape May Warbler
Yellow Warbler
Black-poll Warbler
Red-breasted Nuthatch
Brown-headed Nuthatch

GAME BIRDS

In cabinets within an inclosure near the camp were shown our game birds, such as the web-footed wild fowl and shore birds which may be hunted, grouse, marsh birds or waders, and water or sea birds, as follows:

Wild Ducks and Geese

American Merganser
Red-breasted Merganser
Hooded Merganser
Mallard
Pintail
Black Duck
Widgeon
Green-winged Teal
Blue-winged Teal
Shoveler
Wood Duck
Redhead
Canvas-back
Broadbill
Lesser Scaup Duck
Whistler
Buffle-head
Ruddy Duck
Old Squaw
Harlequin
American Eider
King Eider
Black Coot
Sea Coot
White-winged Scoter
Canada Goose
Greater Snow Goose
Blue Goose
White-fronted Goose
Brant
Whistling Swan

Shore Birds

Woodcock
Wilson Snipe
Upland Plover
Black-bellied Plover
Golden Plover
Semi-palmated Plover
Belted Piping Plover
Wilson Plover
Piping Plover
Killdeer
Willett
Greater Yellow Legs
Summer Yellow Legs
Turnstone
Red Phalarope
Northern Phalarope
Avocet
Oyster Catcher
Long-billed Curlew
Jack Curlew
Hudsonian Godwit
Sanderling
Black-necked Stilt
Dowitcher
Knot
Stilt Sandpiper
Solitary Sandpiper
Spotted Sandpiper
Red-backed Sandpiper
White-rumped Sandpiper
Least Sandpiper
Buff-breasted Sandpiper

Grouse, etc.

Ruffed Grouse
Quail
Spruce Grouse
Mongolian Pheasant
English Pheasant

Marsh Birds or Waders

Great Blue Heron
Little Green Heron
Black-crowned Night Heron
Yellow-crowned Night Heron
Egret
Brown Pelican
Bittern
King Rail
Virginia Rail
Yellow Rail
Clapper Rail
Carolina Rail
Little Black Rail
Florida Gallinule
Mud Hen

Water or Sea Birds

Loon
Black-throated Loon
Red-throated Loon
Horned Grebe
Holboel Grebe
Pied-billed Grebe
Puffin
Dovekie
Cormorant
Double-crested Cormorant
Black Guillemot
Brunnich Murre
Paresitic [*sic] Jaegar
Kittiwake
Gannet

Black Skimmer
Sooty Shearwater
Great Black-backed Gull
Ring-billed Gull
Claucus Gull
Herring Gull
Laughing Gull
Bonapart Gull
Black Tern
Gull-billed Tern
Wilson Tern
Roseate Tern
Least Tern
Black-capped Petrel
Leach Petrel
Wilson Petrel

FUR AND GAME ANIMALS

All of our fur and game animals were represented as follows:

White-tail or Virginia Deer
Black Bear
Lynx
Wild Cat
Red Fox
Gray Fox
Beaver
Raccoon
Skunk
Otter
Fisher
Cottontail Rabbit
Martin
Mink
Black Squirrel
Gray Squirrel
Red Squirrel
Fox Squirrel
Flying Squirrel
Chipmunk
Musk Rat
Opossum
Varying Hare
Porcupine

Our deer were represented by a fine buck, a doe mounted in a reclining position, and a small white doe. Arranged among bushes in the snow scene at the side of the camp this family was most lifelike and pleasing in appearance. White deer are very unusual, but not unnatural. One of them is killed in this State about every two years.

Moose and elk are introduced animals with us now, and, as it is illegal to kill any, life size specimens could not well be shown. However, very good heads were exhibited as a part of the decoration of the camp. Albinos of muskrat and porcupine were exhibited. Such freakish specimens attract more attention than those of usual growth.

RARE SPECIES

In addition to the animals scheduled above were specimens of some species that are probably extinct in the Adirondacks, viz., a gray wolf and a panther. The gray wolf was an excellent specimen loaned by General E. A. McAlpin, of New York city. It was killed about eight years ago on his preserve in the northern part of Hamilton county, and none have been seen since. The panther was killed about twenty-eight years ago by Hon. Verplanck Colvin in the southern part of Hamilton county, and is the last one heard of in the State of New York. The black bear was an unusually fine specimen, killed in Sullivan county. It was mounted to order by Mr. Fred Sauter, of New York city, for this exhibit, and without doubt was the best representative of this species at the Fair. Experts in the art of taxidermy and naturalists were enthusiastic in its praise.

The great blue heron was loaned by Mr. Grant E. Winchester, of Saranac Inn. It was a very good specimen and was mounted by Mr. H. H. Miner, of Saranac Lake, N. Y.

The animals were placed about the camp under the trees in connection with the collection of birds in positions as true to life as possible in the available space, making a picture of woodland life delightful to the eye and interesting to every person that visited the Palace of Forestry, Fish and Game.

FISH

The fish exhibit consisted of eighty-six mounted specimens, representing seventy-two species, most of them prepared specially for this display by the best workmen in the country. Substantially all the food and game fish were shown. In preparing this collection no attempt, with one exception, was made to show abnormally large specimens. The intention was to show the average fish true to life in color, size and contour. Both fresh and salt water species were represented. The collection, which is undoubtedly the best in the country, comprised the following species:

Sea Lamphrey
Common Sturgeon
Short-nosed Sturgeon
Horned Pout
Long-nose Sucker
Common Sucker
Hog Sucker
Golden Sucker
Fallfish
Carp
Eel
Sea Herring
Hickory Shad
Frostfish
Common Whitefish
Smelt
Tullibee
Atlantic Salmon
Red-throat Trout
Brown Trout
Rainbow Trout
Lake Trout
Brook Trout
Grayling
Pickerel
Northern Pike
Shad
Menhaden
Spanish Mackerel
Pompano
Bluefish

Crappie
Calico Bass
Rock Bass
Sunfish
Small-mouth Black Bass
Large-mouth Black Bass
Wall-eyed Pike
Weakfish
Red Drum
Kingfish
Tautog
Rosefish
Tomcod
Haddock
Ling
Cusk
Summer Flounder
Flatfish
Muscallonge
Northern Muscallonge
Striped Mullet
Common Mackerel
Bonito
Sauger
Yellow Perch
White Bass
Striped Bass
White Perch
Sea Bass
Scup
Spotted Weakfish
Croaker
Bergall
Spadefish
Whiting
Cod
Burbot
Hake
Halibut
Sand Dab
Gar Pike

In addition to the above-mentioned specimens there was shown an interesting collection of shell fish, including different varieties of oysters, together with the enemies of the same, such as the drill and starfish. A number of exhibits showing curiosities of oyster growth were in this collection.

The fish were displayed in six cabinets constructed to order for the exhibit. They were lined with black plush, thus forming a strong contrast with the colors of the various pieces.

The land-locked salmon mentioned above is one of the finest pieces extant, not only in relation to size but also in the mounting of the same. It is owned by Hon. J. P. Allds, Norwich, N. Y., and was kindly loaned by him for this exhibit.

A great northern pike that weighed twenty-five pounds when caught was in the collection. It was loaned by Mr. Ferris J Meigs, of New York city, and was caught in Follensbee pond, in the Adirondacks, by Miss Juliet Wilbur Tompkins in 1902. This is the largest pike, sometimes erroneously called pickerel, within the knowledge of the Forest, Fish and Game Commission.

GENERAL NOMENCLATURE

All the specimens of animals, birds and fish were properly and uniformly labeled, giving the names the various species are generally known by, and also the scientific nomenclature adopted by naturalists. The importance of this matter of nomenclature was demonstrated very early during the Fair. The song birds being very small no labels were placed upon them at first, as the labels were in some instances larger than the birds. The fact that visitors examining the specimens would often search for the attendant in order to obtain information as to the names of the different birds exhibited proved the necessity of clearly labeling all specimens. On the other hand there seemed to be a general misunderstanding as to some species of fish, various names being applied to the same species. Visitors were constantly requesting information on these points. The northern pike are by many people called pickerel and sometimes when in water with pickerel are mistaken for muscallonge. The distinguishing marks were frequently explained to interested visitors.

FORESTRY

One of the most scientific and practical features of the New York exhibit was that made by the Forestry department. It was prepared to show the method by which the Forestry Commission is reforesting large areas of State land that have been denuded by repeated fires.

A FOREST NURSERY

The most important part of this was a fully appointed forest nursery, located out of doors close to the northeast corner of the Forest, Fish and Game building. Its neat rustic fence, made of white cedar poles, enclosed an area Of 7,200 square feet (120 feet long by 60 wide) and contained about 80,000 little trees alive and green. The soil being of heavy clay, it was covered to the depth of six inches with good loam before any seeds were sown.

About one-third of the nursery was arranged in beds each sixteen feet long by four feet wide with paths three feet in width. In two of these beds seeds were sown of Scotch pine, Norway spruce, hardy catalpa and American elm, half a bed being given to each species. The seeds were sown about the first of May. They germinated well, and the little trees grew thriftily, the catalpa reaching a height of eighteen inches before the Fair closed. A bed of Norway pine showed the plants on half the bed crowded together in a thick mat as if grown from seed sown broadcast; on the other half arranged as if from seed sown in rows across the bed, both methods of sowing seed being followed in actual practice. Four beds were given to two-year-old plants—Norway spruce, white pine, European larch and Scotch pine. These were also arranged as if grown from seed sown broadcast.

These beds, excepting the seed bed for broad-leaf species, were all shaded with neat screens made of lath to shelter the tender plants from the hot rays of the southern sun.

In actual nursery work, after conifers have remained in the seed bed for two years, they are transplanted into other beds, being spaced four or five inches apart, where they remain for two or three years more before they are placed finally in the forest. Six beds were devoted to showing this feature of nursery work. For this purpose four-year-old plants were used, of the following species Norway pine, Norway spruce, white spruce, white pine, European larch and Scotch pine.

A sample plantation which occupied nearly half the nursery showed how the plants are, in actual practice, placed in the forest. White pine, Norway spruce and Scotch pine were the species used. These were about three feet high and were spaced about four feet apart.

To show how the broad-leaf species are raised for shade trees, for planting along the highways of the State, for farmers' wood lots, for sugar groves and hardwood forests, ten drills, stretching entirely across the nursery between the beds and the sample plantation, were planted with scarlet oak, red oak, honey locust, hard or sugar maple, red or soft maple, basswood, white ash, black walnut and hardy catalpa, a row being given to each species. These were one year old and were spaced about six inches apart.

The names of the species were printed plainly on neat board labels ten inches long by five inches broad. The nursery was kept free from weeds, and was watered each evening during a long drought which began about the first of September and continued till the Fair closed.

Thousands of people visited the nursery, attracted to it not only by the beauty of the small green trees arranged in such interesting manner, but also because of the instruction it afforded in the science of forestry. Foresters, botanists, seedsmen, and others interested in trees in a scientific or practical way, many of whom were from abroad, gave the nursery close scrutiny.

The forester in charge who prepared the nursery, Mr. A. Knechtel, B.S.F.E., of Albany, N. Y., was kept constantly busy answering the numerous questions not only concerning the exhibit, but also in regard to the important work being done by the Forestry Department in restoring the forests upon the denuded non-agricultural lands of the State.

In a corner of the nursery stood two interesting cross-sections of white pine and white spruce, twenty-three inches and sixteen inches in diameter respectively, each having forty annual rings plainly visible, showing that in forty years, under favorable conditions, trees of these species can be grown from seed to the given diameters.

FORESTRY TOOLS AND INSTRUMENTS

Within the building were exhibited thirty-nine instruments and tools used in forestry practice, a collection of the seeds of eighty-four native forest trees of the State, and the photographs of eighty of our more important trees showing the same in leaf and in winter. In connection with each pair of photographs was a life size illustration of the bark of the tree, together with specimens of the leaf, flower and fruit.

INSECTS AFFECTING FOREST AND SHADE TREES

The exhibit of insects affecting forest and shade trees was prepared by E. P. Felt, D.Sc., New York State Entomologist, and was a small, though representative collection, designed to show the life, history and habits in particular of the more injurious forms of insects affecting shade and forest trees in New York State. A special effort was made to depict, so far as possible, the life, history, habits and methods of work of the forms possessing economic importance and to show whenever possible the natural enemies of value in keeping these species in control. This collection was arranged in a specially designed case having a series of three nearly horizontal trays thirty-seven and one-half inches by eighteen and one-half inches upon each side, and an elevated central portion bearing two nearly perpendicular ones upon each side, the middle being occupied by a glass case containing an attractive natural group. A brief account of the exhibit under appropriate heads is as follows:

Insect galls. This collection, occupying two nearly perpendicular trays and representing the work of fifty-three species, was devoted to the peculiar and varied vegetable deformities produced by insects. These structures are always of great popular interest, and the insects causing the same present biologic problems of unusual attractiveness.

Forest insects. The species affecting forest trees in particular were exhibited in three horizontal trays occupying one side of the case. This section was devoted principally to representing the biology and methods of work of this exceedingly important group.

Shade-tree insects. Like that representing forest insects, the exhibit of shade-tree pests was very largely biologic. It occupied three horizontal trays and a nearly vertical one of the exhibit case, and was devoted to species which are destructive largely on account of their depredations upon shade trees.

Adirondack insects. This was a small collection occupying one of the nearly perpendicular trays, and comprised over one hundred species. This portion of the exhibit represented the more characteristic forms occurring in the Adirondacks.

Natural group of forest insects. This group occupied the central glass box and contained thirty-one species of insects or representations of their work upon wax models of their food plants, namely, white birch, red oak, elm and maple. Eleven species of beetles, fifteen of butterflies and moths, two of the bee family and three of the bug family were to be seen upon the plants or on the ground at their base. This group gave an excellent idea of the appearance of insects when amid their natural surroundings.

COLORED PLATES

A series of quarto and octavo colored plates illustrating the work and various stages of some of the more important depredators upon forest and shade trees, was exhibited in two double-faced frames attached to the top of this case. The more important insects included in this group were the following: Sugar maple borer, elm snout beetles, twig girdler or twig pruner, white marked tussock moth, gypsy moth, brown tail moth, bag worm, forest tent caterpillar, elm leaf beetle, oyster scale, scurfy bark louse, San Jose scale, elm bark louse, cottony maple scale. One plate was devoted to characteristic insects affecting oak, and another to those depredating upon hard pine.

SPECIMENS OF NATIVE WOODS

The forest product of the State was represented by a collection of specimens of all the native woods of New York, built into panel work, showing both sides. Each species was represented by two specimens and each of the four surfaces was finished in a different manner. One surface was highly polished, one oiled, one planed and one rough. Ninety-one species of native and nine species of introduced woods were exhibited in this manner. Displaying the several species in four different ways enabled the discriminating observer to study and compare the various woods profitably. The manner of labeling was greatly appreciated. Some students copied all the labels, each spending many hours on this task.

The kinds of timber that grow in this State from which a five-inch board can be sawed and which were represented as described, are as follows:

Cucumber Tree
Tulip Tree
Basswood
Linden
Holly
Striped Maple
Hard Maple
Silver Maple
Red Maple
Box Elder
Staghorn Sumach
Kentucky Coffee Tree
Honey Locust
Red or Canada Plum
Wild Plum
Green Ash
Sassafras
American Elm
Rock Elm
Slippery Elm
Wild Red Cherry
Wild Black Cherry
Wild Crab Apple
Mountain Ash
Cockspur Thorn
Black Haw
Scarlet Fruited Thorn

Shad Bush
Witch Hazel
Sweet Gum
Flowering Dogwood
Pepperidge
Persimmon
Black Ash
White Ash
Red Ash
Scarlet Oak
Black Oak
Pin Oak
Jack Oak
Hackberry
Red Mulberry
Sycamore
Butternut
Black Walnut
Bitternut
Shagbark Hickory
Mockernut Hickory
Pignut Hickory
King Nut Hickory
Small Fruited Hickory
White Oak
Post Oak
Burr Oak
Chestnut Oak
Chinquapin Oak
Yellow Oak
Swamp White Oak
Red Oak
White Pine
Red Pine
Pitch Pine
Jersey Pine
Yellow Pine
Jack Pine
Tamarack
White Poplar
Crack Willow
Weeping Willow
Lalanthus

Chestnut
Beech
Ironwood
Blue Beech
Black Birch
Yellow Birch
White Birch
Red Birch
Canoe Birch
Yellow Willow
Black Willow
Peach Willow
Aspen
Large Toothed Poplar
Swamp Cottonwood
Balm of Gilead
Cottonwood
Red Cedar
White Cedar
Arbor Vitae
Black Spruce
Red Spruce
White Spruce
Hemlock
Balsam
Lombardy Poplar
Wild Apple
Yellow Locust
Horse Chestnut
Blue Willow

These specimens of wood were built into panel work in seven frames of the following seven species of wood, respectively:

Maple
Cherry
Chestnut
Rock Elm
White Oak
Black Ash
Black Birch

LABELING OF SPECIMENS

Each specimen was labeled on both sides, with the common or popular name and also the botanical name. Most of the pieces were from a collection that the Commission exhibited at the Paris Exposition in 1900, which was there awarded a gold medal. In preparing the exhibit the collection was enlarged so as to represent all our native woods, and built into new frame work of substantial and attractive design.

WOOD PULP

A complete collection of the several kinds of wood pulp manufactured in New York was also a part of the exhibit, as follows:

Ground Spruce pulp
Sulphite Spruce pulp
Sulphite Balsam pulp
Sulphite Poplar pulp
Sulphite Basswood pulp
Pulverized Pine pulp
Pulverized Poplar pulp

Ground and sulphite pulp is used in the manufacture of paper and many household articles of utility. Pulverized pulp is used in making linoleum and dynamite.

Although wood pulp was shown in some other exhibits, no one else made any attempt to show a complete collection of all the various kinds of pulp manufactured.

Articles of utility made of pulp, such as wash tubs, pails, measures, cups, pitchers, etc., fifty-three pieces in all, were shown in connection with the display of pulp.

BY-PRODUCTS OF THE FOREST

By-products of the forest were also displayed on a piece of circular shelving with a suitable caption. The articles in this collection were as follows:

Crude wood alcohol
Refined wood alcohol
Columbian spirits
Acetic acid
Refined acetic acid
Glacial acetic acid
Acetate of lime
Gray acetate of lime
Pine needle extract
Light wood tar
Heavy wood tar
Creosote
Tannic acid
Pine pitch
Spruce gum (raw)
Refined spruce gum
Basswood honey
Black walnuts
Wood ashes
Charcoal
Chestnuts
Hickory nuts
Beechnuts
Hazel nuts
Maple sugar (cakes)
Maple lozenges
Maple kisses
Maple sugar (pulverized)
Maple syrup
Mocker nuts
Butter nuts
Sassafras
Witch hazel

There was no other exhibit of this nature at the Fair.

SUMMER RESORTS

On one side of the space occupied by the exhibit was a high wall which was covered with green burlap. On this wall were three groups of large photographs, one of the Thousand Islands, one of Adirondack and one of Catskill scenery.

In the Thousand Island group in addition to a collection of typical island scenery, was a large picture of the Thousand Island House at Alexandria Bay, N. Y., furnished by the owner, O. G. Staples; a picture of the Hotel Frontenac on Round Island loaned by the owner, and a very large colored picture of the excursion steamer "Ramona," on tour through the islands, loaned by the Thousand Island Steamboat Company, Cape Vincent, N. Y.

The Catskill pictures consisted of photographs of mountain scenery and waterfalls, prepared specially for this exhibit. A fine group of scenes was furnished by the Catskill Mountain Railroad of Catskill, N. Y., showing the Otis Elevated road, the Mountain House, etc.

The group of Adirondack views contained pictures of a number of the largest hotels in that region, and collections of mountain and water scenery. One group was of Lake George scenery. A large picture of Wawbeek Hotel, on Upper Saranac Lake, was furnished by J. Ben Hart, of Wawbeek, N. Y. The Delaware and Hudson Railroad Company kindly loaned a large panoramic picture of Lake Placid and mountains of that locality.

Many of these pictures were in colors. They were appreciated by a great number of people that had visited the several summer resorts represented.

AN OPEN HUNTING CAMP

A model of a hunting camp of the open style, of which there are many in the Adirondacks, was displayed. It was constructed of spruce with the bark on, and the floor was covered with balsam boughs, which exhaled a delightful odor noticeable several yards from the camp.

A large rustic table made of a cross section of a cedar tree with the roots of a tree for the standard and legs of the table, was loaned by Mr. Ferris J. Meigs, of Tupper Lake, N. Y. The tree from which the cross section was taken showed by its growth of rings that it was more than four hundred years old.

DETAILS OF EXPENDITURE

For the purpose of making this State Forestry, Fish and Game exhibit, the Louisiana Purchase Exposition Commission generously set aside the sum of $18,000. Being unable to secure as much space as was needed, and for the additional reason that the salaries of some of the persons collaborating on the exhibit were provided for in another manner, it was not necessary to use all of the funds available.

Dividing the disbursements into ten representative accounts, the amount expended was as follows:

Animals and birds	$2,211 56
Fish	1,792 51
Insects	644 52
Plants for nursery, etc.	392 69
Woods, instruments, by-products, etc.	1,119 28
Sportsman's Camp and furnishings	1,507 92
Wall pictures	278 93
Freight and express	697 10
Installation	2,481 76
Maintenance and repacking	3,717 81
Total	$14,844 08

Had the exhibit been prepared without recourse to materials on hand and by a separate force paid from the funds of the Louisiana Purchase Exposition Commission it would have undoubtedly cost the State not less than $20,000, but the fact that considerable material was available from former exhibits, and from the office of the Forest, Fish and Game Commission, and the further fact, as above stated, that some of the collaborators received their compensation from the funds of that Commission, enabled the State to make the elaborate and exhaustive exhibit that it did in this department at the figures shown above.

THE ROSTER

The exhibit was prepared under the direction of Colonel William F. Fox, Superintendent State Forests.

Following is a roster of the persons employed at the exhibit:

Arthur B. Strough, Special Agent in charge
Abraham Knechtel, Forester
Charles C. Hembree, Attendant
Victor Mahlstedt, Gardener

AWARDS

The awards were all conferred upon the Forest, Fish and Game Commission or upon State officials. The juries in the Departments of Forestry, Fish and Game were made up of eminent specialists, and their work was done in a thorough and painstaking manner. They expressed themselves in complimentary terms on the various features of the exhibit, and the result of their deliberations cannot but be gratifying to all who are interested in the advanced work of the Empire State in forestry, in forest preserves and in the protection of our native fish and game.

List of the Awards Classified Under the Several Groups of the Official Classification

GROUP ONE HUNDRED TWELVE

Appliances and Processes Used in Forestry

Collective exhibit of progressive forestry. Grand prize
Seeds of the trees
Instruments and tools used in forestry
Forest nursery and demonstration plantation
Photographs
Native trees with botanical specimens
Forest insects

William F. Fox, for services in the forestry exhibit. Gold medal
Arthur B. Strough, for services in forestry exhibit. Silver medal
Abraham Knechtel, for services in forestry exhibit. Silver medal
E. P. Felt, D. Sc., for services in entomological exhibit, forest insects. Silver medal

GROUP ONE HUNDRED THIRTEEN

Products of the Cultivation of Forests

Model sportsman's camp and outfit. Gold medal
Exhibit of woods, by-products, etc. Grand prize
William F. Fox, for services on sportsman's camp exhibit. Silver medal

GROUP ONE HUNDRED TWENTY-ONE

Products of Hunting

Collective exhibit of animals and birds. Gold medal
Arthur B. Strough, for services on game and sporting exhibit.
Silver medal

GROUP ONE HUNDRED TWENTY-TWO

Fishing Equipment and Products

Collective exhibit of fish. Grand prize
John D. Whish, for making collection of fish. Silver medal

A summary of the awards is as follows:
Three grand prizes
Three gold medals
Six silver medals

The exhibit in this department differed somewhat from the State exhibits in other departments in that, with the exception of a very few articles, which were loaned by private parties to complete or supplement the collections, the showing was exclusively a State exhibit.

SOME SURPRISING FACTS

The exhibit as a whole was immensely popular from the very first day. The people visiting the Exposition were largely from the southern and middle western states, and seemed very generally to believe that New York's forests, fish and game has passed away with the advance of civilization. Most of them were greatly surprised to learn that one-fourth of the State is wild land, which will in all probability always be devoted largely to forests, and that the State has so many wild deer that 6,000 of them are killed annually without any apparent decrease of the number.

The sportsman's camp served the purpose of advertising the great Adirondack region as a summer resort, and a great many visitors expressed their intention of visiting that locality in the near future.

Probably one of the best features of the exhibit was the work shown by the Commission in progressive forestry. This State being in the van of the forestry movement was looked to to point out the path of professional forestry, and if no other award had been made than the grand prize by the scientific jury that served in that Department, we would feel as though our efforts has been appreciated and that our labors had not been in vain.

[Illustration: IGOROTE VILLAGE, PHILIPPINE RESERVATION]

CHAPTER XIV

Mines and Metallurgy Exhibit and Schedule of Awards

MINES AND METALLURGY EXHIBIT By H. H. HINDSHAW
Special Agent of the
State Museum

[Illustration]

As in previous expositions at which the State of New York has been an exhibitor, the scientific exhibits were made through the organization of the State Museum. Dr. F. J. H. Merrill, the director of the museum, assigned to the writer the duty of preparing the exhibit to be made under his direction. The available time and money entered largely into the settlement of the question of what form the exhibit should take.

SCOPE OF EXHIBIT

It was thought best to confine the scope of the main exhibit to the technologic and commercial aspects of geology and mineralogy. A judicious selection of materials made to show the mineral wealth of the State was considered more desirable than to make merely a large display. Many of the materials exhibited were taken from the State Museum collections, supplemented where necessary by such additions as could be obtained within the required time.

The benefit derived by the State from such exhibits is often much more apparent than that which is to be derived by the individual exhibitors, and on this account the Commission is particularly indebted to those firms and individuals which went to considerable expense in preparing exhibits along lines which were intended more to represent all phases of an industry rather than to show the products of a single firm.

Those deserving especial mention in this connection are The Solvay Process Company, of Syracuse; The H. H. Mathews Consolidated Slate Company, of Boston; the Helderberg Cement Company, of Howes Cave; The Hudson River Bluestone Company, of New York; the Medina Sandstone Company, of New York, and the United States Gypsum Company, of Chicago.

INSTALLATION

The cases used were taken from the museum, and suitable stands for the building stone and other exhibits were constructed in Albany. On account of the weight of the specimens exhibited the floor had to be strengthened. This work, as well as the building of platforms and partitions, was done under contract by Messrs. Caldwell and Drake.

The exhibits of mineral resources may be divided into the metallic and non-metallic groups.

IRON

In the first division in our State, iron is by far the most important and probably the one with which the people of the State are least acquainted. A few years ago New York stood near the head of the iron producing states. The depression in the iron industries, commencing about 1888, and the discovery about that time of the seemingly inexhaustible deposits of rich ores in the Lake Superior region, however, resulted in shutting down nearly all of our mines. For the last few years little attention has been paid to them, and they seem to have been popularly supposed to have been worked out. The Exposition gave an opportunity of showing this supposition to be incorrect, and recent investigations show that the deposits are of much greater extent and value than was known in the eighties. With but one or two exceptions none of the mines then worked are exhausted, and immense bodies of valuable ore have not been touched. Most of the non-mining localities were represented by specimens from the museum collections. Messrs. Witherbee, Sherman & Company exhibited a series of ores and concentrates from Mineville, the Arnold Mining Company, magnetites and martite from Arnold Hill, and the Chateaugay Ore and Iron Company, specimens from Lyon Mountain.

MAGNETITE

A series of magnetite and associated rocks from the Tilly Foster and other mines were supplemented by a model of the Tilly Foster mine which was loaned to the museum for this purpose by the Columbia School of Mines.

HEMATITES

The St. Lawrence and Jefferson county hematites were represented by large specimens of ore and by a series of associated rocks and minerals, including some beautiful specimens of millerite, chalcedite, etc. These hematites are mined in a belt about thirty miles long reaching from Philadelphia, Jefferson county, into Hermon, St. Lawrence county. They are known as the Antwerp red hematites, and, being very easily smelted, are mixed with more refractory ores.

The Clinton or fossil ores extend in a belt across the central part of the State and are mined in the vicinity of Clinton, Oneida county, and in Ontario and Wayne counties.

The limonites shown from Dutchess and Columbia counties included some fine specimens of stalactitic ore.

Carbonate ores were shown from Columbia and Ulster counties, where there are extensive deposits on both sides of the Hudson river.

MAGNETIC SEPARATOR

A feature of the iron ore exhibit was a magnetic separator supplied by the Wetherill Separator Company, of New York. This was kept at work on the magnetite ores from Mineville, and was of great interest not only in showing the method of concentrating the magnetic ore, but also in saving the phosphorus which occurs in the form of the mineral apatite and which is of considerable value in the manufacture of fertilizers. A large quantity of ore was donated for this purpose by Messrs. Witherbee, Sherman & Company.

LEAD

Lead, generally associated with zinc and sometimes copper, has been mined on a small scale from very early times in Ulster and Sullivan counties, and more recently in St. Lawrence county. Many other localities have yielded small quantities of these minerals.

A set of specimens was exhibited by the Ellenville Zinc Company, consisting of strikingly beautiful crystalline masses of quartz galina, sphalerite and chalcopyrite and specimens of the rare mineral, brookite. There was also shown in the same case concentrates from the Ellenville mine of lead, zinc and copper made both by jigging and by magnetic separation, and a collection of ores and associated minerals and rocks from Rossie and Wurtzboro.

NON-METALLIC MINERALS

A large part of this exhibit consisted of construction materials, stone, slate, brick, tiling and cement. Most of the building stone was exhibited in the form of ten-inch cubes arranged on three pyramidal stands. Only a few of these were especially collected for this Exposition. Many more which were considered desirable could not be obtained in time on account of the inclement weather conditions of the preceding winter.

GRANITES

The granitic rocks included granite, gneisses, syenites and norite. This series only inadequately represented the New York granites. Among the most striking examples shown were the coarse grained red granite from Grindstone island in the St. Lawrence river, the Mohican granite from Peekskill, Westchester county, which is being extensively used in the Cathedral of St. John the Divine in New York city, and the dark green labradorite rock known as the Ausable granite from Keeseville, Essex county. There are many interesting granite deposits, especially in the Adirondack region, which have not been developed.

MARBLES

The marbles included some fine examples of decorative stone from South Dover, Dutchess county, the black marble from Glens Falls, monumental and building marbles from Gouverneur, St. Lawrence county, and white building marbles from southeastern New York.

LIMESTONES

Limestones of excellent quality are quarried in a great number of localities and were well represented, some of them showing as fine a polished surface as the true marbles.

SANDSTONES

The State is also rich in sandstones of good quality. The Potsdam sandstone forms an almost complete belt around the Adirondacks and is an excellent building stone. Its color is from white to pale red, and in many places it is an extremely hard quartzite. Specimens were shown from Potsdam, St. Lawrence county.

The white sandstones of Washington county have been extensively used for refractory purposes in the manufacture of steel, being almost free from iron. The Medina sandstones are quarried in the neighborhood of Medina, Albion and Lockport. While a pure white stone occurs at Lewiston, the Medina stone is generally of a pinkish red color. It is extensively used as a building stone, particularly in Buffalo and Rochester. It is valuable for paving, curbing and flagging. The Medina Sandstone Company exhibited a piece of wall work to show the various methods of finish, including a finely carved lintel. A number of cubes were exhibited from various quarries.

The sandstones of southern New York occurring in the rocks of Devonian age are generally fine grained and blue or greenish in color and are known as bluestones. Most of the quarries are in the counties of Greene, Ulster, Broome, Delaware and Sullivan. They are described in New York State Museum Bulletin 61 by Harold T. Dickinson. There is a great variety in color and physical properties of stone from these quarries. It is used as building stone and for trimming, and some of it is especially valuable for large platforms. A large proportion of the output is in the form of flagging and curbstone.

The Hudson River Bluestone Company exhibited a piece of wall built into the base of the pyramidal stand holding the sandstone cubes. This was designed to show the ease with which it can be worked and included some finely carved lettering. The main entrance to the exhibit was paved with flags and tiles of this material.

SLATE

With the sandstones were shown some ten-inch cubes of slate cut from the quarries of the H. H. Mathews Consolidated Slate Company, of Boston, which operates a number of quarries in Washington county. The slate belt covers an area of about 320 square miles, the larger part of which is in Washington county, N. Y., but which extends across the line into Rutland county, Vt. This is probably the richest slate region in the world. The beds are of great thickness, belonging to two distinct geologic formations. They are folded on one another in such a manner as to present the workable beds in long parallel ridges.

On account of its great strength and easy working qualities new uses are constantly being found for slate. One of the most striking features of the slate exhibit was a mantel built of rough slabs of dark red slate showing the cross fracture to have a fine satiny texture. This was a copy of a mantel designed by Lord & Hewlet, of New York, and built in a Poultney, Vt., residence. The main slate exhibit consisted of a stand supporting a slated roof, one side of which was covered with unfading green slates one inch thick, such as were laid on Senator Clark's New York residence. The other side was covered with rough thick slabs of unfading red. The sides of the stand were covered with the regular trade slates in four sections—red, green, purple and variegated. The uses of slate for construction purposes were shown by slabs and panels on the upper part of the stand.

CEMENT

The cement exhibit was made by the Helderberg Cement Company, of Howes Cave. One side of the exhibit stand was devoted to Portland and the other to natural cements. Barrels and bags of finished cement formed the base of the structure on which were glass jars containing the rock in its stages of manufacture, with a series of photographs of the works and of buildings of cement. On account of the rapidly extending applications of cement a large section outside of the building was set aside for exhibits of the uses of cement, and the exhibit was designed mainly to show the manufacture, the materials used and the method of their treatment.

GYPSUM

Gypsum was shown by a fine series of specimens contributed by the United States Gypsum Company from their mines in western New York. This material, like cement, is rapidly being adapted for a variety of purposes, especially in the finish and ornamentation of buildings, and the exhibit, encased in one of the square plate glass museum cases with its cut and polished cubes of raw gypsum, selenite crystals, jars of stucco colors and examples of plaster casts, made a very attractive exhibit. In another case there was exhibited gypsum in various forms from other sources.

SALT

The salt exhibit was made up from a very complete set of specimens in sample jars taken from the Museum collections, and a large number of packages from the manufacturers. The salt of New York is obtained from the salina formation in the western part of the State. The industry is of great importance. The deposits are described in State Museum Bulletin 11 by Dr. F. J. H. Merrill. One of the most interesting varieties shown was the solar salt, which has been made on the Onondaga Salt Reservation, Syracuse, since 1788. Blocks of rock salt were shown from the Retsof and Livonia shafts.

Most of the salt produced, however, is from wells bored down through the rock salt beds, and is pumped up in the form of brine and evaporated by artificial heat.

SOLVAY PROCESS COMPANY

The Solvay Process Company, of Syracuse, made a splendid display of soda ash. The plant of this company uses an immense amount of salt which is obtained from the Tully districts and carried by pipes to Solvay. The raw materials used were shown in the lower sections of two cases especially constructed for the exhibit, which also held a set of barrels and other packages in which the soda is shipped. In the upper sections were shown a series of large glass jars with the various products. These were supplied with a series of labels completely describing the process of manufacture and the chemical changes which take place. Above the case there was a set of photographs of the works, illustrating the social life of the work-people employed and the growth of the establishment.

USEFUL MINERALS

The exhibit of the useful minerals of the State was principally prepared by H. P. Whitlock of the Museum staff. One case contained a set of the abrasive materials, the most important of these being garnet, which is found in great quantities in the Adirondacks. Crude garnet from several mines, the ground and cleaned garnet, and grades of garnet paper were shown. A small millstone to represent the celebrated Esopus grit, emery ore from Peekskill, and quartz and sand from many localities were also exhibited in this case. Another case was filled with feldspar, mica and quartz, which usually occur associated with each other in the form of pegmetite dikes in the crystalline rocks of the Adirondacks and the Highlands of the Hudson. These materials are not as yet very extensively mined but an increasing demand for them is bringing to light many promising localities.

GRAPHITE

Another valuable mineral which occurs in the State in great quantities is graphite. Specimens of both the crude ore and manufactured graphite were exhibited. The deposits of this material in the form of graphitic limestone cover miles of territory, but more satisfactory processes for its concentration are needed to make it available for use, especially in the higher grades.

MUSEUM PUBLICATIONS

The Museum exhibited a set of its publications on geologic subjects, a set of published maps and maps specially prepared for this exhibit to show the distribution of useful minerals, and a number of enlarged photographs.

PALEONTOLOGY

The exhibit of the Department of Paleontology consisted of a set of its publications on the paleontology of the State of New York—35 volumes—covering the period 1847-1904, and a set of wing frames with many of the original drawings and plates used in their illustration.

SPECIAL FEATURES

The most striking feature of the exhibit was an immense slab of Potsdam sandstone from Bidwell's Crossing, Clinton county, which was part of the premoidial or cambrian beach laid down about the shores of the Adirondack continental nucleus. The slab shows the trails of animals crossing in all directions, especially those known as clemactechnites, said by Dr. J. M. Clarke to have been made by a a simple primitive type of mollusk. The slab, weighing over fifteen tons, was moved in six sections and put together for exhibition.

Restorations in plaster of paris of the fossil crustaceous eurypterus and hughmilleria were also exhibited.

CLAYS

The exhibition of clays and clay products was made by the State School of Ceramics, at Alfred, N. Y., under the direction of Professor Charles F. Binns, and included some large vases, the work of students.

The State of New York has long held an important place in the brick trade on account of its unlimited quantities of clay along the Hudson river, which have not only supplied much of the brick used for building in New York city, but bricks have been shipped from this source long distances by water. The finer varieties of clay have not been worked to any extent except on Long Island, but other conditions have resulted in the establishment of potteries at Brooklyn, Syracuse and other points, using almost exclusively clays imported into the State. The beds of feldspar and flint now being exploited in the Adirondacks will materially help to put this class of potteries on a firmer basis.

The center of the exhibition space was devoted to a pagoda designed to show the kinds of brick manufactured in the principal localities. The roof afforded an excellent place to exhibit earthenware tiling.

The General Electric Company exhibited a case of insulators, many of them of special types, from their Schenectady pottery. Insulators were also exhibited by Pass & Seymour, of Syracuse, and the Empire China Works, of Brooklyn.

PETROLEUM

The petroleum exhibit was made under the general direction of Secretary and Chief Executive Officer Charles A. Ball. An extensive series of crude and refined oils and by-products occupied a case showing on both sides. On this was installed a model of a tower and drilling machinery such as is used in sinking oil wells. The records printed on the labels furnished data which made an important addition to our previous knowledge of the New York oil fields.

In addition to those heretofore mentioned, the following gentlemen assisted as indicated in the preparation of the exhibit, and are entitled to no small credit for the valuable assistance rendered.

E. E. Engelhardt was engaged in the acquisition of the salt exhibits.

J. S. Bellamy collected the petroleum exhibit under the immediate direction of Secretary Ball.

C. F. Binns collected the exhibit of clay products under the immediate direction of the State Commission.

W. C. Richard assisted in installing the exhibit.

Frederick Braun installed the slab of Potsdam sandstone.

The following members of the staff of the State Museum also assisted: H.S. Mattimore, C.A. Trask, E.C. Kenny, D.D. Luther and Joseph Morje.

Catalogue of Exhibitors in the Department of Mines and Metallurgy, with the Award, if Any, Received by Each

GROUP ONE HUNDRED SIXTEEN
Minerals and Stones
Adirondack Pyrites Co., Gouverneur
  Pyrites: crude and concentrates
Alfred Clay Co., Alfred Station
  Brick
  Tile
Algonquin Red Slate Co., Truthville
  Mineral paint
Alps Oil Co., Alma
  Crude oil
Applebee & Baldwin, Scio
  Crude oil
Arnold Mining Co. Bronze medal

Iron ores
Attica Brick and Tile Co., Attica
  Brick
Atwood & McEwen, Andover
  Crude oil
J.J. Barron, Three Mile Bay
  Limestone (Trenton)
H.H. Barton Son & Co., North Creek and Minerva
  Garnet and garnet paper
Herman Behr & Co., North River. Silver medal
  Garnet and garnet paper
Milo M. Belding, Gouverneur
  Marble
Bellamy & Elliott, Scio
  Crude oil
Frank Bennett, Staten Island
  Diabase
J. B. Berridge, Hudson
  Limestone (Helderberg)
H. Boice & Co., Rondout
  Bluestone
A. F. Bouton, Roxbury
  Red sandstone (Catskill)
Burhans & Brainard, Saugerties
  Bluestone
Eugene Campbell, New Baltimore
  Limestone (Helderberg)
Canton Marble Quarry, Canton
  Marble
B. & J. Carpenter, Lockport
  Limestone (Niagara)
Celadon Roofing Co., Alfred
  Tile roofs
Church & Bradley, Alma
  Crude oil
Church & Co., Wellsville
  Crude oil
Clark, Tracey & Co., West Union
  Crude oil
Conner Paint Mfg. Co
  Mineral paint
Consolidated Wheatland Plaster Co., Wheatland
  Gypsum

Land plaster
Corning Brick, Tile & Terra Cotta Co., Corning
Brick
Delaware Milling, Mining & Mfg. Co., Roxbury
Mineral paint
Albert Dibble, Belvidere
Bluestone
Joseph Dixon Crucible Co., Ticonderoga
Graphite
Duford & Son, Chaumont
Limestone (Trenton)
Ellenville Zinc Co., Ellenville
Lead and zinc: zinc blende, chalcopyrite, galena, lead, zinc
and copper concentrates
Empire China Works, Brooklyn
Insulators
Empire Gas and Fuel Co., Ltd., Willink
Crude oil
Empire Marble Co., Gouverneur
Marble
Empire Salt Co. Silver medal
Salt
Extra Dark Marble Co., Gouverneur
Marble
Foery & Kastner, Rochester
Limestone
D. R. & H. Fogelsinger, Buffalo
Limestone (Onondaga)
Franchot Bros., Scio
Crude oil
R. Forsyth, Grindstone Island
Granite
General Electric Co., Schenectady. Gold medal
Insulators
Genesee Salt Co., Pifford
Salt
Glens Falls Co., Glens Falls
Limestone (Trenton)
Adelbert Gordon, Batchellerville
Mica
Feldspar
Gouverneur Garnet Co., Gouverneur
Garnet

J. B. Gray, Geneseo
   Oil sand and crude oil
Ezra Grinnell, Port Gibson
   Plaster of paris
   Land plaster
Grumply Oil Co., Rexville
   Crude oil
Helderberg Cement Co., Howes Cave. Gold medal
   Cement
D. C. Hewitt, Amsterdam
   Limestone (Calciferous)
High Falls Pyrites Co., Canton
   Pyrites
Horan Bros., Medina
   Sandstone
Horseheads Brick Co., Horseheads
   Brick
L. W. Hotchkiss, Lewiston
   Sandstone (Medina)
Hudson River Bluestone Co., Ulster county. Silver medal
   Bluestone
International Graphite Co., Ticonderoga
   Graphite
International Pulp Co., Gouverneur
   Talc
International Salt Co., Ithaca
   Salt
Interstate Conduit & Brick Co., Ithaca
   Brick
Jamestown Shale Paving Brick Co., Jamestown
   Brick
Jewettville Pressed Brick & Paving Co., Jewettville
   Brick
R. Jones, Prospect
   Graphite
J. F. Kilgour, Lordville
   Bluestone
F. H. Kinkel, Bedford
   Feldspar
   Quartz
A. Gracie King, Garrisons
   Granite
Francis Larkins, Ossining

Granite
B. B. Mason, Keeseville
  Norite
Masterton & Hall, Tuckahoe
  Marble
H. H. Mathews Consolidated Slate Co., Washington county. Gold
  medal
  Slate
G. J. McClure, Ithaca
  Bluestone
J. H. McCutcheon, Lancaster
  Brick
James McEwen, Wellsville
  Crude oil
J. C. & A. McMurray, Olean
  Brick
Medina Quarry Co., New York city. Silver medal
  Sandstone
M. Mervine, Whitesville
  Crude oil
Morris & Strobel, LeRoy
  Limestone
Mount Eve Granite Co., Mount Eve
  Granite
Mutual Gas Co., Andover
  Crude oil
National Salt Co., Ithaca and Warsaw. Silver medal
  Salt
National Wall Plaster Co., Fayetteville
  Crude gypsum
  Plaster of paris
  Land plaster
James Nevins & Son, Walton
  Bluestone
New York State School of Clay Working and Ceramics, Alfred
Silver medal
  Clay products
New York Hydraulic Pressed Brick Co., Canandaigua
  Brick
New York State Museum, Department of Paleontology. Grand
prize
  General Exhibit in Paleontology, including publications, slab
  of Potsdam sandstone, restorations of fossils

New York State Museum. Bronze medal
  Plaster Model of Tilly Foster Iron Mine
New York State Museum. Gold medal
  Publications on Geology, Mineralogy, Topography, Quarrying,
    Mining, Metallurgy, Development of Water Resources, etc.
New York State Museum. Gold medal
  Collection of Minerals and Building Stones
New York State Museum. Silver medal
  Ten Geologic maps of the State of New York and special
    parts thereof
  Relief Map of New York
  Hypsometric Map of New York
  Road Map of New York
  Sixty-four photographic enlargements illustrating New York
    State mineral resources and other geological features; size,
    11 by 14 inches
New York State Museum. Silver medal
  Collective Exhibit
Northern New York Marble Co., Gouverneur
  Marble
North River Garnet Co., Ticonderoga
  Garnet
Oakfield Plaster Manufacturing Co., Oakfield
  Gypsum
Onondaga Coarse Salt Association, Syracuse. Silver medal
  Solar salt
Ontario Talc Co., Gouverneur
  Talc
D. Parmatir, Potsdam
  Sandstone
Pass & Seymour, Syracuse
  Insulators
Peter Pitkin's Sons, Portageville
  Bluestone
Potsdam Sandstone Co., Potsdam
  Sandstone
A. L. Pritchard, Pleasantville
  Marble
Queen City Brick Co., Buffalo
  Brick
Quick & Co., Alma
  Crude oil
Remington Salt Co., Syracuse

Salt
Retsof Mining Co., Retsof and Livonia
  Rock salt
W. Rielly, Cobleskill
  Limestone
E. P. Roberts, Cortland
  Granite
Robins Conveying Belt Co., New York city
  Belts and conveyor on separator
Rochester Brick & Tile Co., Rochester
  Brick
Rossie Metallic Paint Co., Rossie
  Mineral paint
Rudolph & Dotterwich, Allegany
  Crude oil
D. G. Scholten, Gouverneur. Bronze medal
  Marble
Scio Oil & Gas Co., Scio
  Oil sand and crude oil
C. R. Scott, Alma
  Crude oil
Scott, Fuller & Fay, South Bolivar
  Crude oil
George W. Searles, White Lead Lake, Herkimer county
  Infusorial earth
J. Shanahan, Tribes Hill
  Limestone
J. Shear & Co., Schenectady
  Sandstone
Solvay Process Co., Syracuse. Grand prize
  Salt products
Solvay Process Co., Syracuse
  Limestone (Onondaga)
South Dover Marble Co., South Dover
  Marble
St. Lawrence Marble Co., Gouverneur
  Marble
A. D. Symonds, Elmira
  Bluestone
The Tanite Co., Cortland
  Emery
Evan T. Thomas, Prospect
  Limestone

F. Thomas, Troy
  Mineral paint
Loren Thomas, Waterloo
  Marble
James Thornton Estate, Alma
  Crude oil
Ticonderoga Graphite Co., Ticonderoga
  Graphite
Tonawanda Brick Co., Tonawanda
  Brick
W. B. Underhill Brick Co., Croton Landing
  Sand
Union Salt Co., Watkins
  Salt
Union Talc Co., Gouverneur
  Talc
United States Gypsum Co., Oakfield. Grand prize
  Gypsum
  Statuary of plaster of paris
United States Talc Co., Gouverneur
  Talc
James Van Etten, Granite
  Millstones
Vosburg Oil Co., Bolivar
  Oil sand and crude oil
Vossler Bros & Quick, Alma
  Crude oil
Warsaw Bluestone Co., Rock Glen
  Bluestone
Watertown Marble Co., Watertown
  Marble
Watkins Salt Co., Watkins
  Salt
Wells & Hall, Ogdensburg
  Mineral paint
Wetherill Separating Co., New York city. Gold medal
  Wetherill magnetic separator, Type E, No. 3, working on
    New York magnetic iron ores
L. H. White, Saratoga Springs
  Granite
White Crystal Marble Co., Gouverneur
  Marble Ashler
Williamson & Co., Northport

Sand

Witherbee, Sherman & Co., Mineville. Silver medal
  Iron ore

Worcester Salt Co., Silver Springs. Silver medal
  Salt

[Illustration: VARIED INDUSTRIES BUILDING AND PLAZA ST. LOUIS]

CHAPTER XV

Social Economy Exhibit and Schedule of Awards

SOCIAL ECONOMY EXHIBIT By DELANCEY M. ELLIS Director
of Education and
Social Economy

The Department of Social Economy being closely allied with the
Department of Education, and its exhibit being installed in the Palace
of Education, it was placed under the general charge of the Director of
Education, whose title was changed to the Director of Education and
Social Economy.

APPROPRIATIONS

The following appropriations were made for exhibits in this department:

State Commission in Lunacy, —————————— $1,800
State Board Of Charities, —————————— 1,200
State Department Of Prisons, —————————— 2,000
State Department Of Labor, —————————— 1,000
Craig Colony for Epileptics, Sonyea, —— 500
General expenses, —————————————— 1,000

Total, ————————————————————————— $7,500

From the last named appropriation was paid the expenses for the exhibits of the State Department of Health and the State Department of Excise, and such other institutions or associations as were properly included in this class.

PREPARATION OF EXHIBITS

All of the exhibits of State Departments were prepared by the departments contributing them, and in the case of the State Commission in Lunacy and the State Board of Charities the exhibits were installed by a special representative. This also is true of the exhibit of the State Department of Prisons, which required the constant attendance of an expert to demonstrate its workings.

During the latter part of the Exposition period William T. Arms, an attache of the State building, was detailed to the Department of Social Economy, and dividing his time among the several State exhibits, added materially to the pleasure and knowledge of visitors concerning New York's institutions.

PLAN OF ARRANGEMENT

The Exposition authorities determined that the exhibits in the Department of Social Economy should be collective; that is, that all the work in the Department of Charities and Corrections from whatever source should be installed together; the same to be true of general betterment movements, hygiene, municipal improvement, etc. This plan precluded the installation of the State's exhibit in this department in one place with a dignified installation, as in the other exhibit departments, and made necessary the placing of the exhibit in several different parts of the building according to the subdivision of the classification under which it fell. Perhaps from the standard of general utility the arrangement was all that could be desired, but from the standpoint of the State it is of doubtful value, as such a disposition of the State's exhibit made no single part of it of any considerable size, nor as impressive as had the State's work in this department been shown together.

No State in the Union approaches the Empire State in its progressive policy in the care of the insane, the destitute and delinquents, in the solving of labor and excise problems, and had the exhibit in this department been installed together, a most effective and striking lesson would have been taught.

STATE COMMISSION IN LUNACY

The exhibit of the New York State Commission in Lunacy was the most suggestive and comprehensive of any shown in the Department for the Insane, and was designed primarily to show the difference between the ancient and modern methods of treating these unfortunates. Two rooms were shown, the first of which represented the primitive methods adopted for treating insanity. The room was barren, dark and not over clean. At the front was shown one of the old peep-doors taken from the Utica Asylum. It was of massive construction and contained a small aperture covered by a heavy wooden blind, through which the attendant could observe the doings of the patient, or, more properly speaking, the prisoner. Within stood one of the so-called Utica cribs built of heavy wood, over which was a cover of wooden bars. In this crib the patient was obliged to remain in a recumbent position, the cover closed and locked. Near by stood a restraining chair, a whirling chair, a straight jacket and shackles, all representing ancient methods of "quieting" the victims of the dread disease.

Adjoining was an airy room, clean and inviting, made cheerful by growing plants and attractive furniture, with every modern appliance for the care of an invalid, resembling closely a room of the better class in a general hospital. There was an entire absence of any kind of restraint. A neat iron bedstead, rocking chairs, invalid table, wash stand, book case with books, and in fact every comfort and convenience was at hand. In this room were also shown the uniforms worn by the nurses and attendants in the State hospitals for the insane, and a series of reference books upon the subject of insanity, The exhibit was supplemented by a series of handsome photographs completely illustrating the various State hospitals for the insane, the daily life of the inmates and the expert attention which they receive.

Glass cases contained a large amount of industrial work done by the inmates. This chiefly consisted of sewing and embroidery. A feature of the exhibit was an oak cabinet containing a series of specimens showing cross sections of the brain prepared at the Pathological Institute in New York city. It was of decided scientific value and interest. Near by was a miniature tent hospital, a complete model of the hospital for the care of insane patients afflicted with tuberculosis which is now in operation at the Manhattan State Hospital, Ward's Island, N. Y.

A striking feature was a copy of the famous oil painting, "Dr. Pinel Freeing the Insane at La Salpètrière after the close of the French Revolution." It most graphically told the story of the complete revolution in treating this dread disease.

STATE BOARD OF CHARITIES

The exhibit of the State Board of Charities was installed under four different subdivisions of Group 139 (Charities and Corrections) of the official classification.

1. Class 784. Destitute, neglected and delinquent children 2. Class 785. Institutional care of destitute adults 3. Class 787. Hospitals, dispensaries and nursing 4. Class 789. Treatment of criminals

The exhibit of the Board in the department for the care of juvenile delinquents was comprehensive in its make up. Photographs of the various State institutions devoted to this purpose were shown, clearly demonstrating the superiority of these institutions as to buildings, equipment and maintenance. These photographs were supplemented by an exhibit of industrial work of the inmates.

The State Industrial School at Rochester and the House of Refuge for Juvenile Delinquents at Randall's Island both contributed some exceptional work in wood carving and wrought iron.

In addition to this were shown the uniforms worn in the different institutions and also specimens of the scholastic work which the children are doing.

The State Board of Charities also assumed the responsibility for, and partially prepared, the exhibit of various charity organization societies within the State, by far the most elaborate of which was the exhibit of the Charity Organization Society of New York city. By means of photographs, administrative blanks and reports the great work which this organization is doing was clearly revealed.

The work of the Board in the care of destitute adults was demonstrated by means of a complete set of photographs of the county alms houses of the State of New York. From two to four pictures of each institution were shown, giving a very clear idea of their scope and equipment. These photographs were supplemented by a statistical blank containing valuable data as to the value of the plant, number of employees, of inmates, and such other information as would be useful to the public.

The exhibit of the work of the Board as related to general hospitals of the State consisted largely of a series of photographs, supplemented by valuable statistical matter.

The Board also prepared an exhibit from the various State prisons, the industrial work of which is under the jurisdiction of the State Prison

Commission. This exhibit contained photographs of the members of the State Prison Commission, photographs showing the interiors of the different prisons, reports, etc., and revealed the fact that the Empire State is in the front rank in inaugurating reform movements looking toward the health, safety and moral uplift of the inmates.

STATE DEPARTMENT OF PRISONS

The exhibit of the State Department of Prisons probably received as much attention from the public as any single State exhibit prepared. It consisted of a demonstration of the workings of the Bertillon and finger print systems for the identification of criminals. An ornate installation of solid oak, handsomely carved, was built by the inmates of the State Prison at Ossining, and was carried to St. Louis and erected upon the space assigned to this department.

Throughout the season Captain J.H. Parke, an expert on the finger print system, and E.E. Davis, Jr., an expert on the Bertillon system, were present to demonstrate the workings of these systems to Exposition visitors. But few are familiar with the operations of the Bertillon system, and the finger print system is as yet practically unknown.

New York State is the pioneer State of the Union in putting into practical operation the finger print system for the identification of criminals, and it is the only State in which it is at present in use. Although there is a National Bureau of Identification at Washington, D. C., which is conducted through the co-operation of the chiefs of police of many of the large cities throughout the country, it cannot be said to be a department of the United States government, and its system is far from as perfect as that of the Empire State.

STATE DEPARTMENT OF LABOR

Probably in no State of the Union does there exist a labor department organized upon such extensive lines as is that of the State of New York. Recently three bureaus were merged forming the State Department of Labor. These were the Bureau of Labor Statistics, the Board of Mediation and Arbitration and the office of the Factory Inspector. The exhibit consisted of a complete set of reports of these various bureaus, and of the department erected therefrom, supplemented with a series of graphic charts bearing upon every phase of the labor question, and comparing the economic condition of the Empire State with that of other States of the Union and various foreign countries. The exhibit was a valuable sociological contribution. An especially strong feature was four monographs, entitled "Typical Employers' Welfare Institutions in New York," "Labor Legislation in New York," "The Work of the State Department of Labor," and "The Growth of Industry in New York." These were printed in such quantities as to permit of their distribution among visitors to the Exposition. The graphic charts were reproduced in half-tones and inserted in the monographs.

The exhibit was carefully studied by students of sociology generally as it is recognized that the State of New York speaks with a voice of authority upon questions of this nature.

STATE DEPARTMENT OF EXCISE

The question of controlling the liquor traffic is one of lively interest throughout the civilized world. The exhibit of the State Department of Excise was so prepared as to clearly demonstrate the superiority of the system of State control in licensing this traffic as administered under the New York State Liquor Tax Law. The exhibit consisted of a series of graphic charts showing this statute's moral benefit to the people of the State by reducing the number of drinking places more than twenty per cent and increasing the amount collected from liquor licenses from about three million to about eighteen million dollars annually. By means of a key, which accompanied the charts, the visitor was enabled easily to trace the development of the law since its first enactment and to see the efficiency with which it is enforced.

STATE DEPARTMENT OF HEALTH

The exhibit of the State Department of Health was made up of a complete set of reports of the department, supplemented by administrative blanks used in the enforcement of the Health Law, and photographs showing the offices of the department, the anti-toxin laboratory and other features of the department's work. A full set of blanks used in the collection of vital statistics and sample specimens of anti-toxin and anti-tetanus, which are distributed without charge by the department, completed the exhibit.

CRAIG COLONY

The exhibit of Craig Colony consisted of a model designed to show the ideal institution for the care, education and treatment of epileptics, towards which Craig Colony in its development is working. The model was skillfully constructed and cost considerably more than the appropriation made by the Commission, the balance being paid from private sources.

MISCELLANEOUS EXHIBITS

The New York State exhibit in the Department of Social Economy also contained an exhibit of the Woman's Institute at Yonkers, a philanthropic organization providing for the care of needy families in their homes and promoting several general betterment movements. The exhibit consisted of photographs, blanks and statistics bearing upon the work of the organization.

Close by was an exhibit of the George Junior Republic at Freeville, a unique institution for the care of juvenile delinquents and carried on along the lines of a civic organization. The exhibit consisted of interesting photographs showing the buildings and the plant, also specimens of blanks and samples of the money in use in the institution, and a general account of the work since its inception.

One of the most interesting exhibits was that of the Bank of New York, New York city, which is one of the oldest banks in the United States, having been organized in 1784 and having since enjoyed a most prosperous career. In addition to photographs, original by-laws and figures concerning the present condition of the bank, was exhibited the first ledger of the institution, which contained the accounts of Aaron Burr, Robert R. Livingston and other noted contemporaries. In addition were shown requisitions of Alexander Hamilton, then Secretary of the Treasury, for loans to the government, and other interesting historical documents.

The State Library prepared and exhibited an interesting compilation of sociological legislation and literature which was designed to show the advanced work done by the library in that direction.

Exhibits were also in place from the Church Association for the Advancement of the Interests of Labor; the Eastman Kodak Company, of Rochester, N. Y.; the Blacksmith and Wheelwright; the Sugar Trade Review, and a volume published by the Mercantile Publishing Company containing a directory of manufacturers and valuable trade statistics.

Catalogue of Exhibitors in the Department of Social Economy, Arranged by Groups, with the Awards, if Any, Received by Each

GROUP ONE HUNDRED TWENTY-NINE

Study and Investigation of Social and Economic Conditions

Blacksmith and Wheelwright, New York city. Silver medal
  Publication
Church Association for the Advancement of the Interests of Labor,
New York city. Silver medal
  Photographs
  Statistics
Division of Sociology, New York State Library, Albany. Silver medal
  A comparative index of sociological legislation and literature
Manufacturers' Publishing Company, New York city. Silver medal
  Directory of Manufacturers
Willett & Gray, New York city. Silver medal
  Sugar Review

The following awards were made to exhibits not a part of the collective State Exhibit:

American Book Company, New York city. Grand prize
  Text books on economics
R. G. Dunn & Company, Commercial Agency New York city. Silver medal
  Statistics
  Photographs
Richmond C. Hill, secretary Board of Trade, Buffalo. Silver medal

GROUP ONE HUNDRED THIRTY

Economic Resources and Organization

Charles Hemstreet, New York city. Silver medal

GROUP ONE HUNDRED THIRTY-ONE

State Regulation of Industry and Labor

State Department of Labor, Albany. Grand prize
Graphic charts
Reports
Monographs

The following award was made to an exhibit not a part of the collective State Exhibit:

American Institute of Social Service, New York city. Gold medal
Charts
Photographs
Statistics

GROUP ONE HUNDRED THIRTY-TWO

Organization of Industrial Workers

State Department of Labor, Albany. Grand prize
 Graphic charts
 Reports
 Monographs

GROUP ONE HUNDRED THIRTY-FIVE

Provident Institutions and Banks

National Consumers' League, New York city. Grand prize
  Charts
  Printed matter
  Garments.
Bank of New York, New York city. Grand prize
  Historical ledger and documents
  Statistics
  By-laws
  Pictures

GROUP ONE HUNDRED THIRTY-SIX

Housing of the Working Classes

The following awards were made to exhibits not a part of the collective State Exhibit:

J. B. & J. M. Cornell Company. Gold medal
Model Household Nursery. Gold medal
New York city, tenement house department, Lawrence Veiller,
    collaborator. Grand prize
Niagara Development Company, New York city. Silver medal

GROUP ONE HUNDRED THIRTY-SEVEN

The Liquor Question

State Department of Excise, Albany. Grand prize
Graphic charts
Statistics

GROUP ONE HUNDRED THIRTY-EIGHT

General Betterment Movements

National Consumers' League, New York city. Gold medal
Charts
Printed matter
Garments
New York Training School for Deaconesses. Bronze medal
Photographs
Prospectus
People's Institute, New York city. Silver medal
Photographs
Prospectus
Reports
Woman's Institute, Yonkers. Silver medal
Photographs
Charts
Statistics
Administrative blanks
Reports
Young Women's Christian Association, New York city. Silver
  medal
Reports
Statistics
Administrative blanks
Art work

The following awards were made to exhibits not a part of the collective State Exhibit:

American Institute of Social Service, New York city. Grand prize
General Electric Company, Schenectady. Gold medal
Institutional charities, collective exhibit. Gold medal
Prepared and installed by American Institute of Social Service
  St. Bartholomew's Church, New York city
  St. George's Church, New York city
  Washington Square M. E. Church, New York city
  Church of the Ascension, New York city
  Marcy Avenue Church, Brooklyn
  Westminster Presbyterian Church, Buffalo

Mohawk and Hudson River Humane Society, Albany. Gold medal
Siegel-Cooper Company, New York city. Gold medal
J. H. Williams Company, Brooklyn. Silver medal

The following awards were made to collaborators:

Dr. William H. Tolman, New York city. Gold medal
Dr. William W. Stillman, Albany. Gold medal
Mrs. Florence Kelly, New York city. Gold medal

GROUP ONE HUNDRED THIRTY-NINE

Charities and Corrections

Brooklyn Bureau of Charities. Gold medal
    Photographs
    Statistics
Buffalo Charity Organization Society. Gold medal
    Photographs
    Statistics
Charity Organization Society, New York city. Grand prize
    Reports
    Charts
    Statistics
    Photographs
    Maps
    Administrative blanks
Cornell University, Department of Philanthropy and Finance, Ithaca.
 Gold medal
    Graphic charts
Craig Colony for Epileptics, Sonyea. Gold medal
    Model of institution
George Junior Republic, Freeville. Gold medal
    Photographs
    Charts
    Statistics
    Reports
Manhattan State Hospital East, Ward's Island, New York city.
Gold medal
    Photographs
    Statistics
Newburg Associated Charities. Silver medal
    Photographs
    Statistics
New York City United Hebrew Charities. Gold medal
    Photographs
    Statistics
State Board of Charities, Albany. Grand prize
    Reports
    Statistics

Photographs
Industrial work
Administrative blanks
State Commission in Lunacy, Albany. Grand prize
  Rooms showing ancient and modern treatment of insane
    patients
  Reports
  Industrial work
  Model tuberculosis hospital
  Pathological specimens
State Commission of Prisons, Albany. Gold medal
  Photographs
  Reports
  Statistics
State Prison Department, Albany. Grand prize
  Working exhibit of Bertillon and Finger Print systems for
    identification of criminals
Woman's Institute, Yonkers. Silver medal
  Photographs
  Charts
  Statistics
  Administrative blanks
  Reports

The following awards were made to collaborators:

Robert W. Hebbard, Secretary State Board of Charities. Gold
medal
T. E. McGarr, Secretary State Commission in Lunacy. Gold medal
Edward T. Devine, New York city. Gold medal

The following awards were made to exhibits not a part of the collective
State Exhibit:

Association for Improving the Condition of the Poor, Brooklyn.
  Silver medal
Asylum of the Sisters of St. Dominie, New York city. Silver medal
Brooklyn Society for the Prevention of Cruelty to Children, Brooklyn.
  Silver medal
Catholic Home Bureau, New York city. Gold medal
Children's Aid Society, New York city. Gold medal
Committee on the Prevention of Tuberculosis, New York city. Grand prize
Department of Finance, New York city. Grand prize
Department of Public Charities, New York city. Gold medal
Hebrew Sheltering Guardian Society, New York city. Gold medal

Rev. Thomas L. Kinkead, Peekskill. Gold medal
Lincoln Hospital and Home, New York city. Silver medal
Long Island College Hospital, New York city. Silver medal
Missionary Sisters Third Order of St. Frances, New York city. Gold medal
Mission of the Immaculate Virgin for the Protection of Homeless and
    Destitute Children, New York city. Silver medal
Mount Sinai Hospital for Children, New York city. Silver medal
New York Catholic Protectory, New York city. Gold medal
New York Charity Organization Society, New York city. Grand prize
New York Foundling Hospital, New York city. Silver medal
New York Juvenile Asylum, New York city. Gold medal
New York Society for the Prevention of Cruelty to Children, New York
    city. Gold medal
Orphans' Home, Brooklyn. Silver medal
St. Vincent's Hospital, New York city. Silver medal
Seton Hospital, New York city. Silver medal
Sisters of Mercy, Gabriels. Gold medal

The following awards were made to collaborators:

Miss Lillian Brandt, New York city. Gold medal
Homer Folks, New York city. Gold medal
Dr. D. C. Potter, New York city. Gold medal

GROUP ONE HUNDRED FORTY

Public Health.

Rochester, City Department of Health. Gold medal
  Charts
  Statistics
  Photographs
State Department of Health, Albany. Grand prize
  Reports
  Administrative blanks
  Photographs
  Statistics

The following award was made to a collaborator:

Dr. George Goler, Health Officer, Rochester. Gold medal

The following awards were made to exhibits not a part of the collective State Exhibit:

Adirondack Cottage Sanitorium, Saranac Lake. Grand prize
Dr. Simon Baruch, New York city. Silver medal
Department of Health of the City of New York. Grand prize
Allen Hazen, New York city. Gold medal
Dr. S. Adolphus Knopf, New York city. Gold medal
Kny-Scheerer Company, New York city. Grand prize
Kny-Scheerer Company, Department of Natural Science, New York city. Gold
    medal
Sanitorium Gabriel, Saranac Lake. Gold medal

The following awards were made to collaborators:

Dr. E. L. Trudeau, Saranac Lake. Grand prize
Herman Biggs, M. D., New York city. Gold medal

GROUP ONE HUNDRED FORTY-ONE

Municipal Improvement

The following awards were made to exhibits not a part of the collective State Exhibit:

American Institute of Social Service. Silver medal
Photographs illustrating municipal conditions
City of New York, Art Commission. Gold medal
City of New York, Aqueduct Commission and Department of Water
  Supply. Gold medal
City of New York, Children's School Farm. Silver medal
City of New York, Department of Street Cleaning. Grand prize

The following awards were made to collaborators:

Mrs. Ruth Ashley Hirschfield. Gold medal
Model playground and nursery
George W. Waring in recognition of services in the establishment
  of the system used in the Department of Street Cleaning, New
  York city. Gold medal

THE FOLLOWING IS A RECAPITULATION OF THE AWARDS MADE TO THE STATE OF NEW YORK IN THE DEPARTMENT OF SOCIAL ECONOMY.

Grand Prize.

Group 129.................	1
Group 131.................	1
Group 132.................	1
Group 135.................	2
Group 136.................	1
Group 137.................	1
Group 138.................	1
Group 139.................	7
Group 139, Collaborators...	1
Group 140.................	4
Group 140, Collaborators...	1
Group 141.................	1
	—
Total....................	22
	===

Gold Medal.

Group 131.................	1
Group 136.................	2
Group 138................	10
Group 138, Collaborators...	3
Group 139................	18
Group 139, Collaborators...	5
Group 140.................	5
Group 140, Collaborators...	2
Group 141.................	4
	—
Total....................	50
	===

Silver Medal.

Group 129 7 Group 130 1 Group 136 1 Group 138 5 Group 139 13 Group 140 1 Group 141 2 —— Total. 30 ==== *Bronze Medal.*

Group 138 1 ===

Grand prizes. 22 Gold medals. 50 Silver medals. 30 Bronze medal. 1 —— —- Grand total. 103 =====

[Illustration: PALACE OF EDUCATION AND SOCIAL ECONOMY FROM FESTIVAL HALL]

CHAPTER XVI
Financial Statement

EXPENDITURES

GENERAL ADMINISTRATION

Secretary and Chief Executive Officer—
salary (33 months) ———————————————— $10,449 17
Secretary and Chief Executive Officer—
traveling expenses and maintenance at
St. Louis ————————————————————— 6,528 08
Clerk hire, assistants, stenographers, etc.——— 7,143 00
Rent of New York office ————————————— 450 00
Maintenance of Albany office after close of
Exposition ——————————————————————— 550 80
Office fixtures, desks, tables, chairs, etc. 571 19
General traveling expenses of employees
and other officials and expense of
maintenance at St. Louis ————————————— 3,367 38
Printing and engraving, stationery and
office supplies, including all engraving
for functions given by Commission ——————— 4,461 98
Express, freight, cartage, telephone (local
and long distance) and telegraph ——————— 1,481 65
Petty cash, including postage, car fares,
messenger service, sundry supplies, etc . ——— 3,615 07
Railroad and hotel expenses of individual
members of Commission for attendance
at meetings in New York and St. Louis:
    Edward H. Harriman ——————————— $321 00
    William Berri ————————————————— 552 45
    Edward Lyman Bill ———————————— 828 10
    Louis Stern ————————————————— $97 80
    James H. Callanan ———————————— 1,591 38
    Frederick R. Green ——————————— 768 55
    Frank S. McGraw ————————————— 880 92
    Mrs. Norman E. Mack ——————————— 1,592 45
    John K. Stewart ————————————— 1,013 39
    John C. Woodbury ————————————— 1,087 40

John Young ———————————— 1,928 75
Cyrus E. Jones ———————— 35 50
——————— $10,697 69
Railroad, hotel and other expenses of the
Commission attending the dedication ceremonies
at St. Louis, April 30, 1903 ——————— 1,722 80
Railroad, hotel and other expenses of the
Commission for meeting held at St. Louis
in December, 1903 ————————— 1,260 50
Miscellaneous expenditures not included in
above ——————————————— 1,565 33

Total expenditures ——————————— $53,864 64
============

Receipts:
Rebate from Planters' Hotel ————— $60 00
Rebate on insurance ——————— 369 81
Interest on deposits of funds
in treasurer's hands ——————— 403 66

Total receipts ————————————— $833 47
============

NEW YORK STATE BUILDING, CONSTRUCTION

Caldwell & Drake, contract for construction of building and extras ——— ——————————————— $61,634 85 Embellishment of building, models for Quadrigae, statuary, coat of arms, etc., and mural decorations ——— ——————————— 11,133 64 Enlarging and placing sculpture ——— ———— 5,000 00 Organ case ——————————————— ———— $3,500 00 Furniture, carpets, shades, screens, etc. ———— 19,750 55 Electroliers, electric fixtures, etc. ————— 5,077 73 Appointments, watchman's time clock, fire protection, refrigerators, gas logs, electric heaters, etc. ————————————————— 1,189 90 Landscape gardening —————————————— 3,694 30 Architects' fees — ————————————————— 5,128 70 Architects' expenses ——— ————————————— 1,783 90 Insurance on building ——— ————————— 2,444 20 —————————— Total expenditures —— ——————————————— $120,337 77 ============ Receipts: Sale of building and furniture ————————— $7,025 00 ============

NEW YORK STATE BUILDING, MAINTENANCE

Superintendent—salary ———————————— $1,225 00
Hostesses and matrons—salaries ——————— 3,232 50
Attendants, postmaster, watchman, porters
—salaries ———————————————— 20,696 59
Janitor service ————————————— 2,682 50
Allowance for maintenance of superintendent,
hostesses, matrons, etc., at St. Louis ——— 1,902 10
Equipment, including table and bed linen,
dishes, light renewals, canopies, electric
fans, etc. ——————————————— 4,486 91
General supplies, renewals, livery, cartage,
baggage transfer and laundry ——————— 7,721 29
Light and water —————————————— 4,974 90
Caterers' bills, floral decorations, music,
illuminations and other incidentals for all
functions given by the Commission, including
New York Week, Dedication Day and
other occasions elsewhere enumerated,
also for restaurant charges of all members
of the Commission while at the Exposition ——— $17,444 79
Expenses of the Governor, his staff and
legislative party, including transportation
and hotel bills in connection with New
York Week observance ——————————— 3,982 62
Special illumination of building in honor of
visit of President Roosevelt ———————— 250 00
Total expenditures ———————————— $68,599 20

Receipts
Rebate on gas, livery and safe ———————— $70 00

EDUCATION

Director of Education and Social Economy
—salary (20 1/2 months.) ———————————— $3,422 20
Traveling expenses of Director, Advisory
Committee and employees ——————————— 1,815 93
Clerks, stenographer, attendants, draughtsman
and other employees—salaries ——————————— 4,403 98
Allowance for maintenance of Director and
attendants at St. Louis ——————————— 2,719 74
Printing and stationery and binding of
exhibit work ——————————————— 807 01
Supplies—material for preparation of
exhibit ——————————————————— 1,690 00
Installation-booth, facades, cabinets,
counters, cases and appointments ——————— 7,096 52
Express, freight, cartage, postage, telephone
and telegraph —————————————— 793 73

Total expenditures———————————————— $22,749 11
===========

Receipts:
Amounts received from cities, etc., on
account of binding exhibit material,
sale of installation and appointments $666 50
==========

FINE ARTS

Employees—salaries ——————————————————— $280 00
Storage of art works, packing, handling, repairing, etc. ——————————
———————————— 3,129 09 Express, cartage, etc., to and from St. Louis
3,139 04 Insurance on art works ——————————————————— 2,423 00
Printing and supplies ———————————————————— 173 26 Postage,
telephone and telegraph and miscellaneous expenditures ——————————
———— 155 56 ——————————— Total expenditures —————————————
———————————— $9,299 95 =========== Receipts: Rebate on insurance
————————————————————————— $42 13 ===========

AGRICULTURE AND LIVE STOCK

Superintendent—salary (19 months) ————— $3,166 55
Superintendent—traveling expenses ————————— 1,115 87 Allowance
for maintenance of Superintendent and assistants at St. Louis —————
————— 1,380 00 Assistants, attendants, laborers, etc.— salaries ———
————————————————————— 5,579 54 Miscellaneous traveling
expenses for collecting exhibit material ———————————— 1,120 93
Cost of grain, vegetables and dairy products for exhibit ——————
————————————— 2,425 92 Installation—booth, counters, cabinets,
show cases, etc. ————————————————— 4,110 44
Refrigerator show cases for butter and cheese ————————————
————————————— 1,500 00 Printing and stationery ——————————
————————— 42 45 Express, freight, cartage, including on live stock for
exhibit, cold storage, telephone, telegraph and postage ——————————
————— $2,230 62 Miscellaneous supplies ——————————————
—— 612 13 Total expenditures ————————————————————
$23,285 45 Receipts: Sale of exhibit material ———————————————
$592 10

HORTICULTURE

Superintendent—salary (18 1/2 months) ———————— $3,111 06
Superintendent—traveling expenses ———————— 1,021 81 Assistants,
attendants, stenographer, labor, etc. ————————————————
———————— 4,631 31 Allowance for maintenance of Superintendent and
assistants at St. Louis ———————— 1,840 00 Miscellaneous
traveling expenses, collecting fruit ————————————————
———— 858 90 Cost of fruit for exhibit, cold storage, etc. 2,579 81
Installation—booth, facade, tables, cases, etc. ————————————
———————————— 3,711 26 Office rent, supplies, etc. ————
———————— 736 72 Printing and stationery ————————————
—- 181 19 Freight, cartage, express, telephone, telegraph and postage ——
———————————— 1,580 62 Total expenditures ————————
———————— $20,252 68 Receipts: Rent of plates and sale of
installation ———— $253 50

FOREST, FISH AND GAME

General traveling expenses, collecting exhibit material ————
———————————— $1,890 22 Cost of exhibit material ————
———————— 5,782 49 Allowance for maintenance of special agent and
assistants at St. Louis during Exposition period, and for packing and
returning exhibit ———————————————— $3,183 73
Installation—flooring, cabinets, show cases, frames, etc. ————
———————————— 3,283 42 Printing and stationery ————
———————— 262 81 Freight, cartage, express and storage ————
361 07 Miscellaneous supplies ———————————— 97 40
Total expenditures ———————————— $14,861 14 Receipts:
Sale of floors ———————————— $15 00

MINES AND METALLURGY

Clerk hire and labor ——————————————— $901 08
Traveling expenses, collecting exhibit and
  maintenance of attendants and assistants
  at St. Louis ————————————————— 2,631 59
Excavating fossil trails ————————————— 180 91
Installation—flooring, cases, cabinets,
  counters, etc. ————————————————— 2,155 22
Freight, cartage, express, etc. ———————— 1,187 94
Postage, telephone and telegraph —————— 91 22
Printing and stationery ——————————— 122 78
Supplies ——————————————————— 207 44
Other miscellaneous expenditures —————— 254 18
  Total expenditures ———————————— $7,732 36

SOCIAL ECONOMY

Charities:
Services of assistants preparing
   statistics, etc. ———————————————— $148 25
Supplies, photographs, etc.———————————— 549 56
Freight, express and cartage ———————————— $52 25
Printing and stationery ———————————————— 16 58
   Total ————————————————————————— $766 64
Model of Craig Colony —————————————————— $500 08
Excise:
Preparation and installation of charts ————— $276 32
Labor:
Preparation of graphic charts ———————————— $505 15
Printing, engraving, binding, etc. ——————— 201 45
Traveling expenses ———————————————————— 44 50
   Total ————————————————————————— $751 10

Lunacy:
Services of assistants ———————————————— $86 00
Photographs, supplies, etc. ——————————— 1,291 58
Traveling expenses ———————————————————— 23 71
Freight and cartage ————————————————————— 40 28
   Total ————————————————————————— $1441 57

Prisons:
Traveling expenses and maintenance of
   attendants at St. Louis ————————————— $2,000 00

SUMMARY

Receipts:

Appropriation, chapter 421, Laws of
1902 ———————————————————————— $100,000 00
Appropriation, chapter 546, Laws of
1903 ———————————————————————— 200,000 00
Appropriation, chapter 640, Laws of
1904 ———————————————————————— 40,000 00
From General Administration, as per
above schedule ———————————————— 833 47
From State Building, construction ———————— 7,025 00
From State Building, maintenance ———————— $70 00
From Education ————————————————— 666 50
From Fine Arts ———————————————— 42 13
From Agriculture and Live Stock —————— 592 10
From Horticulture ——————————————— 253 50
From Forest, Fish and Game ———————— 15 00

Total ——————————————————————— $349,497 70

Expenditures:

General Administration ——————————— $53,864 64
State Building, construction ———————— 120,337 77
State Building, maintenance ———————— 68,599 20
Education ————————————————— 22,749 11
Fine Arts ———————————————————— 9,299 95
Agriculture and Live Stock ———————— 23,285 45
Horticulture ———————————————— 20,252 68
Forest, Fish and Game —————————— 14,861 14
Mines and Metallurgy ————————————— 7,732 36
Social economy
  Charities ———————————————— $766 64
  Craig Colony ———————————— 500 08
  Excise ——————————————— 276 32
  Labor ————————————————— 751 10
  Lunacy ———————————————— 1,441 57
  Prisons ——————————————— 2,000 00
      5,735 71
Balance returned to State treasury ———— 2,779 69
Total ——————————————————————— $349,497 70

9 789356 784895